WE RISE

WE RISE

XIUHTEZCATL MARTINEZ

with Justin Spizman

RODALE.

RODALE *wellness*

Live happy. Be healthy. Get inspired.

Sign up today to get exclusive access to our authors, exclusive bonuses, and the most authoritative, useful, and cutting-edge information on health, wellness, fitness, and living your life to the fullest.

Visit us online at RodaleWellness.com
Join us at RodaleWellness.com/Join

Rodale books may be purchased for business or promotional use for special sales. For information, please email BookMarketing@Rodale.com.

Printed in the United States of America
Rodale Inc. makes every effort to use acid-free ∞, recycled paper ♻.

All photos courtesy of Tamara Rose with the exception of the following:
Vanessa Black, xiv; Jade Begay, 161, 162, 171; Diana Bray, 137; Chris Castro, 121; EarthGuardians.org, 235; Amir Erez, 105; ©JHenryFair (www.jhenryfair.com), 134, 142; Razz Gormley, 94; Brian Hardin, 9; Paul Hilton, 76, 79; Robin Loznak, Our Children's Trust, 46; Jeff Orlowsky, 84; Cassidy Rass, 191; Ietef Vita, 118

Thanks to Lighthawk (www.lighthawk.org) who piloted the plane for the photo of a fracking wastewater holding pond on page 142.

Book design by Amy King
Researcher: Russell Mendell

Library of Congress Cataloging-in-Publication Data is on file with the publisher.

ISBN-13: 978–1–63565–067–9 hardcover

Distributed to the trade by Macmillan
4 6 8 10 9 7 5 3   hardcover

We inspire health, healing, happiness, and love in the world.
Starting with you.

To the youth who don't have a voice and
to future generations who will inherit the Earth

CONTENTS

PART III: THE GAME PLAN

PROLOGUE

UNcharted TERRITORY
A New Chapter in My Life

There are moments in our lives that help shape the way we see our world. They shift our perspectives and help us understand our immense potential to define our future. The first 17 years of my life have led me to believe that everything happens for a reason. Maybe that's why I didn't feel at all phased as I looked out into the audience of world leaders from more than 100 nations. I'd been given a stage at a pivotal moment in history, and I saw the world needed fresh perspectives if we wanted to make real progress on climate solutions. We've spent the last 20 years pointing the finger and passing off responsibility. We are in a place where we can't afford to wait for others to solve this problem for us. We have all the tools we need...the only thing missing is the will to help us get there.

My name is Xiuhtezcatl (pronounced 'Shoe-Tez-Caht'). I am 17 years old, and I'm doing everything I can to fight for change in a collapsing world. In 2015, I had just finished middle school, and the state of the climate was descending into chaos. That year, global temperatures were the hottest in recorded history, sea levels had reached an all-time high, and greenhouse gases had never been more present in our atmosphere. Climate scientists worldwide were alarmed by how much faster the ice caps were melting than previously projected.

In response, world leaders were preparing to meet in Paris for the most important conversation on climate in our history. This was the COP 21 United Nations Climate Change Conference, and we weren't about to let our voices be excluded from this pivotal moment in history. In the climate movement, we talk a lot about tipping points, and we know that we're running out of time to act before climate change becomes irreversible.

Earlier that year, on Earth Day, I was featured in a short film called *Kid Warrior*. This was a documentary telling the story of my life and my work as the Youth Director for Earth Guardians, a global movement working to empower the younger generation to use our voices and create positive solutions. The film was meant to inspire other young people to get involved, connect, and engage in climate action and other important social issues of our time. I also wanted to show the world that my story is more than just activism . . . that I'm just a regular kid chasing big dreams in a crazy world.

After the *Kid Warrior* short hit the Internet, e-mails from young people flooded Earth Guardians, asking how they could get involved and start Earth Guardian crews of their own. I was swamped with interviews, speaking invitations, and media opportunities. One of those invites came from Susan Alzner, head of the United Nations Non-Government Liaison Service and by far my favorite person working at the UN. She's helping build bridges to connect the UN General Assembly and voices of the people, by identifying civil society attendees and speakers for high-level events, conferences, and summits. One of her topics of interest was climate change, and she got wind of Kid Warrior and the Earth Guardians movement, leading to me.

While I was kind of surprised that the UN heard about me through social media, it was pretty remarkable to get an invite to address the general assembly. My intention was to plant the seeds and lay the foundation of hope for the upcoming Paris climate change conference, while representing the many youth voices that won't be heard by the UN. I was only the second nongovernment person to address the general assembly.

Kathy Jetnil-Kijiner was first. She addressed the United Nations in 2014. At the time, she was a 26-year-old woman from the Marshall Islands, a small island nation that sits about 6 feet above sea level and is already experiencing the impacts of climate change. Rising sea levels and severe storms have come extremely close to destroying these beautiful islands.

In her speech, Kathy indicated that, no matter how hard it might be, we have to solve the issue of climate change. In a truly emotional and beautiful moment, she recited a poem to her infant daughter, promising the little girl that she would do everything she could to protect her from rising seas. She entitled the poem "Dear Matefele Peinam," and here are the first few verses:

> dear matafele peinam,
> you are a seven month old sunrise of gummy smiles
> you are bald as an egg and bald as the buddha
> you are thunder thighs and lightning shrieks so excited for bananas, hugs
> and
> our morning walks past the lagoon

> dear matafele peinam,
> i want to tell you about that lagoon that lucid, sleepy lagoon lounging
> against the sunrise
> some men say that one day that lagoon will devour you

> they say it will gnaw at the shoreline
> chew at the roots of your breadfruit trees
> gulp down rows of your seawalls
> and crunch your island's shattered bones

> they say you, your daughter
> and your granddaughter, too
> will wander rootless
> with only a passport to call home

> dear matafele peinam,
> don't cry
> mommy promises you
> no one
> will come and devour you

no greedy whale of a company
sharking through political seas
no backwater bullying of businesses with broken morals no blindfolded
bureaucracies gonna push
this mother ocean over
the edge ...

She concluded to a standing ovation, leaving many attendees in tears. The beauty of her poem is that it wasn't just about facts and figures, it told a relatable story about a mother's love for her child and an unwavering will to protect her in the face of big challenges. I knew I had big shoes to fill after learning about her speech and just how deeply she touched the world leaders in attendance. I was excited to be the second person and youngest ever to address the United Nations General Assembly. The voices of the people needed to be heard, and I was up for the challenge.

It seems like the majority of people are disconnected from what actually occurs at the UN. With more than 20 years of world leaders talking to each other about climate change, nothing had been solved. For the UN, climate change is topic of bureaucratic debate, whereas for many communities, it's a life-or-death situation. I felt like I had the opportunity to offer my perspective from the front lines of watching climate change decimate our planet. Whether it was feeling the tremendous impact of fracking on the water and air in my hometown of Boulder, or traveling to North Dakota to stand in solidarity at Standing Rock, or protesting against the Keystone XL Pipeline, or visiting damaged rain forests, oceans, and glacier melting sites, I have learned about the impact of climate change one powerful experience at a time.

Looking back, I now know that that speech was the culmination of an incredible period of growth in my life. My voice had just dropped, I was sprouting up, and I was taking my fight to a much bigger stage. I usually don't memorize speeches; most of the time, I just speak from the heart. But, this was no ordinary speech. The UN wanted me to write out every word I was going to say. I have always viewed the words on the page as more of a road map to the places I might go.

The night before I boarded the flight to New York, I finished a draft of the speech. My badass mom, Tamara Rose, came with me on this journey. She's endlessly supportive and my partner in crime in this movement. She does a great job of keeping the pressure out of it, always looking out for my best interests. I know she is proud of me, but she doesn't add any expectations to the moment. She did want me to memorize the speech while I was on the plane though. As we began our ascent into the clouds, I reviewed my speech a few times, but after about 30 minutes or so, I figured I should just relax. I fell asleep, and I didn't wake up until the captain came over the intercom system, indicating our initial descent into New York City.

As we got off the plane, my friend Vanessa Black, who made *Kid Warrior,* and her camera crew were there to film my journey to the UN. Vanessa took us directly to Manhattan, over the Brooklyn Bridge, and to this small suit tailor in the city. It was a pretty funky place. A tailor met me and started taking my measurements. That was the first time in my life that I had ever put on a suit. The tailor shuffled jackets on and off of me and fit me for a shirt and shoes to match my suit. To that point, most of my activism was very grass roots, community-driven, and localized for the most part. This was an entirely different kind of thing than I was used to.

I was both pretty tired and hungry at this point, and I wanted to enjoy some of NYC's best eats. My mom was stressing a little that I didn't have my speech memorized, and I could appreciate her concern, but I was just chilling, knowing that I was ready for the moment. I think my exact words to her were, "Mom, don't worry. I got this." I can only imagine how reassuring that might sound coming from a 15-year-old kid who had just put on his first button-down shirt that wasn't plaid.

June 29, 2015, arrived. As we approached the front entrance to the UN, there was a ridiculous amount of security. We were issued a number of clearance badges, and were eventually connected with Susan Alzner, who greeted us and showed us around. We took our seats in the audience, and I remember sitting through a number of different speakers who took the stage before me. It wasn't engaging at all—the room was lifeless. I tried to sit up straight, so as to not wrinkle my suit or mess up my long hair. I was a little nervous; this was bigger than anything I'd done before.

About 20 minutes before I was scheduled to speak, we were ushered to the side of the stage. We continued to wait, and I surveyed the room filled with chairs, each with a different little placard in front of it, designating the country represented by that seat. The room went silent, and I heard a UN representative start to introduce me. He wasn't the first to mess up the pronunciation of my name. To his credit, he tried a couple of times, but it just wasn't happening for him. As I approached the podium, I looked out into the audience. The atmosphere still felt stale and stuffy. I knew I needed to bring some life into the room.

I unrolled my written speech, took a deep breath, and started off with a prayer in my native language. As you can imagine, not everyone in the room spoke the same language, so there was a booth set up with translators repeating everything for the diplomats in various dialects. Because my prayer was in Nahuatl and it isn't a spoken language, it totally threw everyone off. I could just imagine what the interpreters were saying. Probably something like, "What the hell is happening right now? Nobody recognizes this language." The UN required strict preparation for its speakers, and, in the first 30 seconds, I was already breaking the rules and going off script. Classic.

It only took the audience a few moments to realize that a 15-year-old kid was standing in front of them. I had their attention now—all eyes were on me.

I left the written words behind and spoke what I needed to say from my heart. I used the speech as an outline to freestyle the content. Looking out at the audience and recognizing the importance of this moment, I knew I had an opportunity to say more than what was on the page. By the end, I was totally off- script, and I was flowing with it. It felt perfect. My friend Paul Basis tells me that the power in your words is in the space between them. I took my time so people could feel everything I said. By the time I said what I came there to say, I had gone 3 minutes over the time I was given.

Getting off the stage after you speak to a bunch of people in suits is always a strange feeling. I felt like I said what I wanted to. Besides,

Xiuhtezcatl at the United Nations

the people in that room weren't the ones I was really speaking to. Speeches don't change the world, movements do, but the words and the messages that come through can spark a flame to ignite a movement.

Following the speech I felt the tremendous potential of what this moment could be. While this felt like a powerful culmination of 10 years of passion and dedication, I knew it was just the beginning of a next-level journey—to fulfill the promise of my words would take many more years of hard work. So often people compromise themselves in order to accomplish their political objectives. The goal of my speech was to defy that. I don't ever want to have to be something that I'm not to make a difference in the world. I gave that speech because I wanted to show the world that a kid with a passion and a voice could make a difference, regardless of who he is or where he comes from.

I was able to show up in a fully authentic way, in a place where such blunt honesty is rare. Whether or not my words sunk into the people in the room, my message would resonate to those frustrated by a bureaucracy that had failed to meet the needs of the people. In my speech, I told the audience: "Don't be afraid to dream big." The failure of global leaders to solve this crisis is direct result of their lack of imagination. If we want a sane climate policy, we the people have to push them beyond what they see as politically possible.

Sadly, the UN didn't dream big enough with the Paris Climate Conference that followed my speech several months later. Their efforts fell short of the concrete actions needed to curb greenhouse gas emissions substantially. What progress was made in Paris many fear will be thwarted by a Trump administration, which says they plan to cancel the agreement.

For many of us, waking up on November 9th felt as if we were entering a national nightmare. But I've learned that big dreams often come from total nightmares. The UN was formed in response to the tragedies that occurred during World War II. So I can only imagine that we are primed and ready for something larger than previously imagined. I know that change occurs through each of us. It is the manifestation of our collective efforts. This book is a resource to transform a broken system and build a new one in its place. It will help to paint the picture, demonstrate the struggle, and then outline a solution.

We're up against a lot, but together we've got this. Movements can begin with one idea, one spark of inspiration, and one action. They catch fire when we unite around them. Each of us has a part to play, no matter how small. The solutions we create in our communities are the foundation for something bigger than us all.

Every generation leaves a legacy. The tools to create one are in your hands. Think of this book as a map to help you find your way when you get lost. The ending remains unwritten, because the actions we take will shape the world that the next generation inherits. This book is for the frontline fighters, the people who won't take no for an answer, and for those who believe in change and are seeking guidance to create it. This book is for the straight-A students, the high-school dropouts, the single moms, the rebels, the farmers, the architects, the healers, the poets, the entrepreneurs, the leaders, and those who have not yet found their voice. My faith lies in the amazing people I've met along this journey who won't stop fighting for what we believe in. Another world is possible.

Together we can do this if we just put boots on the ground and pool our time and energy to heal the world one leaf on one tree in one forest in one city in one state in one country at a time. It isn't going to happen overnight, but it can happen if we make the most of each day. Every little bit helps. Local efforts can create global waves. Throughout this book, you'll find helpful conversations about the most important social issues of our time. At the end of the conversations, I will outline steps and resources you can take and use to join in and make a difference.

So keep this book by your side as you navigate the road ahead. Keep it in your backpack, near your bed stand, or in your hybrid. Write in it, highlight it, even rip out the pages and give them to your friends. Please pass it around, and share the guidance and suggestions in the pages ahead. I want you to love reading this book as much as I loved writing it. This is my way of spreading the word as quickly as possible. This book is just the beginning of the movement for change, but I know there are difference-making resources in the words to come. It means the world to me that I have the opportunity to outline my plan to save the Earth that has given so much to each of us. I am one of the many. And so are you. I look at you as my teammate and partner in this battle. We got this if we just work together.

So with that said, please dream big and read on.

PART I

ROOTS OF REVOLUTION

"We are all indigenous to the Earth."

—Xiuhtezcatl Tonatiuh

CHAPTER 1

Indigenous Roots
Connecting with the Ways of My Ancestors

*"Man does not weave this web of life.
He is merely a strand of it. Whatever he
does to the web, he does to himself."*

—CHIEF SEATTLE

I've always been proud of who I am. Of where I came from. As a little kid, my dad would tell me to be grateful that I had a culture and ceremony to connect to, because a lot of people don't get to experience that. From my long hair, to my name, my connection to my ancestors was an important part of my life. I grew up in ceremony, fascinated by the stories of my people. I was astounded by the complex history and philosophy. My obsidian eyes beamed at my father as he sang me songs and told me stories of where we came from.

MEXICA ORIGIN

I am Mexica. It's written in my name and the red road I walk. My people are often referred to as the Aztec. History tells us that the Aztec people came from a mythical place called Aztlán, along with six other tribes that migrated to the four directions. My people traveled north, and, for more than 200 years, they roamed to many different places, mixing with and learning from other tribes until they found the prophetic sign that they had searched for. An eagle perched on a cactus. They knew that this was where they were to lay their roots, and in 1325, they founded the great city of Tenochtitlan, which means abundance or the prickles of the cactus. It was during this time that they began to call themselves the Mexica people, and the empire they built was a culmination of hundreds of years of gathered knowledge. This eventually became modern-day Mexico City.

Our people grew to greatness. We were builders, farmers, cultivators, and intellectuals. Our society and economy were well conceptualized and extremely organized. We developed great systems of agriculture, incredible architecture, art, science, astronomy, and philosophy. My father often speaks of the magnificence and mastery of the art of our ancestors, from our carvings to our ceramics and our paintings, to name only a few. We were known to the world by the incredible accuracy of our calendar, astronomy, and architecture. Over the course of the 15th century, only the Incas in Peru built larger empires than ours.

After many years of growing their empire, the Spanish conquistador Hernán Cortés found our great city and eventually overthrew the Mexicas by extreme force, capturing Tenochtitlan (Mexico City) on August 13, 1521. This brought the last great Mesoamerican civilization close to an end. This colonization and genocide has been a scar within the history that Mexica people still carry. The Spaniards had no mercy and had very little interest to learn from us or our culture. They came to conquer, to take our riches, and to enslave our people. They destroyed everything that belonged to us that they didn't want. They burned our belongings and tried to silence our voices. This left us with very little, and we began our struggle for cultural and spiritual survival. We lived a forbidden life and were no longer allowed to carry our identity or practice our ceremonies, rituals, and language. Our knowledge and cultural heritage had to be kept out of site and brought into our hearts and homes, leaving a great gap between the history written by the conquerors and the history passed down generation to generation by our ancestors.

The Mitotiliztli or "sacred dance" was one of the strongest cultural and spiritual expressions of our people. But, like everything else, we had to mask these ceremonies and dances as tributes to the Catholic saints. That was the only way we could dance publicly without fear of having our legs or hands mutilated as punishment. Times were hella tough for us back then.

For many hundreds of years, we continued to struggle. Our ancestors secretly passed our culture and stories down to the younger generations to keep our culture alive. In the early 1900s, throughout Mexico, there was tremendous discrimination, oppression, and hatred toward indigenous people. In response, many decided not to pass the language, culture, and heritage onto their children as their own parents had, in fear they would recognize the same oppression they had lived. While the bloodline continued, the passing on of the traditions ended with my great grandparents when my great grandma chose to not pass on our language to my grandfather. It wasn't until around the 1950s that the ceremonies and rituals started to appear again in public, slowly coming out and being accepted by the Mestizo (mix-blooded) and mostly Catholic religious society.

My Grandfather Xolotl

In modern Mexico City, once known as Tenochtitlan, traditional Mexica groups started to emerge slowly and occupy the public spaces with their tradition and ceremonies. That is when our family and many people reconnected to their ancestry. My grandfather, Xolotl, worked to help revive the culture and rekindle some of the many traditional dance groups across Mexico. We were once again able to practice our ancient traditions, honoring the Earth, dancing to the spirits, utilizing our sacred instruments we once hid, and wearing our colorful regalia. The prayers of our ancestors were answered, as they said this day would again come and we would revive our culture out of the pain and brutality that we had endured for centuries. This was a new time of great hope for the Mexica.

FROM GENERATION TO GENERATION

My people withstood disaster and despair, weathered tremendous conflict and threats from the outside world, and came alive through art, culture, science, and social evolution. That was the backdrop for the birth of my father, who was born in a small town called Santa Cruz, Acalpixca, in Xochimilco, Mexico City.

My father grew up embracing the ceremonies, practicing the dances in their plazas on a daily basis. His life was deeply rooted in this culture, and it showed him the importance of maintaining a connection to the earth. Many of these teachings were passed onto me. I learned that everything around us is affected by the way that we live, and our actions create a ripple effect, like a stone dropped into a pond of water.

I understood at an early age that we have a responsibility to be caretakers of the land. I had strong indigenous roots. From birth, my parents have raised me with these traditional Mexica practices and beliefs. My first real connection to my tradition occurred when I was just 6 weeks old. My parents often tell me stories of how I got my name, Xiuhtezcatl Tonatiuh.

My mom remembers:

> When Xiuhtezcatl was 6 weeks old, he received his name in the Black Hills of South Dakota. The naming ceremony took place at World Peace and Prayer Day.

Xiuhtezcatl's grandfather, Xolotl Martinez, had traveled to Mexico to bring his name, which was chosen based on the Aztec calendar, from the elders in Mexico. Arvol Looking Horse, a Lakota chief and carrier of the White Buffalo Calf Pipe helped Xolotl do this ceremony. When Xiuhtezcatl was born, his grandfather chose his name based on his Tonalamatl (an astronomical, philosophical, and numerical study based on the Mexica calendar and the time and place of birth). He then determined his name based on what he saw and understood. Xiuhtezcatl means "Turquoise Mirror," representing a reflection of the sky. Tonatiuh references the sun. At the ceremony, Xolotl stood next to Arvol. They held Xiuhtezcatl and presented him to each direction. As they did, we all shouted out Xiuhtezcatl's new name toward the north, the south, the east and the west. After that, they took Xiuhtezcatl, his father, and I to join them in a sweat lodge. The elders were awaiting our arrival. When I entered with him, I kind of panicked because they brought 52 hot rocks into the sweat lodge. For a second there, I thought they were going to cook my baby. I passed Xiuhtezcatl to the first elder, and he held him over the hot stones and made a prayer in his native tongue. This continued until each elder in the sweat lodge did the same. He finally returned to me, and the elder indicated that I could now take him out. He told me that they would pray for him. While I was relieved we weren't going to be inside that hot sweat lodge anymore, I was happy for the incredible blessing he just received. We sat outside the sweat lodge by the fire and listened to the prayers and songs they were singing inside for Xiuhtezcatl.

After I introduce myself, many people ask if I have a nickname, or if there's an easier way to pronounce Xiuhtezcatl. I've never taken up a nickname because my name is more than just a title. It's part of who I am, in the same way that my long hair is. While I don't remember the moment, the story of how I got my name will stay with me forever.

Since I could walk, I began learning my people's ceremonial dances and participating in important events and sacred runs to reconnect with our roots. When I was just 7, the Hopi people planned a sacred run to Mexico City in honor of the water, and to bring attention to the global water crisis many were experiencing. They put a call out to the world for people to send water from their regions that the Hopi would run with all the way to the heart of Mexico City to present at the World Water Forum. Many indigenous brothers and sisters joined in this run, carrying prayers for the healing of the water in their minds and their hearts. My grandfather, Xolotl, and hundreds of our Mexica brothers and sisters received these runners in the ceremonial place in Mexico called Teotihuacan, honoring them with ceremonies and dances.

My grandfather made a commitment to the Hopi people during that ceremony that they would run from Mexico City back to Hopi carrying the sacred fire. In our tradition, when you bring together the water and the fire, it is called the atlachinolli, and it represents new life. This run was in honor of new life and strengthening our commitment to protecting the sacred elements that give us life. This was the second big run that I had participated in as a child. My Grandfather and 30 other Mexicas carried the fire and the water, running several weeks from Mexico City to the US border. There, our family and many other indigenous runners met them. Border patrol didn't let many of the runners from Mexico cross into the US, including my grandfather. Only a small handful (mostly youth) were allowed to cross, and they were prepared to carry the sacred elements and prayers all the way to Hopi land in Arizona. I was 7 at the time, my brother was 5, and my mother was pregnant with my little sister. We stopped at reservations along the way to present the fire and the water in ceremony and gather more runners.

I remember sleeping on the floor in people's houses, riding in the back of pickup trucks, showering in school gyms, and running through the desert, doing my best to keep up with my dad. By the time we arrived outside of Hopi, we were 75 runners strong. We were permitted to enter the first Hopi Mesa running on their old sacred trails. These people lived at the top of a massive plateau, and as the runners approached the reservation, hundreds of elders and people lined the cliffside far above us. They formed lines that we ran through, the elders using feathers to bless us with water as we passed. We continued through all three Hopi mesas, ending in the ceremonial place of the Second Mesa. It was the first time the Hopi opened their ceremonial ground for another culture to enter and offer their dances.

A Mexica Ceremony at Hopi

We were received on a hot, sunny day and presented the elders of that village with the fire that had been carried all the way from Mexico City. We then entered the plaza and set up our altar. My father lead the ceremony and dance. After 2 hours of dancing in the dry heat, I got heatstroke. I'll never forget these experiences while I was growing up—running for weeks in prayer and participating in these incredible ceremonies are deeply a part of who I am today.

THE STRENGTH OF OUR ROOTS

Even though I was born in the United States, I spent quite a bit of time over the course of the first 5 years of my life in Mexico. Spanish was my first language. I participated in all-night ceremonies on the top of the pyramids and in the plazas. I remember other sacred runs we did in

Mexico to special locations, like the birthplace of Quetzalcoatl (one of our great leaders). We lived in my grandparents' home, which had no running water and very little light or electricity. It was a simple life, and we spent our days traveling from ceremony to ceremony. We lived on the money we made from the art and jewelry we sold in the plazas.

While I didn't travel again to Mexico until November 2016, we continued our dances and ceremonies here in the United States. When I returned to Mexico, I was very focused on ceremony and bringing back memories from my early childhood. I deepened my knowledge of the philosophy, the history, and the symbolism of my heritage. Being on the land of my people, I could feel a certain vibration that I hadn't felt before. I felt like I was home, a place where I belonged, knowing that my people fought and died so that I could return to this place and practice the ceremonies of my ancestors.

My experience in Mexico reminded me that part of being indigenous is understanding a connection to the water we drink, the air we breathe, and the earth we walk on. While we might come from different walks of life, places in the world, and religious or spiritual beliefs, it is in our nature to want to fight for the health of the planet. This life is a gift, and it is our responsibility to respect and protect that which gives us life.

My father taught me every time we went out in nature, to a forest or a river, to the ocean or to the mountains, that we should leave behind an offering to honor that land, whether we left a song, a little bit of tobacco, or a piece of hair. From the time that I could walk, I was also learning that our dances, songs, and traditions are completely linked to the Earth. Every step in every dance represents a different element, a different animal, or a different part of our tradition. As human beings, we are the caretakers of the land.

I've been going to a Lakota ceremony called Sundance my whole life. When I was 5, I went to one here in Colorado with my family, and close to 100 other warriors. While the dancers spent 4 days in prayer and ceremony, my father and I sat with the drummers and sang songs to support the dancers. On the 4th day, after the ceremony had come to an end, the Chief gathered everyone to sit in front of the supporters who had brought hundreds of gifts for everyone to choose from. They called this the Giving Ceremony. There was everything from beautiful blankets

Xiuhtezcatl at the Giving Ceremony

and trinkets to animal skins and tons of toys for all the kids running around the camp.

The Chief called the children up first to choose gifts, and about 30 of us ran toward all the items laid out in the grass. While all of the kids went for the colorful toys, I walked straight toward the Chief and dancers, choosing a beautiful deerskin lying on the ground. I picked it up, threw it over my shoulder, and walked back to sit with my dad. It was at least three times my size.

The chief and dancers began to laugh at the gift I'd chosen, joking that my dad put me up to it. Honestly, I genuinely thought that it would be way doper to bring home a huge deerskin than a squirt gun. I also took myself way too seriously when I was little, way more than I do now anyway. The chief approached my father at the closing celebration of the Sundance and said that it was very unusual for a child to choose a gift like that, and that particular deerskin once belonged to him, so I had to be sure to take special care of it. The chief's wife told my mom, "Xiuhtezcatl will have a strong path in his life." After we returned home, I slept on that deerskin for as long as I could, until it started falling apart.

Moments like these helped shape the life that I'm living, and made me who I am. My connection to my ancestry and my connection to the Earth have helped define my identity and my view of the world, and they continue to shape the path that I walk. I'm painting my legacy in honor of everything my ancestors fought for and in hope for the world that I will pass onto the next generation.

LIVING A SACRED LIFE

I know we can reverse the damage caused by hundreds of years of neglect and thoughtless action, but only if we return to a way of living that recognizes that all life is sacred. The future of the planet needs to be shaped by an important balance of technology, media, innovation, and indigenous wisdom. If you study the many tribes and their beliefs of hierarchy, there was a tremendous sense of respect for women and elders. Women were commonly honored as the providers of life and as caretakers, and seen as equals to men. Mexica people believed in an important balance between the masculine and feminine energy, and it is necessary in order for our communities to thrive.

A respect for our elders has always been a part of family traditions. It's customary to care for our parents and grandparents in the way that they cared for us our whole lives. That was just a part of life for my family. My great-grandmother turned 93 this year. She can barely see, doesn't have many teeth left, and is one of the most beautiful people I've ever met. My family in Mexico all help take care of her. When I came back to live in the US, I was shocked to see that the cultural norm is to put your grandparents in retirement homes the moment that they can't take care of themselves. Even if it's a really nice retirement home, separating ourselves from our elders breaks a connection within families and to the knowledge and wisdom they have to offer. Keeping our elders close forges a relationship between the older and younger generations that I believe is missing from some cultures.

We've been so focused on growth, progress, and development that we've forgotten who we are. Humanity has left behind a lot of what makes us human, most importantly our connection to the Earth. Reconnecting to these ancient teachings can help us to strike a balance between growth and development and the health of our planet.

A Mexica Solstice Ceremony

Flowers and Songs

One of the most important pieces of wisdom my father ever shared with me was a poem in our language. It says, *"Ti nechcayo to tiuhxochime, ti nechcayo to tiuhcuicame"* These words are from one of our great leaders, Nezahualcoyotl, who was recognized for his vision and the ways he so beautifully expressed the presence of mankind on Earth and the magnificence of life. These words translate to, "At the least, we should leave flowers, at the least we should leave songs." What this poem is saying is a reflection on the legacy of our people. When our empire falls, when our days of power come to an end, the true greatness of the Mexica will live on in the hearts and minds of its people. The only thing that will outlast the glory of our nation is our culture, our ceremonies, and our ways of life, written in the songs that we teach our children, passed down to the heirs of this culture. The legacy of my people is one of flowers and songs. Handed down by my father, along with the responsibility to keep this legacy alive in the hearts and the minds of our people—that is where the power to shape our world lies. The power to determine our legacy and to pass on all that those before us fought for.

CALL TO ACTION: AUTHENTIC SPIRITUALITY, NOT CULTURAL APPROPRIATION

Spirituality is something that everyone is losing. It is part of us. But, when we put it aside, we don't allow it to grow, and it is something very vital for harmony on this planet. At this time, our children, our seeds, don't have that spirituality that they should have to feel connected to this Earth and understand that there is a spirit in everything. That spirit needs to be honored and cared for.

My good friend Lyla June Johnston is a young Navajo leader who is constantly offering amazing examples of bringing spirituality into her movement work. She helps organize the Black Hills Unity Concert, which is more like a ceremony than a festival. Artists and musicians donate their time to bring attention to the Sacred Black Hills that need to be returned to the Lakota people. She brought that same grounded spiritual presence to her work, supporting the protest at Standing Rock to stop the Dakota Access Pipeline. She says, "Our ancestors believed that we are merely vessels through which spirit would work, and so, an activist leader without prayer is like a vessel without water."

From Gandhi's satyagraha in India to the Civil Rights Movement to Standing Rock, spirituality has been an essential part of movements. Spiritual connection can be a powerful anchor for our movements, if it's done in an authentic way. Some European Americans have taken things from indigenous spirituality without permission or gratitude. At times, they then distort the message to suit their own needs. For a long time, nonindigenous people have used indigenous knowledge and wisdom to profit or enhance their own social status. This is not the way the teachings were intended, and it's important to address and bring an end to cultural appropriation. When many people hear the phrase "cultural appropriation" they think of offensive team mascots like the Redskins, or the terrible trend of young people wearing native headdresses to festivals. Sometimes, it's not that obvious, though, and well-intentioned people can cause harm when they adopt spiritual practices.

Here are some tips for avoiding cultural appropriation, while exploring spiritual connection:

Explore your own ancestral traditions. We are all indigenous to this Earth, and many people, even Europeans, have Earth-based spiritual practices in their lineage that have been forgotten by their families. Do the investigative work to track back your lineage to the days before the colonization of your people.

Always ask permission. When you participate in spiritual traditions that are not your own, be respectful. Many people that don't have a spiritual way or have lost their connection to it are spiritually hungry. Understand that this is someone else's home, and, even if you were hungry, you wouldn't just walk into someone else's home and take food from their fridge. It's important to knock on the door and ask to first be invited in. Once you're in someone else's spiritual home, be humble, ask for guidance, and follow the instructions of your hosts.

THE VOICE OF OUR ANCESTORS
An Interview with Xolotl Martinez

Xolotl Martinez is Xiuhtezcatl's grandfather and the patriarch of the family.

ME: How did you get connected to your culture, and what is the importance of it?

XOLOTL: The vision and connection that I have to our culture was given to me by my grandparents. It is what has given me my path, and I thank them for that ancient wisdom. They taught me to respect and appreciate the plants and traditional medicine, our Nahuatl language, the customs, the food, and the celebrations—all this was vital for my life and spiritual path.

ME: What is the importance of transmitting our culture?

XOLOTL: Understanding that this is an ancient culture, it is our responsibility to re-create and teach the youth and children that we come from a culture rich in values and beauty. And so, in this way, they can continue being connected to the ancient wisdom and learn to live according to this lineage with their customs and traditions that have a base respect to life itself.

The Mexica culture is one of the greatest of the world, because the antiquity (old age) richness and value to humanity. The Nahuatl language is recognized for its extended reach to the Americas, being one of the most spoken in the old world. For the decedents of this culture, it is a privilege and pride to have this tradition and be part of this great culture of the world.

The world doesn't know the depth of the Mexican culture, since we only hear the negative aspects written in the history books. Little is known of its greatness, harmony, creativity, skill in the fine arts, philosophy, and values.

ME: Where did my name come from?

XOLOTL: We all have a name and with it comes our destiny—when your name was chosen and given to you, it came with your destiny. We gave you your name with the intention to bring you light, guidance and knowledge from your ancestors. We live in a world of multiple dimensions. Xiuh is the shine, the blue light that emerges from the universe, the color of the energy that comes from the universe, the blue of the fire from the stars, a reflection of the sky. The second part of your name, *Tezcatl*, is the mirror or the reflection. Blue turquoise mirror, reflection of the sky, and blue reflection of the celestial gourd are all a part of your name.

It is important for us to stay connected to the ceremonies, which helps you to awaken the consciousness the world needs. The more youth and children are united, the more we can create a change. We all need to work together to promote and protect Mother Earth.

CHAPTER 2

Kid Warrior

Developing Purpose at a Young Age

I genuinely believe that we are here for a reason. Everyone is a small part of a really big puzzle. I started to find my place at a younger age than you'd expect from most people. Even in the first few years of my life, I could tell something was wrong with the world. It didn't take a climate scientist to see the way we as a society were living wasn't sustainable. To me, it was an obvious problem and apparent everywhere I went, because everything we do is contributing to it. I learned from my parents that everything is connected, and what we do to the Earth, we do to ourselves.

Even as a little boy, who could barely see over the counter, I saw the desperation in the planet I loved. I wanted to do something about it. I might have been small, but I wanted the world to hear. It didn't really have anything to do with being an "activist." I just wanted people to understand how I felt, and hold adults accountable for what they were passing on. From a 6-year-old's perspective, it pretty much looked like the adults had messed up the world that I was growing up in. Throughout my childhood, there were a bunch of important moments that that helped me find my voice and empowered me to make a difference.

WRITING MY OWN STORY

The first time I stepped on stage was at a climate change rally in Boulder, Colorado. I made the decision to speak because I saw it as an opportunity to hold adults accountable for the current state of our environment. I arrived at the rally with a folded-up piece of paper in my hand, the speech I had worked hard to memorize. I gazed up to the microphone towering over me and waited for someone to come lower it, so I could speak. I started the speech the same way I would at the UN almost 10 years later, by reciting a Mexica prayer. After I finished, I explained to the audience that I had just said a prayer in my native language, giving thanks to all the elements—water, fire, earth, and air. I told them, "I was giving thanks to them to give us life, to give us energy, and to give us strength." I was kind of nervous, but afterward, everyone said that they couldn't tell. People still tell me to this day that I had fire in my eyes, and a lot of intensity very unique to a 6-year-old. After I introduced myself, I told the audience my age and that I was a boy, feeling a need to clarify because of my long hair.

I explained to the audience that when I was 5 years old, I wanted to go with my little brother to shut down all the factories. But when I turned

Preparing for Ceremony

6, I realized that it was us who were buying from the factories. I asked them to change their lifestyles and to be more conscious of their consumption, while passing on these lessons to their children.

After giving that speech, I gradually continued to get more involved. With my family, we started to learn more about local and global issues and how our decisions affected the environment, as well as the impact political leaders have on protecting us from climate change.

I remember when Obama ran for President in 2008. I made a video to try to get undecided voters to vote for him, because I believed that he would be a president that we could hold accountable for making decisions that would slow the destruction of our planet. We needed someone that could excite young people and get them off their couches to actually do something.

Looking back at those first few speeches, I realize that I came across as much more serious than I am now. These days, there are few moments where I'm not cracking jokes or goofing off, but when people saw me speak as a little kid, I came across as fiery and determined. I was exposed to such big issues at a young age, and it was a lot for a 6-year-old to come to terms with. I know now that, to deal with shit this serious, it's best to not take yourself too seriously.

During those early days in Boulder, I found one of the most important things a human being can find—my voice. Giving those early speeches motivated me to learn more, because I realized that people would listen and feel inspired when I spoke. That desire is what led me to sit down with my parents and watch Leonardo DiCaprio's documentary on the global environmental crisis.

AN URGENT CALL TO ACTION: THE ELEVENTH HOUR

Just one year after I spoke to the crowds in Boulder, I was in our living room in tears, unable to fully understand what I was seeing. My parents were watching a documentary called *The Eleventh Hour.* Leonardo DiCaprio narrated as the documentary cut between scenes of environmental collapse, rising sea levels, super vivid images of extinction, and massive storms washing away cities. Looking to my parents, I couldn't help but ask them, "How could we let this happen?" I just couldn't understand how we could live our lives every day without even thinking about the mess we humans created. The planet was falling apart, while people went to school and to work without considering the impact that their actions are having on the Earth. This documentary showed me that our lifestyles are killing our only home. I was completely devastated.

Watching that documentary changed a lot for me. I realized that it didn't matter how old I was, I needed to speak out about what was happening to our planet. I had to do everything I could to protect this planet that was in so much danger. It felt like a huge turning point for me. I began to put together everything I had learned from my sisters and my mom about taking action in the world and everything my father taught me about our connection to the Earth.

When the film ended, I cried in the arms of my father. I knew that I wanted to take this emotion, this pain, and this sadness that I had for our planet and do something about it. I felt a sense of true purpose as the urgency of this crisis sunk in.

Discovering My Community: The Earth Guardians

I wouldn't be the person I am today without the support my family and my community. They created the perfect platform to make a difference before I was even born. In 1992 in Maui, Hawaii, my mom started an organization called Earth Guardians (EG). EG worked to address the local environmental problems, like burning sugar cane, the degradation of the coral reefs in the ocean, and protecting aquatic life. All of my siblings were involved in it, as well as my aunts, uncles, and cousins.

In 1995, the Dalai Lama gave the first generation of Earth Guardians the Children's Torch of Hope, which 25 Earth Guardian youth carried on a 6-month tour to events in 29 states. They gathered letters from youth at all these events, calling on world leaders to stand up for their future, eventually delivering them to the United Nations for the UN's 50th anniversary. On the tour, they used hip-hop music and dance to tell the stories of the work they did. Earth Guardians eventually settled into Boulder, Colorado, and my oldest sister took over leadership of the crew. She organized high-school students and huge local events. My sister and her friends would have meetings in our basement, and I would always run around the outside of the house and peek through the window underneath the stairwell to spy on them. I would eavesdrop on their conversations as they planned events and talked about Earth Guardians. When they saw me, I would run away. I pretended that they hadn't seen me. I literally thought I was a ninja when I was a kid.

I can still remember an event we did to try and educate people on the dangers of plastic in our oceans. We tried to persuade people to bring their own reusable bags to the store instead of getting a plastic one every time. We set out a little table in the front of the grocery store and put some pamphlets with educational facts on display. Being this cute little kid, they chose me to man the booth and talk to people as they walked into the store. I would walk up to shoppers and ask if they had brought their own bag or planned on using the plastic ones provided by the store.

I wasn't aware of it at the time, but I was absorbing everything happening around me. My family went to marches to support causes we cared about, and I would ride on my dad's shoulders. My father would also open up many of these events with prayer and dance. Being engaged in the community was a normal part of my family life, and at the same time, we were never far from nature since we lived near lakes, forests, and the Rocky

Xiuhtezcatl and His Brother at Work

Mountains. It reminded us of what we were fighting to protect.

When I turned 9, my sister passed the torch of leading the local Earth Guardians to me. The issue that got us started was learning that our local government was going to add two new chemicals to this list of pesticides that they already were spraying in parks all over Boulder. While this was a small-scale issue compared to global climate change, I knew that I wanted to take this on. I told my friends that I wanted the youth to be a part of rising up and meeting this challenge. There were a lot of other organizations working on the cause, and we played our role by throwing a youth press conference where we could speak out on the issue. There were around 15 speakers, all under the age of 13.

I was so excited because, for the first time since I'd taken on the leadership role, I wasn't the only young person standing up. After the press conference, we went into the hearing with our city council and our mayor, where they were hearing public testimony about the use of pesticides. For the first time ever, my little brother, Itzcuauhtli, decided he wanted to get up in front of people and share his voice. When it was his turn to speak, they had to grab a box for him to stand on, since he couldn't reach the microphone. He said, "I shouldn't be here right now speaking to you. I should be outside playing in the park. But, because you guys aren't doing your job well, I have to come and tell you how to do it." The room was shaken by his words.

After feeling the pressure from the community, the council decided not to add the new pesticides to the list of existing ones that they already sprayed. They eventually rewrote the entire Integrative Pest Management Plan to find nontoxic ways of dealing with weeds and pests in the city of Boulder. The emotion and the passion we, as kids, brought played a role in getting them to take action. We realized that our size had nothing to do with our ability to effect change.

REIGNITING THE FLAME

Earth Guardians was starting to build momentum. We had a solid crew of kids who showed up every week to plan more dope actions. We met in my house, and, through fundraising, eventually saved enough money to get a little office space. We were designing presentations and speaking about the problems. Each youth had his or her own issue that they were passionate about, whether it was discussing the oceans, pesticides, or climate change. It was such an exciting time for me, because I felt so empowered by the local change that we were creating. It helped ease the pressure of the global crisis we were facing. The small changes and the small steps that we made in my community gave me hope for the future of the world. We were doing everything we could to help combat climate change at the local level. One example of this is an action we took to transition to renewable energy.

I was 11 years old when the Earth Guardians decided to help plan an action to close a local coal power plant. We figured that if we got enough attention and signatures from our community, we could permanently shut it down and keep it from polluting our city. We decided to join in on an international day of climate action, with 4,500 events being planned around the world, all being coordinated by 350.org. We organized with our local 350 Colorado leader, Micah Parkin, and other local groups, like the Rocky Mountain Peace and Justice Center, to make this action happen.

Early that morning, over a couple hundred people of all ages gathered at the Boulder bandshell on their bikes. Food not Bombs had agreed to come and give away free food to people before the long bike ride out to the coal plant. A huge crew of my friends and Earth Guardians showed up. We started off the ride alongside several hundred others. We had so many people, we took over a three-lane highway with all the bikes. We wanted this action to make lots of noise and draw attention from the media to help spread the word.

By the time we got to the coal plant, we were 500 strong. We had a huge rally there. I took to the megaphone to get people fired up about getting off coal and fossil fuels. As a symbolic gesture of the future of energy coming from the sun, we planted a bunch of sunflowers along the fence in front of the coal plant. We were stoked about how the event went. A bunch of media covered us the following day.

A couple of weeks after the action, employees from the coal plant

Biking to Coal Power Plant Action

had pulled all the sunflowers out of the ground and sprayed them with pesticides. We were all pretty upset. So, we went back to the EG headquarters to figure out how best to respond. We decided to have a funeral for the sunflowers, to bring attention to what the power plant had done. We made big coffins out of cardboard boxes, and painted them black. A few days later, we dressed in black and went back to the coal plant. A big crowd of supporters formed as we unloaded the coffins.

We gathered the dead sunflowers and placed them in the coffins and the lined them up along the fence. We gathered in a circle around the coffins of dead flowers and said prayers for our future and sang some songs. This action drew the attention of local media and spread the word to the general public. With this coverage and support, we spent the next several months helping to gather signatures for our petition. After a 7-year process, Boulder has finally phased out the burning of coal at the power plant.

One of the most important lessons I learned at a young age was that global change can begin in your local community, and from there, it can ripple out. This all started with me and some of my closest friends trying to make a difference. We always had fun with it. We didn't know every statistic about climate change, we didn't know every economic and political impact of a fossil fuel infrastructure, but what we did know is that our futures were impacted by the choices of our leaders and by the industries that threaten our communities. We felt as though we had a responsibility to do something about it. So, we did.

One of the benefits of fighting for a cause at a young age is that your ideas have no boundaries. It allows you to use your creativity and imagination to solve problems. We just followed our hearts and did what we thought was right. We didn't listen to anybody who was trying to tell us that we were too young or that our voices didn't matter.

I had to find my voice, discover a sense of urgency, and build my community to make an impact. To anyone who is just getting started: I encourage you to be brave about taking your first steps in using your voice for good. I often see that when we go beyond our comfort zones, the world meets us halfway. The voice of young people is going to be crucial in combating the challenges we face. Whether you're outspoken or shy, you have a role to play in this movement. We can't afford to let the scale of these problems swallow us up. We have to be hopeful. Even the greatest movements had humble beginnings, and it can often be helpful to start small. Find something that you're passionate about fighting for, and keep at it. Once you've found your direction, surround yourself with people who have similar ideas and want to put their skills into action. It's going to take effort from all of us.

CALL TO ACTION: PURSUE YOUR PASSION

The most excited I've ever been about being involved in making a difference is when it came from a place of doing what I love most. Finding ways to make a difference by using your passion brings joy and purpose into your work. Break free from the traditional tactics of activism and evaluate your skill set, as well as the unique and fresh perspective you could bring to the movement. Ask yourself, "What makes me feel alive?" Put your passion into a cause you want to put energy toward, and be creative with your solutions, meetings, events, and projects.

However serious or mature I may appear to be in front of the UN or while giving a TedTalk, I'm still just a 17-year-old kid trying to make a difference, while having a hell of a good time doing it. The events people are most likely to show up for and the crews and organizations people most want to be a part of are the ones that are different, outside the box, innovative, creative, and fun. Not everyone is an outspoken leader, a frontline fighter wanting to risk arrest, or even a skilled organizer, but everyone has a part to play, no matter how small it is. We all can be leaders in our own ways. I've learned that no matter your age, you've got to have fun and be inspired by the work you do. Transforming your passion into action is one of the best ways I've found to avoid burnout and feeling overwhelmed by the movement.

So write songs, design apps, build social media platforms, plant seeds, grow gardens, paint murals, and make the medicine the world needs. We need every piece, and there is something special within you.

For the parents: Help your kids connect with nature. We need a revolution, not just in the streets but in our homes as well. Our youth are growing up with no exposure to nature and no connection with the Earth. Because of this, an entire generation is numb to the realities of the world, disconnected from the beautiful web of life. We need to love something in order to want to protect it. If parents aren't fostering that love of the natural world, kids will lose the chance to resonate with and fall in love with all the beauty around them. You can expose your kids to nature in many different ways, from taking them to the park on a regular basis to going on hikes or walks in the mountains or around town. Get your children to museums to explore the intricacies of the world, spark their natural curiosity, and support them in growing fascinated by the world around them.

CHAPTER 3

Composing Revolution

Creative Passion into Action

"Art is the absence of fear."

—ERYKAH BADU

There are times in my life when I've felt lost within the chaos of move-ments. It's crazy how much is happening, and there is always more to do than there is time to do it. It can be overwhelming. At times like these, my music is my compass. It's the perfect outlet to transform the fears or sadness I feel about a world gone mad into a source of inspira-tion. There is something profound and empowering about song and dance that can't exactly be put into words. After I write something dope, it's as if the weight on my shoulders feels a little lighter. It's impossible to feel alone when I'm rocking out with my crew on stage, and the audi-ence is rocking with me.

It's no wonder that music has been used throughout history not only as an outlet but also as a tool to bring people together for a common purpose. From traditional ceremonies to modern religious practices, from social movements to national anthems, music has a power to form bonds and transform our understanding of the world. Music is both timeless and ever-present.

Rocking with My Homie Richard Wagner on Violin

MARCHING TO THE RHYTHM

For generations, social movements have co-evolved alongside music and art to create a unique flavor that defines that moment in time. When you think about the 1960s and 1970s, you think about songs that relate to peace and love. When Bob Marley was singing "One Love" or John Lennon was singing "Imagine," they used song to break down social barriers, and people of all walks of life were dancing and singing together in the streets. When Marvin Gaye was singing "What's Going On," people were calling for the end of the Vietnam War and questioning US imperialism. The songs fit with the movement of that time. They were a mirror that reflected the most important issues of that time and the hopes of the people.

Some of the greatest social movements in history happened during that time period, and the soundtrack played a vital role. Many of the iconic actions of the Civil Rights Movement were accompanied by powerful songs like "We Shall Overcome" or "Keep Your Eyes on the Prize." The movement was amplified by musical legends like Nina Simone, Joan Baez, Bob Dylan, Billie Holiday, Mahalia Jackson, John Coltrane, and Peter, Paul and Mary.

At the same time, an edgier counterculture music was arising from people like Gil Scott-Heron, whose 1970 song "The Revolution Will Not Be Televised" laid the foundation for a whole new genre of music. His rhythmic poetry was cool and revolutionary, but never commercial. Some would say these were the raw, real, and power-filled seeds for hip-hop music.

ROOTS OF HIP-HOP

While I appreciate all forms of music, I have always connected with hip-hop above all else. Its origins fascinate me. It tells the story of oppression, injustice, and hard times. It also shares a story of overcoming challenges and hope. Just think of the 1970s in the Bronx, where hip-hop was born. This was one of the most dangerous neighborhoods in the United States because of ongoing violence, poverty, and riots. It was not an easy place to grow up, to say the least, and very economically underdeveloped.

Much of the youth had no path, and many seemed destined for poverty, violence, drugs, and jail. One of the few places that they felt like they could make a difference was through avenues like music. As a melting pot of culture intersected, more and more people were speaking out through their talents. The DJs would spin records and have house parties and block parties where everybody would come together to dance and listen to music. Emcees started to spit lyrics at bars, clubs, and on street corners. The message spread, and people connected through music. It was a common denominator shared by all.

Hip-hop continued to grow and change. As the movement evolved, people came together to have rap battles and dance battles and introduced different art forms into the mix. Rappers have always been able to connect the audience to a different world. Sometimes, their expressions bought into the culture of materialism and violence imposed on them from childhood, and sometimes they broke through the surface to the roots of systemic oppression.

KRS-One, who emerged from the Bronx in the mid-1980s, is considered one of the architects of conscious hip-hop. He has always described hip-hop as a verb, not a noun. "Rap is something you do, hip-hop is something you live," he says. His name, which stands for "Knowledge Reigns Supreme Over Nearly Everyone," describes a part of his philosophy: To participate in hip-hop is to put knowledge into action.

The politically charged hip-hop of KRS-One and Public Enemy were among the forces that helped ignite the Golden Age of Hip-Hop in the early 1990s. They were fearless in the issues they would address, tackling topics such as the meat industry, war, and police violence. While many popular hip-hop artists, such as 2Pac, N.W.A., Nas, and Wu-Tang Clan, were considered gangsta rap, they continued to address social issues with their music. This art form was meant to connect with their reality, which included guns, drugs and violence, while offering a critical analysis of the world they had grown up in. The edgier music fit with an edgier movement feeling. Many actions in the 1990s were characterized by riots, angry protests, and the vibe of radical opposition. It was a sharp contrast to the peace and love messages of the 1960s.

This took an even more intense new form in pop culture decades later with the music of Rage Against the Machine, who combined political hip-hop with the antiauthoritarian angst of punk rock and metal. As people raged in the streets about corporate globalization and sweatshops, Rage was dropping the hit single "Guerrilla Radio." The popular music video begins in a sweatshop that mimics a Gap commercial, as the lyrics discuss the exploitation of the developing world. It was 1999, and the same year as the Battle of Seattle, a massive demonstration against the World Trade Organization.

The following year, Rage released another hit music video, directed by Michael Moore, "Sleep Now in the Fire," from the album *Battle of Los Angeles*. In the video, Rage Against the Machine was arrested for performing a free concert on the steps of the New York Stock Exchange, which temporarily shut down business for the day. In a way, the video foreshadowed Occupy Wall Street, exposing the inequities and the problems created by unchecked greed. It shouldn't be a surprise that many of the activists involved with the Occupy movement were inspired by the music of that generation, as the action was radical and anti-establishment. Tom Morello of Rage Against the Machine played multiple times for Occupy Wall Street, including a one-year anniversary show where his band performed the same song featured in the music video that may have inspired the movement.

The era ended in the early 2000s after the World Trade Center bombing. Politically controversial music like that from Rage Against the Machine began to be censored and banned from the radio. Political messages became muted. While people rallied in the streets against the Iraq War, there were only a few popular songs to represent the political climate of that moment. Some songs did break through into popular culture, like the Black Eyed Peas' "Where Is the Love," which was reminiscent of the musical messages of the '60s and '70s.

Hip-Hop Renaissance

As we look to these past examples, a new evolution of music with a message is beginning to emerge around us. Kendrick Lamar's chilling yet empowering song "Alright" speaks of the resilience of the black community to endure centuries of oppression and the current state of police violence. The main line in the song, "We gon' be alright," brings back memories of the chant "we shall overcome," repeated again and again during the Civil Rights Movement.

The same year, 2015, John Legend and Common released the song "Glory," which, like "Alright," bridged the gap between the Civil Rights Era and the modern one. The song was featured in the film *Selma*, which tells the story of the historic fight for voting rights in Alabama led by Dr. Martin Luther King, Jr., and the Student Nonviolent Coordinating Committee (SNCC).

The struggle continues, as the very same voting rights that King and others fought for are being stripped away. In 2013, the Supreme Court overturned the heart of the Voting Rights Act, saying it no longer applied. At that time, many Southern states were taking advantage of the lack of the federal legislation, passing laws to make it harder for minorities to vote.

Music remains a strong tool to understand oppression and combat it. Its ability to reach so many people who wouldn't otherwise get the message makes music a powerful avenue for creating change. Joey Bada$$, one of my favorite young hip-hop artists, is using his platform of millions of fans to talk about important issues. His new politically charged album, *All Amerikkkan Bada$$,* calls out America for turning its back on the black community and its continued oppression of people of color.

Facts and figures can only communicate so much. The power found in song and art is that, sometimes, you can break through an entrenched belief system and connect to the emotions beneath it. From that place of feeling moved, we as humans are able to re-evaluate our ideas and beliefs and develop new perspectives. That is why I use music as a medium for my message.

BREAKING FREE

My music has continued to evolve and become more than a tool for education. It has become a way to express my relationship with the world. I want the listener to understand what it's like to be a teenager taking on the fossil fuel industry and systemic oppression. I want them to see it through my eyes, but I also want them to deepen their own relationship with the subject.

By getting more personal and adding depth to my music, I believe I can connect with people on another level. The title track of my new album *Break Free* exemplifies this new approach:

Performing "Break Free" at YOUTHvGOV Rally

To break free is our only choice,
we march through the streets
silence overpowers the noise
don't let your greatness die
within you
chain me to these pipelines
black lives, indigenous
rights, connected lifelines.
Break free from your
suffering, don't let it change
you,
leave it in the past, know that
stronger is all that made you.

I want people to feel the song, not just listen to it. I want it to evoke emotion that dances the line between "damn, this world is messed up," and "damn, we are so powerful that we can change all this." There is a feeling that we're all in this together. Maybe that's what can save us—that deep humanity that only true expression can uncover.

IGNITING A MOVEMENT

Music is one of the tools that has helped Earth Guardians spread to every corner of the globe. As we traveled, using music to tell our story, people were signing up to start Earth Guardian crews, which are kind of like local chapters of the organization. They were popping up everywhere, in places like New Zealand, Togo, and Bhutan. The global expansion of our organization changed our approach. We created global days of action called Protect Our Future, which allows Earth Guardians to coordinate and highlight particular issues. It took a tremendous weight off of my shoulders when I heard the stories of what other young people on the ground were doing. I began to realize that there were kids like me around the world building the movement and doing incredible things in their cities.

Being engaged felt isolating at times, until I saw the young people who were as passionate as I was joining our movement. The traveling, performing, and giving presentations were beginning to connect a global community of young people primed for action. After every speaking gig or every college that I visited, there was always a group of youths that came up to me afterward and said, "I want to get involved." More and more people began to connect with us and develop a platform for creating change and generating solutions.

Everytime we held a global day of action, incredible stories would come back to us from around the world: In Togo and Ghana, an Earth Guardians crew planted more than 10,000 trees in 2016. In Norway, the Earth Guardian crew is fighting against a recent countrywide plan to kill more than two-thirds of its wolf population living in the wilderness. The Puerto Rico Earth Guardian crew is working to protect their beloved water and marine life, fighting against the use of disposable plastics.

There are hundreds of Earth Guardian crews across the world in more than 30 countries. The seeds that were planted in 1992 when my older siblings and my mom started Earth Guardians in Hawaii were blowing up everywhere and beginning to take root. This was no longer about me and my crew. This was about a global movement of young people on the rise. In a world thirsting for inspiration, this was a much-needed rain in the middle of a drought. Young people were beginning to show the world what was possible. It's incredible how a tiny seed can turn into a giant tree. The energy and intention was there, we just needed to figure out how to direct it. To solve the problems that we saw in the world, we needed to examine the root.

I found myself reflecting on how we got to this point. The impact of climate change did not happen overnight, it was the culmination of hundreds of years of neglect. It is the result of big business, consumer choices, and the corruption of our leaders. If we are to use our creativity and passion to compose revolution, we have to first understand the crisis, and then move the needle toward transformation.

CALL TO ACTION: START YOUR OWN CREW

One of the most important things you can do to spread your message and find your purpose is to find your community. You can help to shift the entire world when you find your activist family. It's important to find people who resonate with your values and are doing something about the injustices in the world that put those very values at risk. Crews are the heart and soul of the Earth Guardians movement. The first step to starting a crew is to sign up on our web site at www.EarthGuardians.org/crews. Once you sign up, you will receive a welcome packet and be asked to agree to our values and principles before getting your crew started.

Once you have a crew, you will be connected to the global Earth Guardians network and be invited to participate in global actions like the Protect Our Future campaign. Below are some tips to get started.

1. Figure out what issue needs attention in your community.

- Identify social and environmental issues and opportunities that light you up.

- Read the local newspaper.
- Focus on current events, political news, and the community spotlight sections to identify the issues and the people involved.
- Attend community meetings (from neighborhood potlucks to city council meetings).
- Reach out to folks who have been involved since the beginning. Ask them to mentor you—intergenerational relationships provide killer resources.

2. Build your crew.

A crew can be as small as you and your siblings or as big as your entire school district. Get your family and friends on board. Engage existing groups who share your focus. Team up. Collaborate.

3. Get social.

Connect with other Earth Guardians and spread the message with the world on social media. **Use these hashtags online:** #EarthGuardians, #GenerationRYSE, # #ProtectOurFuture

- Build a Facebook page for your crew, and on Twitter, Instagram and whatever your Social Media choices are.
- Post pics of your crew and your projects, and share news and ways to engage on our page.

4. Host your first meeting.

Start with one goal (e.g., turn our school into a zero-waste facility).

- What will completing that goal look like?
- Map out an action plan.
- What steps can you take to reach your goal?
- Look for ways that incorporate the skills and passions of your crew.
- Empower your crewmembers to take initiative in areas that inspire them.

Remember: Leaders create leaders. Set a meeting schedule and stick to it.

5. Mobilize your community.

Organize your first community event. We've seen crews hold press conferences and marches to get publicity and membership. We've also seen crews hop right into community actions like tree-planting parties, litter pickup events, and net-zero days. Don't let our framework limit you. We've seen crews tackle big, innovative, long-term projects.

Find out more at Earthguardians.org/crews.

POETRY IN MOTION

An Interview with Kathy Jetnil-Kijiner

Kathy Jetnil Kijiner is an activist and poet from the Marshall Islands. Her most famous poem, "Dear Matafele Peinem," is a work she wrote for her then seven-month-old daughter, explaining to her the never-ending battle to combat climate change. She recited this poem to the United Nations, inspiring and moving the audience to protect our climate to save our children. She started writing poetry when she was just a little child, and poetry is now her chosen language to influence the hearts and souls of those around her. She continues to fight for our planet, starting a nonprofit organization for youth and the environment.

ME: I just want to ask you about your poetry. I think it has moved people all around the world. When did you start writing poetry?

KATHY: I began writing poetry in the 3rd or 4th grade. I just did it to understand the world around me. I think it flows out of me really naturally. I kept writing, just on my own, and didn't really share it with anyone until I got into creative writing courses and stuff. I began to do spoken word when I was a senior, and that's when I saw the potential for sharing and amplifying stories that I see. There are no books of poetry from my island right now. At the time, I didn't grow up knowing many islanders who were writing. I didn't really get to see myself in any of the stories or in any of the media around me. Poetry was really my way of trying to share those stories that I found to be important.

Once I got into spoken word, I got into Poetry for the People when I moved to California for college. There, I was taught that poetry should have a purpose and that it should speak to movements and people. I learned it could speak to our struggles as people of color. In that same kind of line, it was really kind of natural, especially when I moved back home to the Marshall Islands. It was really natural for me to start writing about climate change as the new struggle that our people were facing. It was the latest threat. Yeah, it's really stories that I feel that people don't know, or not enough people know about. Stories that I think are important, but mostly stories of my people that really inspire me.

ME: Awesome, thank you for sharing. I think the speech that you gave at the United Nations really made a difference in the way the world viewed climate change. I think it humanized it. Why do you think people resonated with your story, your perspective, and your words?

KATHY: I think it's exactly what you said. I humanized it. I mean, up until that point, it had been a lot of statistics, it had been a lot of numbers and research and politics that were always at the forefront of the discussion, in my opinion. Yes, we have had speakers from before who were moved by it. But, that's what's really interesting about poetry, right? It's not just that I had a story . . . it was the way I told that story. I think it was the fact that it was poetry, and poetry, when you write it well and you're able to write it, can connect people to an issue.

I think with such a big issue, such as climate change, poetry forces you to slow down. You are aware of every single word that you use in poetry. That awareness, when you bring it to such a huge issue, makes it seem like less of a huge issue. It brings you down to the ground level. There's that, but then there's also, of course, the fact that I'm writing to my daughter. So many of those people in that room, they're older and they're parents or they're grandparents. They've connected with children at some point in their lives. They've been children.

So, the real factor that pushed it over the edge was the fact that I was speaking to my daughter and promising to fight for her, and putting her as the face that we were fighting for. It's so easy to fight for a child, right? We can see that children connect us on another level. What was really cool, that I noticed after I performed, was that before it was such a cold space, but later, after I performed, I was in this cafeteria-like area where everybody was eating after the presentation. Everybody was coming up to me and not just complimenting me, but asking to hold my daughter and telling me about their kids and telling me how much they missed their kids. It just changed the whole conversation. Suddenly, we weren't diplomats, we weren't fighting, and we weren't politicians. They were just parents, too. I think that's another way that the poem had impact.

ME: What message do you have for the next generation of climate leaders?

KATHY: Oh, man. I don't know if I have any words of wisdom. I'm still trying to figure it out. It's hard to figure out. This thing is scary. I was just reading an article that all these scientists have come together to predict that the worst of climate change is about to hit the Pacific in 3 years or 4, which is like 20 or so years before it hits everywhere else. That just really freaks me out, and I'm still processing it. I haven't really figured it out. It's interesting, because I found a youth-oriented organization back in the Marshall Islands. We just did this whole restructuring and training with another nonprofit to help us figure out that nonprofit. We figured out, after talking with them and really processing it, that it wasn't really an environmentalist program, it was a youth environmentalist program, which really changes how I saw it. It made me realize that, yeah, it's really young people that I'm invested in. As you said, I see them as the leaders. They're so passionate and creative. I guess some people would count me as still a young person, but I kind of don't.

I guess the most important thing is to not lose hope, because, once you lose hope, you lose the battle, right? That's it. How are you going to fight if you don't have hope? How are you going to have the energy to go through the daily fight, the daily struggle? It takes so much of your energy and your spirit to fight this fight, and, without that hope, you just won't have the energy to keep moving forward. Yeah, I guess you have to find ways to keep that hope alive. Search for it. I remember after Trump won, man, I had to search for that hope. That was hard. I had to look everywhere to find that hope. I feel like that's probably the most important thing in this struggle, is just maintaining that hope to keep going forward.

ME: What gives you hope?

KATHY: Well, definitely, my baby helps a lot. She loses her shit over bubbles, right? Like, bubbles. She just loves it. The cherry blossoms are in bloom out here, and she totally thinking, "Oh my god, it's snowing flowers." It was just this amazing thing to her. That definitely gives me hope. Just the fact that she can still stare at the world in wonder. That there's still ways to stare at the world in wonder. There's that, but then, besides that, my elders actually give me a lot of hope. There's a woman who I cite a lot in my work. She is a nuclear survivor. She survived the testing of nuclear weapons by the United States on our island. She's had so many miscarriages, and she's so elderly now, and she's had thyroid cancer, and she's lost almost all her family to cancer . . . and she still fights. She still speaks out. She still talks about her experiences and shares her stories. I'm like, man, I have no excuse to not keep fighting. That's definitely those two factors. It's our youth and our elders that give me hope.

ME: Perfect. Beautiful balance there. You've given us a glimpse of what it's like to live on the front lines of climate change. From hearing what you're saying, it's only going to intensify. What is the thing that you most want people to know about the struggle of your people to defend your home?

KATHY: I've been trying to convey to a lot of journalists the importance of land to our culture and how we can't lose that land, because if we lose that land, we lose ourselves, we lose our identity, we lose our roots. Not many people seem to understand that, and it's been kind of hard to really convey it. It has to be like, "Well, explain why you can't just move?" It's like, "Yeah, of course, we can move. But, I want to go back home to my island that is still there."

There's a difference between being exiled and not ever being able to return and just temporarily living away. I guess there's that. What else is there that I would want people to know? Yeah, that land is so important. We would be definitely some of the first to go. We would definitely be some of the first to leave our land. I guess one other thing is that we've felt the pain and loss of losing our island. I felt the pain of losing my culture and identity because of the fact that I was raised in the states, and I lost a lot of language. I had to work really hard, and I'm still working really hard, to this day, to regain all of it. I guess I don't want anybody else to experience that.

We've already lost our islands to nuclear testing. The nuclear testing evaporated our islands. Literally, on the spot. A lot of the islanders can never go back home. We've already felt the pain and loss of some of our islands near my home, and we just don't want to have to feel that anymore with the rest of our islands that remain. I guess that, and mainly just the fact that we are completely rooted to the land. I don't know how to demonstrate that to people, how to really convey that sense of loss that could happen. Yeah, I guess that would be it."

CHAPTER 4

Moving from Crisis to Opportunity

How Did We Get Here?

When I woke up on the morning of November 9, 2016, with the news of Trump's presidency, it felt like awakening to a bunch of ice water being dumped on my head. The feeling sucked, but I knew it could wake us up. For many of us who care about human rights and important social issues, such as climate change, it was shocking. The feeling was awful, but I think something this alarming is necessary to wake people up and get them to face the challenges we can no longer wait to address.

The following day, more than three million people marched in the streets, standing with women and vulnerable communities threatened by a Trump administration. As I marched with my own crew, we walked alongside people who had never taken this kind of action before. In the weeks and months to follow, hundreds of protests demonstrated opposition to a president who denies climate change and threatens the rights of marginalized communities. The resistance was growing, and it became clear to many that sitting on the sidelines of this movement was a danger that we could no longer afford.

The fact is that we had been sleeping for far too long. Our alarm was going off for years, and we failed to answer the wake-up call. Evidence of a changing planet has continued to mount. In 1988, James E. Hansen, former director of the Goddard Space Flight Center for NASA, warned us during a congressional hearing that "scientific evidence is telling us we have a problem . . . a serious problem." He was referring to climate change, an issue that few were talking about at the time. This was the first time we hit the snooze button on climate change.

That was almost 30 years ago, and, since then, the alarm has continued to buzz with greater frequency. Just look at the past 8 years. In 2010, the BP oil spill in the Gulf lasted nearly 3 months and dumped more than 200 million gallons of oil into the ocean, devastating wildlife and impacting the overall health of those on the coast. We've seen hundreds of oil pipeline spills, and the impact of fossil fuels on the climate is becoming more and more evident each year.

Then in 2012, Hurricane Sandy ravaged the East Coast, killing more than 150 people and becoming the second costliest storm in United States history. Scientists believe that Arctic Sea ice melt, in addition to warming ocean temperatures, increased the severity of that storm.

It seemed easy to stay asleep, especially with a president like Barack Obama in the White House. Based on the things he said during his campaign, many thought he would be our champion. When elected, he told us, "This was the moment when the rise of the oceans began to slow and our planet began to heal."

Obama took some meaningful steps while in office. He helped put into place laws that require passenger cars to double fuel economy by 2025, which was a step forward that Donald Trump has now reversed. Obama's administration used the stimulus plan to invest heavily in renewable energy jobs. He rejected the Keystone XL Pipeline and sent the Dakota Access Pipeline back for review. He signed the Paris Climate Accord. Despite his efforts, these actions did not add up to enough, and Congress sought to block him every step of the way.

However, there was another side to Obama's climate policy. He embraced an all-of-the-above energy strategy. In his speech he gave in Cushing, Oklahoma, in March 2012, he seemed to be courting the fossil fuel industry. The speech was held in front of a row of piping, while Obama celebrated the building of the southern leg of Keystone XL. He said, "Now, under my administration, America is producing more oil today than at any time in the last 8 years [applause]. That's important to know. Over the last 3 years, I've directed my administration to open up millions of acres for gas and oil exploration across 23 different states. We're opening up more than 75 percent of our potential oil resources offshore. We've quadrupled the number of operating rigs to a record high. We've added enough new oil and gas pipeline to encircle the Earth and then some."

While the sentiment is that our present leadership in the White House is taking us in the completely opposite direction, we haven't been headed in the right direction for quite some time. Trump said that he believes climate change is a hoax, made up by the Chinese. He appointed climate deniers to crucial posts, like Scott Pruitt as the EPA Administrator and Rick Perry as the Secretary of Energy. Studies show that our current President's climate views and that of his administration not only run counter to science, they are also not aligned with public opinion. Seven in 10 Americans think that climate change is actually happening. Sixty-two percent of voters surveyed by Yale and George Mason universities shortly after the election said that they want Trump to do more to address climate change.

They say the ocean recedes before a giant swell, so maybe we are finally ready to take action like never before. Maybe we needed this wake-up call at this precise moment, because we are running out of time. We're up against the limits of what the world can handle, and the scientific community is officially beginning to freak out with an administration that doesn't recognize basic science. Here are a few of the things they said following the election.

Jennifer Francis, sea ice researcher at Rutgers University: "If President Trump acts on statements he made during the campaign, we are likely to see any federal efforts to curtail fossil fuel burning go up in smoke. . . . Mother Nature did her share to influence this election by dishing up a smorgasbord of record-breaking heat, flooding, drought, and storms—yet, climate change was a nonissue."

Jacquelyn Gill, paleoecologist at the University of Maine: "We have just elected the only climate-denying president in the free world, with a Young Earth Creationist vice-president."

Neil deGrasse Tyson, award-winning astrophysicist and host of Cosmos: "When I meet President Trump, I may first grab his crotch—to get his attention—and then discuss science with him."

Michael Mann, paleoclimate researcher at Penn State University: "[Trump's] building a wall between himself and the evidence of climate change."

We aren't just hearing these concerns from the scientific community. Following the election of Trump, we have seen a groundswell of local political demonstrations. From San Diego to Washington, D.C., to New York to countrywide "Not My President's Day" rallies and town hall meetings, people are standing up in unprecedented numbers to this administration. At a time when the world needs us the most, we are finally awake and ready to jump into action. Electing a president who denies the science of climate change has caused people to realize that we can't stand on the sidelines any longer, while the government strips us of our rights and threatens our future.

We are continuing to see the connections between issues. Studies have concluded that the war in Syria that has killed hundreds of thousands owes its origins at least in part to climate change. A report from the National Academy of Sciences shows how extreme heat and severe drought worsened by climate change drove 1.5 million rural farmers from their homes into Syria's overcrowded cities. Trump's travel ban and Islamaphobic policies attempted to keep the same people fleeing this war from finding refuge in the United States, while he is enacting policies that are likely to create more refugees. If there is a silver lining to all of this, it's that, in the face of this crisis, we're beginning to come together in a way that we never have before.

THE HIDDEN AGENDAS: HOW BIG BUSINESS IS ATTACKING OUR VERY EXISTENCE

Climate change didn't occur overnight. It's the result of hundreds of years of harmful choices and bottom-line practices of businesses operating in the United States and all over the world. The climate crisis began way before people were even aware of it. The Earth's temperature is regulated by a perfect atmospheric composition, which allows the right amount of heat to enter and exit. Since the Industrial Revolution, we have begun to change that atmospheric balance. The use of fossil fuels and industrial agriculture has resulted in the increase of heat-trapping in our atmosphere, causing warmer temperatures and a host of environmental problems.

As time passed, big business increased in size and scale. Industrial factory farming, which produces a substantial carbon footprint replaced local agriculture. Big fossil fuel–guzzling SUVs replaced bicycles, walking, and horseback riding. Maybe most impactful, though, is that traditional and indigenous wisdom that has now been replaced with a cultural disconnection and attitude that more is never enough. We live in a world that teaches us that we should take as much as we can with the little time we have. We can see examples of this in the colonization of the Americas and Africa in the late 15th and early 16th centuries, where resources were extracted and sent back to the motherland to amass wealth. Meanwhile, indigenous peoples were treated as expendable on their very own land.

Big corporations have been aware of their impact for a long time, but fail to take responsibility. Documents show that ExxonMobil knew about the dangers of climate change since 1977. In the 1980s, they helped form a powerful corporate group to spread information questioning climate science. Since then, billions of dollars have been spent on a public-relations campaign to make the general public question climate science and billions more on a legislative agenda to block climate policy. They hired the same PR firm that the tobacco industry hired to convince people that smoking was not bad for your health and didn't cause cancer. They cooked up a similar public-relations strategy to deceive the public, by attempting to counter the scientific consensus that climate change is man-made and is a serious threat.

The line has been blurred by the connections between big business and politics. Politicians are heading where the money is when it comes to their beliefs, their policies, and, sadly, their votes. In 2010, the United States Supreme Court case, *Citizens United v. Federal Election Commission*, opened the floodgates for money in politics, by deciding corporations could give unlimited campaign contributions. This gives an incredible amount of influence to big polluters, like the American Petroleum Institute, so that they can spend as much as they like without a requirement for disclosure.

The decision comes from the legal distinction giving corporations the same rights as people, which protects their freedom of speech under the US constitution. This is intuitively ridiculous, because they are not, in fact, people. They lack a human heart, empathy, and, unfortunately, they don't die from old age. In addition, these corporations are afforded many of the rights of human beings without bearing any of the responsibility. For instance, people go to jail when they commit a crime. But, when corporations violate the laws of this land, they are rarely held accountable for their actions.

Big business has used this gaping loophole to make politicians increasingly beholden to their interests above those of the American people. More often than not, you can follow the money on campaign contributions and see which way representatives will vote. It is not just the climate that is broken, it's our political system made for and by the wealthy and powerful. It can make us feel hopeless at times, but we are doing everything in our power to change that and reclaim our democracy.

THE TRIAL OF THE MILLENNIUM: CHALLENGING THE GOVERNMENT TO PROTECT DEMOCRACY

In 2016, I was featured in *Teen Vogue* magazine. They asked me the question: "Do you love America?" It was a complicated question for me to answer. It's hard for me to have love for a country that was founded on slavery, genocide, and the continued oppression of people of color. As I thought through it more, I realized that I'm incredibly inspired by the potential that this country has to really influence the world in a positive direction. The fundamental principles of democracy rely on standing to

Speaking at the Supreme Court in Washington, DC

hold the government accountable when they fail to represent the voices of their constituents. In fact, if we are really trying to make an impact, we need democracy now more than ever. A lot of the work to change a broken system has to come from within. To play my role in creating that shift, I decided to join a constitutional climate recovery lawsuit against the president of the United States and the executive branch of the federal government.

As I looked around, frustrated by politics and big business, I started to see that corporate influence is eroding our democracy. I believe that as activists in this country it is important to know when to use the existing systems to create change. We had an opportunity to do so from the inside out and infiltrate the system to demand that our government uphold our interests.

Climate change is the crisis of our century and of our generation, but politicians continue to ignore the urgency of the problem. Things have gotten to the point where we need a different course of action. So I jumped at the opportunity to join Our Children's Trust (OCT) in using our legal system to hold our governments accountable for their inaction on climate change. OCT is elevating the voices of youth, to secure the legal right to a healthy atmosphere and stable climate on behalf of present and future generations. They are leading a campaign to implement enforceable science-based Climate Recovery Plans that will return atmospheric carbon dioxide concentration to below 350 ppm by the year 2100. Twenty young people and I joined the federal lawsuit that OCT supports, challenging the actions of the US president and the US government that have caused the climate crisis and violated our constitutional rights. We are demanding that the federal government take science-based action against climate change before it is too late.

We filed this lawsuit in the US District Court for the District of Oregon in 2015. We are alleging that the US government has actually known about the existence of climate change for far too long, and even with the knowledge of all that they would destroy, they kept a promoting a fossil-fuel–based energy system, even when the alternatives for energy were at their fingertips. Their actions promoting and supporting the fossil fuel industry infringes upon our constitutional rights to life, liberty, and private and public property. Those actions also violate the government's public trust obligation to preserve essential natural resources for the benefit of present *and* future generations. Our government is taking away our constitutional rights because of their support of the industries that have created this crisis. We fought numerous motions that were filed by the most powerful fossil-fuel companies and the US government. They combined their endless resources to argue that these suits should be thrown out of court. They claimed we did not have legal grounds to hold them accountable for their actions.

All the plaintiffs traveled to Eugene, Oregon, to attend both of the big court hearings in 2016 and listen to the arguments. It was amazing to see kids between the ages of 8 and 20 intently listening in on the hearing. We wanted the judge to see who we were, so he could put a face to this lawsuit. Each kid had their own unique story linking them to climate change. I remember listening to 9-year-old Levi from Florida speak about how rising sea levels are going to wash away his home. Our heartfelt stories were sources of inspiration, as people saw us taking a stand for our future.

Our personal narratives gave life to the lawsuit, making it more than just a legal argument. The science shows the importance of the transition away from a fossil-fuel–based economy to reduce our greenhouse gas emissions, but human stories give that data life. If we win, we hope the court

Lobbying Congress

will force the federal government to implement a national Climate Recovery Plan to reduce greenhouse gas emissions from the United States so carbon dioxide concentrations in the atmosphere come down from levels over 400 parts per million now, to below 350 parts per million by the year 2100. It is an ambitious goal, but only through substantial action will we prevent catastrophic damage. This is just one example of the power and the will of the youth.

Just 2 days after Trump was elected, the presiding judge in Eugene eventually denied the federal government's motion to dismiss the case. The lawsuit would proceed. On that day, 21 youth prevailed over a multibillion-dollar fossil-fuel industry, supported by one of the most powerful governments on Planet Earth. We filed this lawsuit so people would understand the terrible threat that climate change presents to my generation and to seek a solution. We need to see our government held accountable for the infringement of our rights. We are aiming to have this case come to trial by the fall of 2017. The federal government will find itself on trial for the first time for their role in creating the climate crisis.

Donald Trump is now sitting in the defense chair. His administration is doing everything possible to block us and has even resorted to desperate measures. In June 2017 they filed for a *writ of mandamus* in the Ninth Circuit Court of Appeals. This meant they are asking the higher court to overrule the decision made by the District Court to allow the case to move forward, arguing that it's improper for the "judiciary to decide important questions of energy and environmental policy." Clearly they skipped the political science class where the teacher talked about the separation of powers. One guy who didn't skip that class is Supreme Court Justice Anthony Kennedy. He said a *writ of mandamus* is a "drastic and extraordinary remedy" reserved for "only exceptional circumstances."

We are clearly up against a lot this time, but I find my inspiration from past movements. Throughout history, we've seen people overcome the odds to achieve change previously thought impossible. We've seen empires fall and independence achieved. We've seen oppressive systems abolished and rights reclaimed. People would laugh and call you crazy if you told them 100 years ago that the United States would legalize gay marriage and elect a black president. I also find faith from my own generation; we are motivated and more progressive than ever. Our future hangs in the balance with climate change. So, what better time than now to make a change once thought impossible?

CALL TO ACTION:
BECOME A POLITICAL WARRIOR

If 21 youth leaders can take on both the government and the oil and gas industry in a landmark climate lawsuit, then we have more power than we previously imagined. Young people have the potential to create enormous change. Our political system has been infiltrated by huge amounts of money and we have a responsibility to do our part to bring the power back to the people. The first step in combating a corrupt political system is to make sure we're all paying attention.

First, organize to demand money out of politics. We have to know who is representing our voices. Familiarize yourself with your local and congressional elected officials. An easy way to do this is through the Countable App, which allows you to see who your representatives are, how they vote on certain issues, and even lets you contact them to express your opinions. The fight can begin on the local level where officials are often more accessible.

Then, support candidates who are willing to get money out of politics. The best measure I have found is National Intervention's sobriety test, which finds "sober" candidates who are willing to support anticorruption laws and publicly funded elections. After you've figured out who your elected officials are, you can then use National Intervention's tools to send the sobriety test to your candidates and see which ones are willing to adopt the pledge. Text SOBER to 1-202-600-2653 to get started. Organize your friends, family, and community members to advocate for candidates willing to represent the people and not corporate interests.

Second, resist injustice. Once you've figured out which candidates are committed to getting money out of politics, engage your community in pressuring other candidates to do the same. Ways you can do this include attending and asking questions at their town hall meetings, starting a letter-writing campaign, placing phone calls to their local office, and partnering with the nonprofit organization Indivisible to make sure our rights are protected. Indivisible provides a guide to help you resist Donald Trump's corporate agenda and hosts events and rallies around the country. Localizing political power is an important piece of reclaiming our democracy.

PART II

✕

THE MOVEMENTS AND OUR OPPORTUNITY TO TURN THE TIDE

"We owe it to future generations to be the leaders of today so that they can have a tomorrow."

—Xiuhtezcatl Tonatiuh

CHAPTER 5

Holding Back the Sea
Confronting the Climate Crisis

*"I am not a scientist, but I don't need to be.
Because the world's scientific community has spoken, and
they have given us our prognosis, if we do
not act together, we will surely perish."*

—LEONARDO DICAPRIO

For far too long, we have lived a lifestyle that attacks the very planet that sustains us, leaving our chances for survival in the balance. If we keep this up, we will become footnotes in history, like the dinosaurs before us. Unlike them, we have the opportunity to determine our own fate. The Earth will survive, but without swift action, it will look completely different from the one we've grown to know.

The world is changing right before our eyes. Floods, wildfires, hurricanes, tornadoes, earthquakes, loss of sea ice, the accelerated rise of sea levels, intense heatwaves, and droughts are some of the many frightening effects of climate change. These are no longer solely acts of nature; they are impacted by what we are doing as humans. Even if we do survive this new extreme world, we'd experience a lifestyle filled with constant threats, vulnerability, and a tremendous shortage of natural resources.

We still have an opportunity to shift the trend, but if we don't, all other concerns will become obsolete. Speaking with author and founder of 350.org, Bill McKibben, I began to see that climate change is more than just an issue; it's a lens to view all the issues we face. Everything from our economies to our energy and food systems contributes to a changing atmosphere and is impacted by climate instability. Climate change is what brings all issues together.

The United Nations estimates that 25 million people—about the population of Australia—are currently displaced by natural disasters and other consequences of climate change. The number is steadily growing and is currently larger than the number of people displaced by war. The Red Cross estimates that we will reach 250 million people displaced by the year 2050. There are 7.2 billion people on the planet, so that's 1 in 30 who will be left without a home. Denying climate change is like denying the reality of war. They are both direct attacks on human lives everywhere, yet for some reason we seem to regularly talk about one, and give little attention to the other.

Imagine the global response if one single threat to our existence that isn't as politically polarizing as climate change endangered such a large portion of the world's population. Communities around the world would pool their collective resources in an effort to eliminate that threat, regardless of the cost. However, politicians and corporations continue to operate with a business-as-usual mentality. As long as money is flowing into the corporate boardrooms, they'll put profits before people and progress before the planet. Even then, we cannot just point fingers at big business and crooked politicians, because we have all played a role.

THE UNNATURAL DISASTER

Kathy, the amazing poet who addressed the United Nations the year before me, painted a graphic picture of the feeling of her home being swallowed by water. If global temperatures were to reach just 4° Celsius, it's likely that water would submerge 10 percent of the world's homes. The people most impacted by this catastrophic sea level rise look more like Kathy than the oil and gas billionaires and bankers most responsible for the greenhouse gases in the atmosphere. Those on the front lines of climate change are mostly poor people of color. The communities that have contributed the least to the problem often bear the greatest impacts. Climate change isn't just an environmental issue; it's also a race and poverty issue.

The people who live by the coast aren't the only ones impacted. My home state of Colorado resides 1 mile above sea level. Growing up there, I experienced my own wake-up call about how close to home climate change can be. What scientists call the pine beetle epidemic is one of the biggest impacts we see from climate change in my part of the country. This small insect is eating its way through millions of acres of pine forest. The pine beetle is native to Colorado, but warmer temperatures have allowed the population of these insects to expand, because warming winters are not killing them off at the same rate. We've seen more than 60 million acres of forest die off from New Mexico to British Columbia. In Colorado alone, we have lost more than 70 percent of our lodge pole pines. Many places I used to love to go hiking in the forest as a kid are now dead and won't support a thriving ecosystem for decades.

These swaths of dead trees are the perfect starter for rapidly spreading wildfires. Since I was little, wildfires have been a regular occurrence in Colorado. As I got older, they began to increase in frequency and severity. A good friend of mine lived up in the mountains in Sunshine Canyon. We used to go to his home to play and hang out. But then, the wildfires hit, and just like that, his house was nothing but the concrete foundation. He told me that as the wildfires spread in the direction of his house, they got their dogs, their favorite Legos, and a few prized possessions and just left. They were under a mandatory evacuation. It was intense to return to their home after the fires and see the scorched ground where we used to sleep over and eat blueberry pancakes for breakfast.

Wildfires also continue to increase in Colorado and across the country because of drought and hotter summers. Throughout my childhood, Colorado was constantly breaking records for the worst wildfires in the history of the state. In 2013, we had the worst wildfire on record. If that didn't wake us up, then the worst flood on record 3 months later should have. These disasters destroyed more of our friends' homes,

killed Coloradans, and stranded others who had to be rescued by heli-
copters as they were surrounded by floodwaters. For me, this is more
than a political issue—it is about our survival. It threatens my community and is deeply personal.

If we look around the country, we see similar trends occurring. During the first 34 days of 2017, there were 2,459 wildfires burning about
55,000 acres. On May 1, 2016, a wildfire broke out in Fort McMurray in
Alberta, Canada. This fire was the costliest Canadian natural disaster
ever, with 1,600 buildings destroyed. The fire took two lives, and they
evacuated the entire population of about 90,000. The smoke from the
fire could be seen as far south as Iowa. The unstable climate is setting
the wrong kind of records each year.

It turns out that at the same time climate change is increasing the
frequency of wildfires, it is also bringing more floods. Warmer air holds
more moisture, and over the past 25 years, heavy rainfall events have
increased by 20 percent. Superstorms are also causing more destruction
than ever. Warmer seawater surface temperatures allow storms to maintain and gain speed, causing more destruction when they hit land. Rising sea levels will only increase the damage done by these storms.

No matter how long you've been involved with this movement, the
reality of the situation doesn't get any easier to cope with. A lot of people
would rather turn the other way than face it, but for those like Kathy on
the front lines of climate change, that's simply not an option. For people
like her, resistance is their existence. I recently spoke with the President
of Kiribati, a South Pacific Island, on Al Jazeera's *The Stream*. He shared
with me that his island nation has already suffered significantly from
sea level rise and told me one of the most powerful examples of human
resilience I've heard. He expressed to me that, for his people, "it is too
late." Climate change has submerged his community, has displaced people and taken its toll on Kiribati. Even though his country is likely
beyond recovery, he was not going to stop fighting "to ensure the safety
of these young people and future generations." Kiribati is one of the low-
est carbon-emitting countries on the planet, yet they are fighting to do
their part to make sure that the rest of us don't suffer the way they have.

A large number of the Pacific Islands are projected to be completely
submerged under water in just the next 100 years. But, they are taking

a stand with the message: "We are not drowning. We are fighting." Native warriors are rising peacefully to protect the Pacific Islands from climate change. One of those leaders, Fenton Lutunatabua from Fiji, who helped found 350 Pacific, was also on *The Stream* with me. He went on a tour across 13 different Island nations endangered by climate change, and in every place, he listened to the stories and concerns of young people. He found that, everywhere he went, people had a strong spiritual connection to warrior culture symbolized by the canoe. Together he and other island leaders founded the group Pacific Climate Warriors.

For a year-and-a-half, the group organized climate warrior trainings across the Pacific, and out of these came an action that would help redefine frontline climate leadership. Before travelling to Australia, they spent 2 weeks in intensive workshops to get ready for this action. Once they were prepared, they put a call out for people to join them:

> This journey will be epic. From across 13 Pacific Islands, our Pacific Warriors will travel to Australia, carrying with us traditional hand-made canoes decorated with symbols of support from our homelands. We will use these canoes to lay down a challenge to the fossil fuel industry, and to highlight what we will lose if their reckless contribution to climate change continues. This will be a means of telling the industry, the Australian public, their government, and the global community that climate change is having a real impact and is threatening the culture, health, and environment of our Pacific Islands.

Their first action when they arrived in Australia was to acknowledge and connect with the aboriginal people of that land, who have long been oppressed by the Australian government. This was powerful, because in Australia (like many places around the world), indigenous voices have been sidelined. When it comes to climate change, wealthy and white voices often dominate the conversation and often leave out important issues like indigenous sovereignty.

On October 17, 2014, the morning of the action, the aboriginal people and Pacific Climate Warriors led a ceremony together connecting their struggles. The Pacific Climate Warriors used their traditional hand-made canoes to blockade the largest coal export facility in the world, the Port of Newcastle. My friend Joshua Kahn Russell, who was there, described the scene: "We're in this port where these gigantic, sort of Death Star like vessels, these coal ships . . . I don't even know how to describe how enormous they felt in person, but dozens of them would go through the port each day."

The warriors took to the waters first, steering their canoes to block the massive coal ships from leaving the port. They were followed by hundreds of Australians in kayaks, many from the grass roots direct action group Rising Tide. Imagine hand-carved canoes and tiny kayaks staring down a coal ship the size of the Empire State Building. The police, who were on Jet Skis and boats, were literally ramming and cap-sizing canoes intentionally.

My friend Josh Fox, who was filming that day for the incredible documentary *How to Let Go of the World and Love All the Things Climate Can't Change*, was on the largest canoe, known as *Vanuatu*. While there, a police boat crashed into the canoe and the boat suddenly flipped into the water. In that moment, Josh threw his camera to someone in the police boat who had already been arrested. The guy caught the camera and kept filming as police dragged people out of the water. Miraculous as that sounds, something equally miraculous was about to occur.

The boat was dragged to shore, and people were crying as they watched a coal ship escape port. But the warriors refused to give up, quickly repaired the canoe, and returned it to sea. No other coal ships were allowed to leave the port that day. There were 10 ships in all, carrying 578,000 tons of coal that were prevented from making it to sea that day. It was an incredible victory, and one that demonstrated the resilience of frontline communities. The sea might already be swallowing their homes, but they were not going to go down without doing everything they could.

One of the protagonists of Josh's film, Mika Maiava of Samoa, spoke about why the action was so successful: "You need to win from within, so that even if people look at you like you're losing, you're not losing, because you've already won in your heart . . . [We're] hoping that the energy we give will change somebody else's heart. What we're doing here is a very powerful statement that says 'we stand as Pacific Island nations in solidarity.'"

At the Paris climate talks, we saw it as our responsibility to elevate the stories and demands of the people most likely to be driven from their homes by climate change. We had many actions together where we chanted, "1.5 to stay alive," referring to a proposed cap of 1.5° Celsius of temperature rise, which would still result in the likely submergence of many island nations. We have already raised the temperature almost 1° Celsius, and it's estimated by some that we have already released enough emissions to raise the temperature another 0.5° Celsius, putting us perilously close to the what scientists call the point of no return.

The commitments in the Paris climate agreement, which are nonbinding, are estimated to allow for warming between 2.7° and 3.7° Celsius. While many people were stoked that we had come to an agreement, for the most impacted communities, this will still be disastrous. Some of the so-called solutions outlined in the agreement are a step sideways and not a step forward.

EXPOSING FALSE SOLUTIONS

In our mission to find real solutions, we sometimes fall for something that sounds good but doesn't actually address the problem. There are a number of false solutions being packaged as meaningful steps in the right direction. They cause more harm than good and undermine the real efforts being taken to solve this crisis.

Big business and crooked politicians will always be one of the greatest enemies of our movement. Cap and trade is a market-based approach to controlling pollution by providing economic incentives for reducing emissions. This has allowed for programs like Reducing Emissions from Deforestation and Forest Degradation (REDD). This false solution is a program that looks good on paper, but, in reality, it allows polluting companies to force indigenous peoples off their ancestral lands and receive carbon offsets while claiming to "preserve" that land.

In addition, calling fracking (the process of injecting water, chemicals, and sand deep beneath the surface of the Earth to fracture underground shale formations to extract oil and gas) a climate solution is one of the biggest industry lies you'll hear. I'll go deeper into fracking later in the book, but, in short, big oil and gas has tried to fool us into thinking that fracking for gas has about half the climate impact of coal, because it gives off roughly half the carbon emissions when its burns. However, looking at the full process, fracking often has more of a climate impact than coal because of methane leaks. Over a 20-year period, methane is a hundred times worse as a heat-trapping gas than carbon dioxide. The health impacts of fracking make it a terrible alternative on its own, but combined with the increased climate impact, it is completely the wrong direction for global energy.

While in Paris during the United Nations conference, we took over a space known as COP 21 Solutions. We were invited to perform there and talk about Earth Guardians and the youth movement. The day we were set to perform, we found out that this event was sponsored by some of the biggest European fossil fuel companies. We discovered this because of an action involving people from the Indigenous Environmental Network on the prior day. They scaled exhibits, hung banners, and stood in front of booths with megaphones, calling out the hypocrisy of these corporations calling for false solutions. It was an intense scene, and police carried out a bunch of our allies. For our performance, Earth Guardians had received a number of event passes for our team to attend the event. We decided to give some of the passes to the people from the Indigenous Environmental Network, who were thrown out of the event just 24 hours earlier.

We performed a set for the crowd, and after playing our last song, we called all the Earth Guardians and Indigenous Environmental Network activists on stage. We made a statement about how we were not about to accept false solutions and how we need to get corporate interests out of the climate talks and oil money out of politics. To bring attention to what was going on, we were trying to make enough of a ruckus to get escorted out of the building. We stood in solidarity with the frontline communities affected by fossil fuel extraction as indigenous people and youth representing those most affected by climate change.

COP 21 Paris Action

Joey Montoya, the director of Urban Native Era, who was with us at the action, described the scene as the event organizer tried to stop us: "He awkwardly came on stage and tried to smooth over what just happened. A few seconds later, he gave the signal to the staff to turn the lights off. So, then we started a mic check saying 'no false solutions.' and 'no REDD.'"

From COP 21 in Paris to the communities being impacted by REDD, they are trying to silence the voices of leaders everywhere. For example, according to Ninawa Huni Kui, the president of the Federation of the Huni Kui people in Acre in the Brazilian Amazon, his community can no longer fish, hunt, or farm on their own land. These activities have been declared illegal, and the local police will jail protesters or those who fish, hunt, or farm. In his own words: "Leaders are being criminalized for opposing the [REDD] project, and communities are told that the services provided for education or transportation or health care will be suspended, if they oppose the project."

False solutions threaten our opportunity to pursue real change. We have to remain alert to the hidden agendas and cover-ups manufactured by big business and crooked politicians. The challenges that we face are daunting, but we have to remember that the world we want to see depends on protecting everyone's rights. We cannot rely on our so-called leaders or government bureaucracies to ignite the shift in thought, action, and behaviors we so desperately need. They have failed us for hundreds of years, putting their financial agendas above our communities. Revolutionary, politician, and freedom-fighter Nelson Mandela said, "To deny people their human rights is to challenge their very humanity." We have been challenged, and now we must respond.

CHANGING OUR APPROACH

While we can't completely stop climate change, with concrete action, we can slow rising water and avert further catastrophic disaster. It's all a matter of how quickly we're able to get emissions under control. Even though this is the most critical issue our world faces, the media is mostly silent about it. That's why my little brother, Itzcuauhtli, decided to use silence as a megaphone to uplift the voices of the people most affected that so often go unheard. As a sign of solidarity, he placed green tape over his mouth and didn't speak a single word for 45 days. On December 10, 2014, he asked those around him to join him in a global hour of silence and wear a green wristband to show their support. Social

Silence into Action

media blew up with people around the globe sharing photos of them participating in the silent strike, recognizing their own power as world leaders. His message: "If we act as leaders, then leaders will act."

I was incredibly inspired by his commitment and creativity. I've spent my whole life with this kid, and, trust me, he is one of the most talkative kids you will ever meet. I tried to go silent for just that 1 day, and it was incredibly difficult. I only made it to dinner. He was planning to break his silence at a big event in New York City, but instead, he decided that he wanted his first words to be with his family. I still remember the first thing he said was "I love you, guys" in a roomful of close family and friends. It was hella touching, and a bunch of people started crying. When it comes down to it, this movement is about love.

It reminded of an action my friend Tim DeChristopher took, where he disrupted a federal oil and gas auction by bidding on public lands to keep them from being drilled. His bold action helped protect 22,000 acres of Utah wild lands from destructive oil and gas drilling, and also made him sacrifice 21 months of his life in federal prison. Looking back on his action, Tim encouraged others to join him, saying "With countless lives on the line, this is what love looks like."

It's that kind of love that propels us to do things that we wouldn't ordinarily do. These are the actions that inspire the world, define a generation, and get people to finally pay attention. They are the ideas that are bold enough to reach outside the boundaries of what we believe is possible when it comes to climate action. Education and awareness is where our fight begins. You have to understand the problem, the urgency, and how it connects to your community. We have to have the conversations, do the research, and spread it to others. The solutions are here, and they are spreading, but not fast enough. We're not going to be 100-percent fossil-fuel-free overnight, but if we continue to use creative and out-of-the-box tactics to reach our goals, we can get there faster than we ever imagined.

EDUCATING YOUR COMMUNITY

When people are armed with the truth, they are more likely to act, and act effectively. You can start by educating yourself. There are

Educating My Generation

a lot of amazing resources out there like Union of Concerned Scientists (www.ucsusa.org), Ecowatch (www.ecowatch.com), and many more that are constantly updating their web sites with the latest in climate science. Once you read through these sites and digest this knowledge, start sharing the information with your friends, family, and community. This can include learning how to set up a presentation in your school, your religious institution, or local community center.

One excellent tool for educating in schools is the Alliance for Climate Education (ACE) Assembly, which is a fast-paced multi-media presentation that teaches climate science in a fun and engaging way. The presentation incorporates up-to-date reports from the Intergovernmental Panel on Climate Change (IPCC), while presenting a vision of youth solving the climate crisis. A peer-reviewed study found that, after seeing the presentation, about 60 percent of students were inspired to take increased action to confront climate change, while getting their friends and family involved.

Live the solution. There are a number of ways to cut your own carbon footprint (the amount of carbon dioxide we emit due to our use of fossil fuels) to help be a part of the solution. Earth Guardians has put together a helpful resource with 50 tips to cutting carbon and living more sustainably. A few of my favorites include:

Home

- In the winter, turn down the thermostat and wear warmer clothes instead.
- Avoid using the clothes dryer; hang your clothes out to dry whenever possible.

Eating

- Eat vegetarian—or better yet, vegan. Remember to buy organic.
- Buy locally sourced food, when possible.

Bathing

- Cut your shower time by 20 percent, or take one less shower each week.
- Turn off the water while shampooing your hair or washing your body.

Cleaning

- Use rags or hand towels instead of paper towels or napkins.
- Use nontoxic, environmental-friendly products for cleaning.

Shopping

- Local, local, local! Consider paying a little extra to support a local store or restaurant.
- Shop at secondhand/thrift stores.

Transportation

- Walk, Rollerblade, skateboard, ride a unicycle, or ride a bike.
- Carpool and ride-share, whenever possible.

Activity

- Replace screen time with socializing, creating, learning, creating art, and exercising.
- Start or help with a community garden.

Recycle and Reuse

- "Reduce, Reuse, Recycle"—in that order!
- Recycle old cell phones, mobile devices, and batteries.

In general, these tips help us to use less, recycle, and live in a more energy efficient way. Don't stop with these tips. Keep going. Consider getting an energy audit of your home. Auditors learn about your living habits and find ways that you can save energy, sometimes cutting your energy footprint (and bill!) in half. They can also find simple retrofits you can do to your home that will save energy and money. Energy efficiency is one of the most effective ways to be a part of the solution, and some of the above-mentioned tips would help you to reduce your overall energy use.

Consider your consumption. The consumer-driven market has a tremendous impact on the climate. The more we consume, the more big business will produce and manufacture. If we all demanded electric cars, thee car industry would only build electric cars. Our decisions dictate their actions. We consume an alarming rate of meat in the United States. The meat industry is one of the greatest pollutants of our air and water. We are displacing forests, releasing greenhouses gases into the atmosphere, and using tremendous fossil fuels to create space for cows to live and eat. We then burn a large amount of gas to transport this meat all over the world to fulfill carnivorous appetites. In short, we have to change the way we act and consider supporting the businesses and products that strive to support us.

Create a Climate Recovery Ordinance. Changes in our own lives will not alone be enough to solve climate change. We also need to work locally and nationally to change the system that is creating climate disaster. One way Earth Guardians and Our Children's Trust (OCT) are doing this is with Climate Recovery Ordinances (CROs). CROs are legally-binding documents that ensure that municipalities reduce community-wide greenhouse gas emissions in line with the best available science.

This is a way that Earth Guardians crews and OCT are helping shape local policies to participate in meaningful action and create concrete climate recovery plans for their communities. You can get started by joining or starting an Earth Guardians chapter, testifying at public city council meetings, and petitioning your city council for adoption of locally-tailored climate recovery laws.

Join the movement. Climate change is the crisis that connects us all. More than any time in history, we are all in the same boat. The same emissions are impacting people of every race, gender, and ethnicity in every part of the world. 350.org has organized more than 20,000 climate actions in every country, except North Korea. There are so many ways to plug in to enact solutions, whether it's a march, a rally, or volunteering in your local community. Connect with your neighbors; get creative; utilize art, music, or theater; and do what you love and make that a part of the solution.

Whatever you do, don't stop. It takes an ecosystem of a movement to create change. We all have an essential role to play. I have no doubt that our collective brilliance can transform our communities that can then change the world.

SHIFTING OUR PERSPECTIVE ON CLIMATE CHANGE

An Interview with Bill McKibben

Bill McKibben is an author and environmentalist who focuses on climate change. He wrote his first book in 1989, and titled it, *The End of Nature*. Most people know it as one of the first mainstream books on climate change. Since then, he has written a dozen more books. He is the founder of 350.org, which is the first planet-wide, grassroots climate change movement. Since its inception, 350.org has hosted and organized more than20,000 rallies around the world. Bill McKibben is a true grass roots warrior and frontline defender. I am proud to call him both a mentor and a friend.

ME: This is a two-part, complex question. What does Donald Trump mean for the climate movement? Also, are you concerned about our becoming too defensive in a time where we really need to be making progress in averting climate change?

BILL: Look, I think what Trump represents is a serious break in the momentum that was starting to build in the direction of clean energy. Paris was the high point so far of the globe's efforts to deal with climate change. It wasn't enough; the steps outlined in the Paris agreement were not enough to stop climate change, or even slow it down anywhere near enough. But, it was a beginning. There was a strong sense of momentum beginning to build.

The question now is whether that momentum can be sustained even in the face of Trump. He's going to put a pothole in the road, probably a ditch across the road. He's going to try to build a crevasse across the road that will swallow up all that momentum. Our job is to keep that from happening, if we can. The news is, of course, discouraging. What he's done even just today, with announcing that the automakers are not going to have to live up to their agreement to produce more fuel-efficient cars.

These are the kind of things that do real, real damage over many, many years. And I do think we need to fight very hard against them and play some defense with Mr. Trump, but I also think that you're right to be wary of becoming enmeshed in defense alone. It's also moments like this when we need to lay out a really bold and promising vision of the future, explaining exactly what it is we are fighting for, so that when and where we're able to take political power, no one will have any doubts of what needs to be done.

I think the clearest banner around which to rally now is the calls going forward for 100-percent renewable energy. Jeff Berkley and Bernie Sanders will soon introduce the bill in the senate calling for that. It won't pass, of course, there's no chance of that in the current congress. But, I do think it'll become the rallying cry and help us point the conversation in the right direction so that, when the time comes that Donald Trump is not there, we won't have to waste a lot of time trying to get whoever does take over to understand what the right thing is.

ME: In recent years, the situation with climate change has become worse than ever. How do we communicate the urgency of the problem without having people lose hope in this issue?

BILL: Well, that's a fair question. I have to say that I think there's a degree to which a certain amount of despair and fear are rational responses to the situation we find ourselves in. We're now, as you know, losing the largest physical features on the planet. The Arctic is melting, the Antarctic is melting, and we lost some vast percentage of the world's coral reefs in the last year alone. These are things that rightly give us great pause.

I think that to find hope amidst them, one needs to look at the resistance that's rising, and that is a very hopeful sign. I think the metaphor, the way to think about it is, the Earth is running a fever, and the only antibodies available to fight that fever are us. So, it is good to see those antibodies coming into action all around the world. Make sure there are people rallying, people working, people going to jail, people going to engineering school, people doing all the things that are necessary to try and stop the fossil fuel industry and promote the renewable energy industry, because that's what it's going to take.

When I get to feeling despairing, I go and look through some of the pictures in the Flickr account at 350.org. We've organized, I think, about 20,000 demonstrations around the world in every country but North Korea, and you've been a part of a bunch of them. Most of those people come from places that didn't cause this problem, and yet they are willing and eager to work on trying to solve it. That always gives me the inspiration I need to get back to work.

ME: What is one thing about climate change that you wish people better understood?

BILL: I think people don't understand the speed with which it's happening. I think that even those who view it as a problem tend to think of it as something that will happen gradually and probably in their children's and grandchildren's lifetimes. Instead, it's breaking over our heads as we speak. Getting across that sense of urgency seems paramount to me.

ME: Your article, "Global Warming: A Terrifying New Chemistry," showed the dangers of trading one fossil fuel for another, talking about how cuts in atmospheric carbon dioxide from switching from coal to natural gas are offset by methane emissions from fracking. In reaction to this article, are you seeing any change in the way that nonprofits or politicians are approaching the subject after it was published, talking about switching from one fossil fuel to another?

BILL: I think that politicians have been very slow to grapple with the fact that methane emissions are as dangerous as carbon dioxide emissions. Those politicians who wanted to do something about climate change 5 and 10 years ago, but didn't want to do anything that would be too dramatic and too radical and too upsetting, fixed upon natural gas as the future. They could do that without riling the oil companies too much, because the oil companies were gas companies, too. Exxon's the biggest fracking leaseholder in the country, I believe.

So, politicians like Barack Obama found it a very, very congenial place to land. The problem was that the position was soon undercut and dramatically slowed by emerging science, demonstrating that the leak rates from methane were very high, and by the economists, who pointed out that, in fact, this was damaging to coral and perhaps even more so damaging to wind and sun, and so was prolonging instead of shortening our global warming moment.

ME: Do you think that climate change is more of an environmental issue than it is a human issue? What is the disconnect between those two things that the public doesn't understand?

BILL: I actually don't think of it as either one, and I don't even really think of it at this point as an "issue" anymore. It seems to me that it's a lens through which to view the world. The lens that we have viewed the world for the last century had everything to do with economic growth. If something was going to make the economy larger, then we were for it, at least politically. I think that the lens through which we need to view all the decisions we make and all the planning we do, and really our understanding of the world in the 21st century, needs to be through this lens of the narrowing window that we have to address the greatest threat we've ever come across. To think that environmentalists can solve this problem by themselves is folly. It's much too big. Environmentalists by themselves can muster enough political power to create a national park, or something like that, but not to take on the fossil fuel industry. This one requires the participation of everyone, especially those active in the communities that will suffer first and most from the impacts of climate change.

ME: A lot of people often come to me asking about what individual steps they can take in their own lives. What actions do you recommend for young people looking to make a difference?

BILL: I started 350.org with young people. The other seven cofounders were all college students when we began. I work with young people all the time, and my main message to them usually is: "Don't think of yourself as young people. Don't let yourselves be patronized and patted on the head. You're activists with as much or more right as anybody else to be driving this fight." I tend not to worry about individual action steps very much. Everybody knows the things they should be doing in their homes and lives. The light bulbs, the cars, the whatever. I don't think we're at a point where we can solve this problem with individual actions, so when people ask me that question, I always say that job one is to organize, and job two is to get together with your neighbors and friends and organize, and job three is to organize.

ME: The last question I have is do you have hope?

BILL: I do have hope. Not that we're going to stop climate change, it's too late for that, and there's a lot of damage done already, and more will happen. But, I have hope that human beings are creative and loving and smart enough to wake up to this warning we've been given, and to take real action to build a better world. Hope is not the same thing as expectation. I don't know whether we will or not, but I'm willing to get up every morning and work hard to try and make it so. If enough other people are, then, yeah, we have a shot.

CHAPTER 6

Wilderness Warriors

Where Have All the Wild Things Gone?

*"Biological diversity is messy. It walks, it crawls,
it swims, it swoops, it buzzes. But extinction is silent,
and it has no voice other than our own."*

—PAUL HAWKEN

To get the full scope of what we are doing to the planet, you have to look at the human impact on the ecosystems of the world. It is estimated that 200 species go extinct every single day. *Every single day.* Gone forever. That number is more than a thousand times greater than what scientists call the natural rate of extinction. The last time we saw such a remarkable threat to so many species was 65 million years ago, when dinosaurs went extinct. Many of these species live in rain forests that are thriving environments. They are not the only ones that depend on these biodiverse ecosystems for survival. So do we. When we lose one species, the ripple effect is felt throughout the world. Biodiverse ecosystems produce the most oxygen, sequester the most carbon, and are the ancestral home of many.

Growing up surrounded by the beauty of Colorado's mountains, lakes, and forests, I felt a connection to nature from a very young age. It wasn't just that I was surrounded by nature. My parents raised me to see the magic in everything that lived, from our forests to the water in a river to the life of an insect. My dad taught me that everything is connected. I learned that respect for the natural world must guide our actions in order to live in balance with nature.

In Colorado, the impact of climate change on our forests has been disastrous. Seeing the destruction firsthand changed my understanding about our climate crisis and helped me understand the extent and urgency of this issue even more. In the 16 years that I've been alive, more species have gone extinct than ever before. It seems as though the reality of species disappearing off the face of the planet forever would be enough to wake up the world, yet we, as a society, are still asleep to the human impact that threatens some of the most beautiful and important places on Earth.

The same destruction I notice in my backyard is happening all over the globe. The actions of mankind have thrown entire ecosystems out of balance, threatening their ability to sustain life. Our atmosphere is also destabilized as these biodiverse environments are negatively impacted by human consumption. To that point, the rain forest is one of the most important biomes on the planet for human survival. It's easy to view the rain forest as a far-off place that will never affect your local community. The warriors that have stood to defend these forests are on the front lines of a movement to protect not only their own homes, but the air and water for all of us.

It is crazy to think that 1 in 10 of the world's species live in the Amazon rain forest. In just one hectare of this land, there are more different types of tree species than found in all of North America combined. The Amazon rain forest provides one-fifth of the world's oxygen and one-fifth of the world's fresh water. While the Amazon is just two million square miles long, it offers us an unbelievable abundance of nourishment and resources.

For those of us who like to breathe, what's already in motion should be cause for us to pull the emergency alarm. We've already lost more than half of the world's rain forests, and we are losing approximately 90 acres of rain forest every minute. Most of this destruction is due to heavy industry, like logging, mining for minerals, drilling for oil, and the meat industry. Essentially, we are seeing an aggressive man-made attack on these lush and nutrient rich ecosystems.

The Amazon is not just home to animals and plants. Five hundred years ago, there were an estimated 10 million tribal people living in the Amazon. However, there are only an estimated 200,000 people still living traditionally in the rain forest. For centuries, tribes had lived in harmony with the forest and nature, protecting the balance of a complex ecosystem, while preserving a powerful knowledge of the region, animals, and agricultural benefits like medicinal plants. As we lose these indigenous cultures, we also lose their rich ancestral knowledge and healing power. Indigenous people of the rain forest have not only lived in balance with nature, but they have taken a leading role in defending the world's rain forests.

THE FRONTLINE PROTECTORS

The story of the Kichwa people in the Sarayaku region nestled deep in the Ecuadorian Amazon is one recent example of the determination to defend these lands. Our movements have a lot to learn from their ability to stand their ground despite the powerful financial interests against them. They successfully defended their homes against oil development in

Nina Gualinga Paddles to Paris

one of the most biodiverse regions in the world. Nina Gualinga is only 22 years old, and was born and raised in the Sarayaku region. She is a powerful voice in the movement to assert indigenous rights over extractive industries. In 2012, the Sarayaku region won their fight against Big Oil by suing the Ecuadorian government in the inter-American court of human rights, eventually preventing the local military and major oil companies from clearing the land to drill. This is an important example of a people who believe their lifestyle, which is deeply connected to the land and the planet, is a blueprint for humans to save themselves from the ongoing threat of climate change.

Nina said it best in an online blog in *Huffington Post*:

> Locations where fossil fuel deposits have been discovered are situated directly within the homes and territories of local indigenous peoples. We are actively struggling against exploitation of these reserves. We are struggling for the future of all mankind. Therefore, we deserve the support of international communities. We have persistently been on the forefront of the fight against environmental disaster and climate change. So, why are our voices not being included in the decision-making process at COP20 and at other high-level governmental meetings? It is not only our right but it is also the obligation of governments, state parties, corporations, organizations, and other such institutions to make sure indigenous peoples have a say on our own future.

Until 2008, Mario Santi was the president of the people of Sarayaku. In discussing the resistance, he indicates in a *Yes!* magazine report that "our fathers told us that for future generations not to suffer, we needed to struggle for our territory and our liberty, so we wouldn't be slaves of the new kind of colonization. The waterfall, the insects, the animals, the jungle gives us life. Because man and the jungle have a relationship. For the Western capitalist world, the jungle is simply for exploiting resources and ending all this. The indigenous pueblos without jungle—we can't live."

The battle in the Amazon rain forest continues. At the end of 2015, Nina Gualinga and a delegation of other people from the region set out in a handmade canoe to travel 6,000 miles from their home in the Amazon to Paris for the COP21 conference. They did so with a message of peace, of hope, and a proposal called *Kawsak Sacha*, which means "The Living Forest." Nina explains their motivation for this trip: "I think that indigenous peoples' voices are the voices that should be heard. Indigenous people should be inside the actual negotiations, but we are not. Those who are actually negotiating right now, they might not have to live with the consequences of climate change, but I will. I will have to live with it. My sister, my little brother, and my children, they're all going to have to live with the consequences of climate change. And who are they to decide over my future, over my sister's future, over my children's future?"

SAVING THE WILD THINGS

The feeling of being in a rain forest is the feeling of being surrounded by life. It's home for hundreds of thousands of animals, and their survival is connected to the survival of us all. The magnificence of the rain forest is something powerfully sacred, something so clearly worth protecting. These ecosystems exist in perfect balance until they are destabilized by man-made disruptions. Different regions of biodiverse land are experiencing various threats. The Indonesian forests are under attacked for its palm oil and logging for paper. They are home to 10 to 15 percent of all known species of plants, mammals, and birds. These

Palm Oil Devastation

rain forest habitats are home to some of the planet's most spectacular and endangered wildlife, like the Sumatran tiger and the orangutan.

Sadly, the orangutan population has fallen 50 percent over the past 60 years. There are only about 50,000 orangutans left on this planet. The species has lost over 55 percent of its habitat to palm oil plantations and logging. Palm oil is a hidden ingredient used in half of the packaged food and cosmetic products found on supermarket shelves, from soap to toothpaste. After learning that many of my favorite snacks use palm oil, I had to find alternatives. Palm oil might be one of the cheapest oils on the planet, but the cost to wildlife, to humanity, and to the planet is devastating.

As the world's old-growth forests are damaged and destroyed, we push more species closer and closer to extinction. For example, there are only an estimated 15,000 jaguars roaming the planet, 2,800 northern spotted owls, 100 to 200 Cross River gorillas, and 32,000 boreal caribous, which is down from the hundreds of thousands that roamed the Earth as recently as the 19th century. The stars of BBC's *Planet Earth* series may soon join the list of extinct species in the years to come. Mining, logging, and construction projects invade the homes of these amazing animals, killing the rightful inhabitants of the land.

If we continue to use these crucial environments as manufacturing plants for our personal and consumer needs, we will be the next ones to go extinct.

The Lungs of Our Planet

The rain forests are the lungs of the planet. For humans, lungs play the crucial role of allowing the body to take in oxygen from the air and exhale carbon dioxide. Forests inhale the carbon dioxide we produce and exhale oxygen for us to breathe. We are inarguably dependent on this symbiotic relationship with our forests.

The Indonesian rain forests are one of the most important carbon sinks in the world. A carbon sink is a forest or ocean that absorbs more carbon than it releases. This is crucial to our existence, because carbon sinks create negative emissions and help to reduce and reverse climate change. The Indonesian forests sit above peatlands, which are estimated to store 35 billion tons of carbon. Slash-and-burn agriculture has made Indonesia the world's third-largest emitter of greenhouse gases, as these practices are used to grow palm oil, releasing carbon into the atmosphere. A single acre of peatland can release 15,000 tons of carbon during this transition.

Indonesia isn't alone. The Boreal forest in Canada is home to 22 percent of the world's carbon, actually storing twice as much carbon in its soil as a typical tropical forest. In total, the Boreal forest holds an estimated 186 billion tons of carbon. Nearly 50 percent of the bird species in the United States and Canada rely on the Boreal forest for survival. There is no debate that the old growth forests of the world are key to supporting life on the planet.

But like the Amazon, the forests found in these regions are threatened by heavy industry, in this case tar sands mining. The process of extracting tar sands involves clear-cutting the old-growth forests and scraping the soil, which they refine and process using massive amounts of clean water. Since the soil is gone, the forest will never grow back, and the water is poisoned with chemicals and held in giant open pits. Tar sands development in Northern Alberta threatens an area the size of the countries of Portugal and Denmark combined. When I first saw an image of the destruction created by this massive industrial project from above, I thought, "Damn, this looks like Mordor from the *Lord of the Rings*." Desolate, lifeless, and dark. It was horrifying to think we'd created something on Earth looking like it was spawned out of the dark parts of J. R. R. Tolkien's imagination.

Breathing Life Back into the Rain Forest

Protecting these powerful places starts with education. As we learn more, our action steps become clearer. There are some amazing groups to connect and plug in with, from Amazon Watch to Rainforest Action Network (RAN) to Greenpeace to local nonprofits like Acción Ecológica, who was so powerful in their efforts to protect the Ecuadorian Amazon, that the Ecuadorian government temporarily shut them down. Some organizations, like ClearWater, are helping build rainwater catchment systems for families who lost their clean water due to oil drilling.

When we follow our inspiration after discovering how messed up the problem is, it can open up doors to make a difference. My homie Russell, who works with me at Earth Guardians, first learned about the destruction of the Amazon from oil companies in the film *Crude* when he was in college. The movie tells the story of how ChevronTexaco intentionally dumped more than 18 billion gallons of wastewater and spilled 17 million gallons of crude oil into the Amazon River. All the oil waste was poisoning indigenous communities and killing wildlife. Chevron was refusing to clean up the mess they created, so immediately after seeing the film, Russell began doing research on people working there to clean up the mess. He found the Amazon Mycrorenewal Project, which is using mushrooms to remediate oil spills and e-mailed them about volunteering. Months later, he and his friend Ivon were in Ecuador assisting community president Donald Moncaya and Nicola Peel building rainwater catchment systems with people who had lost their clean water from the pollution.

CORPORATE CAMPAIGNING

At the same time, some people were attempting to deal with the overwhelming waste Chevron had created, and others were trying to get the company to take responsibility for the mess they made. The community was suing Chevron to make them clean up and pay for the damage they caused, and after more than a dozen years, they finally won a $9.5 billion lawsuit, however Chevron has refused to recognize the court's decision and pay up. A group of activists and artists led by RAN began to think of what they could do to shame the company into doing what was right.

Cesar Maxit is an incredible climate justice street artist who was approached by Chevron marketing to put up posters from Chevron's new ad campaign. Before he agreed to take the job, he asked them to send him the designs so he could look at them. After receiving them, he got together with folks at RAN and the group The Yes Men. They designed their own ad campaign that mimicked the Chevron posters, but told the truth about their company. They put out their own designs in a

OIL COMPANIES **SHOULD** CLEAN UP THEIR TOXIC **MESSES**

WE AGREE.

Communities Representing:
Ecuador
Alaska
Salt Lake City, UT

Philipines
Angola
Indonesia

RAN's Spoof Ad Campaign

professional style press release before Chevron could. The media picked it up. Their new ads said things like "Oil Companies Should Clean Up Their Mess. We Agree." This type of activism is called culture jamming. It's creative, exciting, and helps wake people up.

RAN has also created a campaign to help get snack-food companies to stop using what they call conflict palm oil, sourced from slash-and-burn plantations that are destroying habitats of endangered animals. They are targeting 20 of the biggest snack-food companies in the world. Of the 20 companies they are targeting, 15 have agreed to plans to transition to responsibly sourced palm oil. There is still more work to be done to make sure these plans are improved to keep conflict palm oil entirely out of their supply chain. You can learn which companies are still lagging behind and how to get involved at www.ran.org/palm_oil.

CHANGE YOUR HABITS

Not everyone can jump right in with an organization or a campaign. A great place to start is being mindful of what you consume on a daily basis. Palm oil is not just in food, it's also in beauty products and soaps. One company that creates sustainably sourced beauty products is Lush. They use no palm oil in their products, and they have an online palm-oil-free soap recipe that you can make at home. There is also the Palmsmart app that you can use to see which products contain palm oil.

Our consumer choices cannot be where our action ends. It is also crucial that we spread the word and get our friends and family involved, sharing photos, media, and helping the people in your life make conscious decisions about what they consume. Screen a documentary like *Virunga, People of the Zenith, Crude,* or *Racing Extinction* to educate your community about the destruction of our forests and the people defending them. Go into nature, fall back in love with the natural world, and let your commitment stem from that place of connection. What you see may spark a powerful connection that will motivate you into action.

We live in a modern world with a great opportunity to spread the word. Use your social media to share snaps, photos on Instagram, Facebook posts, and e-mail blasts to show your friends, family, and followers the importance of taking action. The people who will inherit this Earth are counting on us to preserve the magic and beauty of the planet. Tipping the scales toward the future we know is possible depends on us reconnecting to the Earth and fighting for what gives us life.

CHAPTER 7

Troubled Waters
Defending Life below the Surface

"The sea, the great unifier, is man's only hope.
Now, as never before, the old phrase has literal meaning:
We are all in the same boat."

—JACQUES COUSTEAU

I don't think it takes much to fall in love with the ocean. In the same way I imagine looking at the Earth from space can make you feel small, I feel a sense of vast unknown looking out past the break of the waves. I was born hundreds of miles from the nearest beach, so part of me has always been jealous of my three older siblings who grew up in Maui, swimming, surfing, and snorkeling pretty much since birth. I love my mountains and forests, but I can't help but wonder if I would've made a better ocean boy. Every time I travel to the coast, I don't leave without going to the water, putting my feet in and letting it wash away the heaviness of the world, even if it's only gone for a second. I've fallen in love with the smell, the sound, and the magic of the world's oceans. And this thing that connects us all, affects us all, this beautiful vast unknown landscape that many people love and rely upon is changing far quicker than we could've ever predicted.

I've been fascinated by life in the ocean from the first memories of playing in tide pools in Mexico when I was 2 years old. After seeing the Great Barrier Reef for the first time on *Planet Earth*, I knew that this was a place I had to visit during my lifetime. My friend Lee has been on the reef since he was 10 years old, and hearing his stories and experiences completely shifted my perspective on our oceans. "I hardly remember any change until I was like 25," he said. "I think if you saw the reef for the first time, you'd say, 'oh, the water is crystal clear and there's some fish swimming around,' and it would look quite beautiful, but having seen it over a lifetime, I remember when there were huge fish everywhere, and it used to take your breath away. You would put your face underwater and the colors were so crazy that it was sort of like euphoric. What's happening now is, as the reef is dying, with all the nitrogen in the water, there's this algae and green stuff growing over all the dead coral skeleton. What used to be a multicolored iridescent coral garden is now just a plane slate gray and green slime growing over everything, and it's so disheartening."

The Great Barrier Reef is one of the wonders of the world, visible from space and also known as the planet's largest single structure made by living organisms. The reef is both a sacred part of the Aboriginal people's culture and one of the most biodiverse places in the world. Just like more of my fellow Coloradans feel connected with the Rocky Mountains, many Australians identify strongly with the Great Barrier Reef.

The same year that UNESCO designated the Great Barrier Reef a World Heritage Site, it also experienced its first mass-bleaching incident. The coral rely on algae for food. However, with rising sea temperatures from climate change, coral is unable to digest the algae, turning bone white and dying off in a matter of months. In just the last 10 years, there have been catastrophic bleaching events that have killed more than half of the coral in the northern part of the reef. After the reef is dead, algae colonize the dead coral, sucking oxygen from the water and giving off carbon dioxide. Agricultural runoff compounds the problem with nitrogen-based fertilizers feeding the algae, as it takes over the dead reef.

Like our rain forests, our oceans are responsible for holding an incredible amount of the carbon dioxide and heat produced by the Earth.

Scientists refer to our oceans as carbon sinks, because of their ability to hold carbon that would otherwise be released into the atmosphere. The oceans have absorbed about 30 percent of carbon dioxide produced by human activities since the 1800s. The increased carbon from burning fossil fuels and the algae takeover has led to a massive increase in acidity. The acidity in turn kills off more of the reef, setting in motion a vicious cycle. In the last 10 years, ocean acidity has increased beyond what we have ever seen. We have drastically overlooked the importance of the role our ocean places in maintaining a stable climate.

PAINTING THE PICTURE OF THE OCEAN

The biggest wake-up call for me personally was actually witnessing images and time-lapses of the collapse of an entire ecosystem. It is heartbreaking to see the transformation of these breathtaking ocean seascapes to barren, lifeless graveyards. Emmy Award–winning director and good friend of mine, Jeff Orlowski, opened a window for the world to peer beneath the surface and experience what so many of us have been disconnected from. Jeff's most recent work, *Chasing Coral*, is one

Coral Bleaching

of the most powerful stories with the potential to captivate the world in defending our oceans.

In late 2016, *Chasing Coral* was screened for Congress, the White House, and the United Nations. I agree with the *New York Times* when they called *Chasing Coral* an "emotional race against time." The documentary shows a team of divers, photographers, and scientists that set out on a daring ocean adventure to discover why coral reefs around the world are vanishing at an unprecedented rate and to reveal the untold story to the world.

I asked Jeff what he learned through the process of making the film, "I thought I knew a lot about climate change, then when I was working on the oceans, I realized that I knew nothing about it. Because the ocean is absorbing the vast amounts of the energy it needs, we don't see the consequences on land because the ocean is absorbing so much. So right off the bat, 93 percent of the energy is being absorbed into the ocean . . . The biggest wake-up call for me was that with climate change in the oceans affecting coral reefs specifically, it's such a different shift than we're seeing anywhere else on the planet."

It's incredible just how much you can learn about climate change just from coral. He also directed the award-winning documentary *Chasing Ice*, chronicling environmental photographer James Balog's journey to take pictures of the melting ice caps in the Arctic. The film blew me away when I saw it in theaters, with the image of massive ice caps breaking off into the ocean.

Jeff laid out the thread that connects the two films. "Both of these documentaries are evidence of climate change. In *Chasing Ice*, we had time-lapses of glaciers to show the audience the change and inevitable impact. We used that same philosophy in *Chasing Coral*. In some ways, it was much easier because you just see all this dead coral. It's based on this one weird, unique phenomenon that coral reefs tend to live at the upper temperature threshold. They live close to the highest temperature at which they can function. But they die as the water temperature goes up just a couple of degrees for an extended period of time. In my assessment, it's the first time that we've seen climate change just full-on kill an ecosystem."

I've learned that whether it's through music, film, art, or writing, telling a story has always been one of the most powerful tools to wake people up. Stories speak to people in a way that science and statistics never will. Jeff's film is a massive step toward telling the story of the collapse of our oceans, in a time where unified action is needed more than ever. Climate change is probably one of the scariest things happening on the planet. We are witnessing the death of one of the Earth's most massive and beautiful ecosystems that has thrived on this planet for thousands of years. We have to be brave enough to face this crisis head-on, and once stories like *Chasing Coral* reach the world, we cannot let anything stop us from fighting like hell so that places like the Great Barrier Reef can be more than a landmark of the destruction of our planet.

PIRATING CHANGE

As climate change threatens our oceans, so, too, does overfishing. Fishing vessels can now go farther, stay out longer, and catch more fish on each trip. Massive ships act as factories, processing and packaging fish while still at sea. New tuna-fishing vessels can now catch more fish in one trip than some countries catch in a year. As a result, we've overfished 63 percent of global fish stocks. Healthy oceans have a similar balance to what we see on land—there is a hierarchy of predators that rely on other species of fish for food. Due to overfishing, we've seen populations of top predators disappearing quickly. Small, faster-growing species are now replacing the larger ones, and they threaten to disrupt the balance and shift an entire ecosystem.

Organizations like the Sea Shepherd Conservation Society (SSCS), established in 1977 and founded by Captain Paul Watson, works to end the destruction of habitat and slaughter of marine life in the world's oceans in order to conserve and protect ecosystems and species. Their mission is to "use innovative direct-action tactics to investigate, document, and take action, when necessary, to expose and confront illegal activities on the high seas. By safeguarding the biodiversity of our delicately balanced ocean ecosystems, Sea Shepherd works to ensure their survival for future generations."

Sea Shepherd focuses primarily on direct action to save critically engendered species, like the vaquita porpoise, endangered sea turtles, pilot whales, and dolphins. Sea Shepherds is confronting illegal fishing head-on, using direct action tactics to investigate, document, and take action. If you've ever seen the show *Whale Wars*, you've seen them in action. They are the modern-day pirates for good. The Sea Shepherd crews are taking action when our governments fail to, while also willing to work with these same governments to help make fishing a sustainable practice.

For years, Sea Shepherds have worked with the rangers of Costa Rica's CoCos Island to protect the Galapagos Marine Reserve. Shark-poaching and long-line fishing has been a problem for decades, and, with the help of Sea Shepherds, rangers have been able to monitor and prevent illegal fishing operations.

I'm inspired by the way that Sea Shepherds does not wait for permission from leaders to act. They come from a place of strong conviction and expect politicians to follow. As a movement, we can all learn from their example of the power of direct action. Often rallies, lobbying, and petitions just aren't enough. That's when it's time to call in the pirates.

OIL AND WATER DON'T MIX

One other huge threat to the oceans is deep-sea oil drilling. The BP oil spill is still recognized as the worst oil spill in United States history. In 2010, there was an explosion on the Deepwater Horizon oil rig located in the Gulf of Mexico. Within days of the explosion, underwater cameras showed the rig was leaking oil onto the ocean floor. This went on for 87 days, until they could cap it off. But the damage was done, as an estimated 4.2 million barrels of oil and gas had already escaped.

As you can imagine, removing spilled oil from the ocean is a difficult task. They used 1.82 million gallons of dispersants on these fragile ecosystems. Chemical dispersants do not decrease the amount of oil entering the environment, but they break down the oil into smaller droplets that can actually release more toxins than the oil alone. The dispersants also push the oil deeper into the ocean where it can have a more harmful impact on marine life. The United Kingdom has banned the kinds of dispersants they used in the BP oil spill because of their negative impacts. Although they were shown to be more toxic and less effective than other alternatives, Nalco, the company that developed these dispersants, has deep ties to the oil and gas industry, which may explain why BP chose them in the first place.

(continued on page 93)

CAPTAIN'S QUARTERS

An Interview with Paul Watson

Paul Watson is a marine wildlife conservation and an environmental activist, who founded the Sea Shepherd Conservation Society, an antipoaching and direct-action group focused on marine conservation and marine conservation activism.

ME: First of all, I want to thank you for all the incredible work that you've done in your lifetime. You've been running expeditions for 35 years with the organization, probably taking the most active role in protecting our oceans. The first question is: What is the biggest change you've seen to marine life over time?

PAUL: It's been 40 years with Sea Shepherds. Prior to that, I spent 7 years with Greenpeace. The biggest changes? I've seen a rapidly diminished biodiversity within our oceans, with much more pollution now, and different kinds of pollution. Now, we're dealing with seismic pollution from fracking and from military testing, low-frequency sonar, which I don't know what the purpose of that is because Al-Qaeda certainly doesn't have any submarines. The problem is that they keep putting all this money into it, and they have to spend it, even though it has no practical application. So, the cost of that is killing whales and dolphins, because it destroys their eardrums and is causing all sorts of problems to other marine life forms.

We also have plastic pollution, which I was writing about 25 years ago. But nobody paid attention. People are finally starting to pay attention to it. One of the most insidious threats to life in the sea right now is the millions of tons of plastic that are floating in the ocean and breaking down and being consumed by wildlife. Nothing is really being done about it.

So, there's quite a difference between say, 1970, 1980, and now. The ocean has become much more diminished. We do this at our own peril, because people still don't understand the relationship between a healthy ecosystem in our ocean and our own survival. I attended the Climate Change Conference in Paris last year, and the subject of the oceans and the oceans' role in climate change was hardly discussed. People didn't even think about that relationship.

Since 1950, we've seen a 40-percent diminishment in phytoplankton populations worldwide. I believe that's because there's a diminishment of other wildlife, especially whales. Whales contribute to the phytoplankton. They're literally the farmers of the sea by providing the nitrogen and iron in their fecal material every day. One blue whale defecates 3 tons a day. You diminish whales, you diminish sea birds, you diminish other marine life, and you diminish phytoplankton. We don't survive if the phytoplankton disappears. That provides about 80 percent of the oxygen that we breathe.

ME: Damn. Seriously. I don't know if you're familiar with the film *Chasing Coral*, but it is just now circulating in different film festivals. Done by a filmmaker named Jeff Orlowski, who also made *Chasing Ice*, it looks at the documenting recession of glaciers in the North Pole. Now he's done this whole project about understanding the climate impact on our oceans, particularly surrounding coral reefs and the massive die-offs and bleaching that's happening. You should definitely check that out when you get a chance.

PAUL: By 2025, we'll see the first disappearance of major ecosystems—the coral reefs around the world. I spent 3 months on the Great Barrier Reef, and I've seen that diminishment. Pretty much most of it is gone right now, and nobody's even been paying attention. The problem is that none of the governments in the world today really take this issue seriously. They talk a lot about it, but they don't really do anything about it. It's out of sight, out of mind. There's no economic or political motivation for them to do anything about it, so they don't.

ME: You've been in a lot of dangerous situations with Sea Shepherds. What do you think is the closest you've ever come to death?

PAUL: There's been a lot of dangerous campaigns here, so I don't really give it much thought. I would say that pretty much all of our campaigns have some element of danger in them. We've been in incredibly dangerous storms, our ships have been rammed, and we've rammed other ships. I've been shot at many times, and certainly threatened, but the thing is that we've never lost anybody. We've never had a single injury in 40 years. I don't really worry about those things. Everybody's going to die someday, so best not to worry about it.

ME: In a nonprofit world that's all about lobbying and advocacy, why did you choose to lead an organization that's focused on direct action?

PAUL: I was with Greenpeace for 7 years. I just got tired of hanging banners and taking pictures. I just don't like protests. It's very submissive. It's like, "Please, please, please, don't kill the whales." They're going to kill them anyway. They don't care what you think. I felt there had to be a better way, so I set up Sea Shepherds as an interventionist organization. We're really an antipoaching organization. When Greenpeace criticized us for what we were doing, I said, "Look, you don't walk down the street and watch a dog being kicked to death and do nothing but hang a banner and take a picture. So, you don't stand there and watch a whale die and just hang a banner and take a picture. You have to intervene."

ME: What message do you have for the younger generation who want to directly be involved in the movement, the revolution, and to make changes to stop environmental destruction and climate change?

PAUL: I think there's a lot more involvement of younger people now than there has been in years past, because people are more and more aware of the issue. The problem, of course, is getting people to care about the issues. I've always felt that if we're going to save ourselves, I don't really worry about saving the planet. The planet will do quite fine without us, probably better off. If we're going to save ourselves, then we really have to harness imagination and courage to fuel the passion. So, I try to encourage people to act on what they're passionate about. Within the context of Sea Shepherds, we have a lot of young people. Once you become 18, you're eligible to become a Sea Shepherd crew member. What we hope to instill in people is that each and every one of us has the power to make a difference. So, people leave Sea Shepherds, and they go on to do other things.

For instance, in 1979, I had a crewmember, a 19-year-old guy named Alex Pacheco. After our campaign down the Sierra, he said, "What are we going to do about laboratory animals, Paul?"

I said, "I'm not going to do anything about laboratory animals, because I'm on a ship here, and I don't know what the hell to do. Why don't you do something about it?"

He said, "What can I do?"

I said, "Use your imagination."

He did. We went back and he got a job in a laboratory in Maryland and exposed everything that was going on there, shut the place down, and eventually founded People for the Ethical Treatment of Animals. This is the kind of thing we like to do in Sea Shepherds. We encourage people to go out and use their own initiative and make a difference.

ME: The state of the planet, the state of our oceans, the state of wildlife is all threatened. Obviously, now more than ever in the history of the world, we're in an incredibly critical point in time. Do you think there's hope to turn things around?

PAUL: If I didn't feel there was hope, I wouldn't be doing anything. I always feel that the answer to a seemingly impossible problem is to find that impossible answer. We find that impossible answer through imagination and passion. In 1972, the very idea that Nelson Mandela would be the president of South Africa was unthinkable and impossible, yet the impossible became possible. So, that's what we really have to look for, is finding that impossible answer. That can be found by taking a stand.

I don't really worry about the future too much, because back in 1973, when I was a medic with the American Indian Movement during the occupation at Wounded Knee in South Dakota, we were surrounded by 3,000 federal officers shooting at us, about 20,000 rounds a night. I went up to Russell Means, who was the leader of the American Indian Movement there, and I said, "Russell, we don't have a hope in hell of winning this battle. Why are we here?"

He said to me, "Well, we're not here because we're worried about winning or losing, and we're not worried about the odds against us. We're here because this is the right thing to do, and this is the right place to be." So, if you take a stand in the present, you can contribute toward a better world tomorrow. You may lose. You don't know, but you have to take that stand in order to find out. I've found over the years that you can jump into these situations where it doesn't look like you can win, and it doesn't look like there's any way out or even that you're going to survive, but you take the plunge, and you come out on the other side unscathed, and many times with a victory.

ME: What are the things that give you hope, for not only the future, but what gives you hope to continue to fight today, in the present?

PAUL: I live my life in accordance with the three basic laws of ecology: the law of diversity, the law of interdependence, and the law of finite resources. I know that no species has ever survived in the history of this planet that has lived outside of the boundaries of those ecological laws. I believe that those ecological laws allow the planet to recover from major disasters, whether it be a meteor strike or whether it be the greed of one species like ourselves. There have been five major extinction events in the history of this planet, the last one being 65 million years ago. We lost 97 percent of everything during the Permian extinction 250 million years ago.

So, now we're in the sixth major extinction, called the Holocene. It's named after us, and we'll lose more plants and animals between 2000 and 2065 than we lost in the last 65 million years. What's that mean? The long version of it is that it takes 18 to 20 million years to recover from a major extinction event, so it'll be a really nice planet 18 to 20 million years from now. The environmental conservation movement is not really about saving the planet. It's about saving ourselves from ourselves. As Pogo, the title character in the comic created by cartoonist Walk Kelly, said, "We've met the enemy, and he is us." It's a daunting, daunting task, because quite frankly, human beings are ecologically insane. Trying to cut through that is very difficult, but like I said, persistence. You do what you do, the best you can do, with the resources that you have available to you within the boundaries of practicality, and you can do amazing things.

ME: One last question. Trump is now in office. The reality of that is that things have gotten harder in a lot of ways for people working in advocacy, working as activists or as nonprofit organizations looking out for the environment. How do you see our role as people that care about the stewardship of this planet, the stewardship of humanity, adapting to a Trump administration?

PAUL: I don't think we have to adapt to it. I think we have to react to it. I actually see the election of Donald Trump in a positive manner. That is, he's shaken up the entire system. The establishment powers have controlled everything for so long that it would have just been the same-old, same-old under Hillary Clinton. Bernie Sanders certainly had given us some hope, but that was dashed. Trump has come in, and he's gotten people so angry, he's gotten people so upset, that more and more people are becoming involved in the process. He's waking people up, and that's a good thing. I'm hoping that by 2018, we'll overthrow the Republican Congress and the Senate because of the stuff that Trump's doing, and that'll be the end to it. In the meantime, we're learning a lot of lessons.

Under previous administrations, the EPA had no teeth. So, what's the difference between his dismantling it and it not having any teeth to do anything at all? People are going to see the contradictions. They're going to see just why we need these rules. Some rules were enforced, of course, but certainly not with a lot of vigor. For instance, Prime Minister Trudeau of Canada is very outspoken on climate change, and of course, Trump denies climate change, but what's the difference between the two? Because both of them do absolutely nothing about it. In Canada, you have the Prime Minister okaying the pipelines and the tar sands and every other thing. He's business as usual, just like his predecessor, but he looks good because he says, "Climate change is a problem. We have to address it." But he doesn't address it. Trump looks bad because he says climate change doesn't exist, but the result is the same.

The carnage was everywhere. It was horrific to see photos and video of fish bellied up and dead in pools of oil on the ocean surface, pelicans and other birds covered in black tar, turtles washed up to the ocean choking to death, and stranded dolphins found on the sand. The death of precious species like dolphins doubled in the 7 months following the spill. There were hundreds of thousands of dead seabirds related to the oil spill. The long-term effects on fish populations are yet to be determined. But we do know that oil can cause heart defects in the larvae in the ocean. The ecosystems within the Gulf of Mexico were devastated. More than 1,000 miles of ecosystem within the Gulf, from Texas to Florida, were impacted by this single oil spill. Scientists and marine biologists are still working hard to track the oil and remove as much as they can from the depths of the ocean.

It's not just the oil spills that are impacting marine life. Seismic air guns are one form of searching equipment used by oil and gas companies to pick the best places to set up shop. They send extremely loud blasts into our waters that repeat every 10 seconds every day for months at a time. The blasts cause whales to go deaf. Since these whales use their sense of hearing to navigate the ocean waters, many whales are now washing up dead on shores. The government estimates that as many as 138,500 whales could be injured or killed in the future along the East Coast of the United States if companies are allowed to continue to explore for oil using seismic testing.

SHELL NO!

There is terrible irony in the fact that melting ice caps from warming temperatures have opened the Arctic Ocean to deep-sea drilling. Since 2009, Shell Oil has been trying to drill in the Arctic, only to be blocked at every turn by brave activists. In 2012, Lucy Lawless, an actress from New Zealand and six Greenpeace activists boarded a ship that was bound for the Arctic to drill and halted its operations. Lawless and the activists were arrested after days atop the 174-foot drilling tower. "I have three kids," Lawless, 43, told the Associated Press. "My sole biological reason for being on this planet is to ensure that they can flourish, and they can't do that in a filthy, degraded environment. We need to stand up while we still can."

Despite the fact that Shell did not have a solid plan to deal with oil spills, they were at it again 3 years later trying to get ships out of Seattle and Portland. In May 2015, hundreds of "kayaktivists" blocked a ship known as the *Polar Pioneer* from leaving port by filling the harbor with dozens of Kayaks. One of my best friends Aji Piper, who is a plaintiff in our federal lawsuit and an active member of Earth Guardians, was there that day and performed at the rally. He spoke to the importance of this victory: "Once they start drilling in the sea, they've already damaged that environment, they've created a hazard zone . . . it was extremely important to stop this before they got the chance."

Just 2 months later, in July, another boat tried to leave a harbor in Oregon, but had to pass underneath a bridge in Portland to get to sea. When they got to the bridge, 13 Greenpeace activists were hanging from the bridge in hammocks, blocking the boats path. They blocked the boat from leaving port for 2 days, impacting an already short timeline for Shell's boat to find oil while the ice was still melted. Shell never found oil on that

Greenpeace Activists in Hammock Blockade

expedition and received a lot of bad publicity as many cheered on the bravery of these activists who stopped a potential disaster in the Arctic Ocean.

In September of that year, Shell abandoned their search for Arctic oil after spending an astounding $7 billion on its quest. The dedication of activists to block the ships and the negative PR the company received had taken its toll. People are willing to put their bodies on the line to do their part to protect our oceans, our climate, and our planet.

FINDING SOLUTIONS
IN THE ALTERNATIVES

Not all of us can become pirates or hang from bridges, but we still need to do our part to help protect our oceans. An easy way that everyone can make a difference is by not using plastic. Not only do plastics come from fossil fuels and pollute the atmosphere, but every minute, a dump truck's worth of plastic goes into our oceans. This pollution problem is destroying wildlife and getting into the fish many people are eating.

Like many other environmental issues, young people are also rising up and taking the lead in protecting our ocean. I met a badass crew of high-school students at a conference in upstate New York that blew me away with one of the projects they were working on to clean up the ocean. Their school is called the New York Harbor School, and they are working on a massive campaign called the One Billion Oyster Project. In the 1600s, the New York Harbor was home to 220,000 acres of oyster reefs, which had sustained the indigenous Lenape people and a pristine, biodiverse ecosystem. By the early 1900s, all the oysters were gone and the water was so polluted that oysters and other marine life could not regenerate. It stayed that way until the Clean Water Act passed in1972, which banned dumping waste in the river, allowing the harbor to support life again.

The New York Harbor School had the great idea to restore the original oyster habitat, and found that, by doing so, they actually filtered pollution out of the water. Working together with volunteers and students, they got local restaurant owners to collect and donate shells to restore the habitat. Because of their hard work, there are now 20 million oysters in New York Harbor, filtering 19.7 million gallons of water, removing 72,500 pounds of nitrogen from the water. Their goal is to restore 100 acres of oyster reef by 2030 to sustain one billion oysters, returning this once-dead harbor back into a thriving ecosystem. You can find out more about their project at www.billionoysterproject.org.

In addition to cleaning up the oceans and reclaiming habitats, some youth leaders are working to prevent the pollution in the first place. Lauren Singer has been able to fit all her waste for the past 5 years into a 16-ounce mason jar. Over that time period, the average American would have produced 6,500 pounds of garbage. She says there are two steps to eliminating waste in one's life.

Evaluate. The first step is to take a look at your daily life and ask yourself the following questions.

- How much garbage (and what types) am I currently producing? For example, food packaging—this can help you determine the places that you can start reducing and looking for alternatives.

- Why am I even interested in decreasing my impact? Is it for the environment, to decrease toxins in my life, decrease clutter, or because I'm totally broke and want to save money? Really understand your motivators, and use them as a place to start decreasing what you use.

- What do I actually use on a daily basis (what is in my daily routine), and what do I not use/need? This can help you determine the things that you can donate and reduce.

- What products do I use that I can get more sustainable alternatives to? For example, choosing glass or mason jars instead of plastic storage containers.

- The most important one: How much and what do I really need to be happy? Really assess why you own and hold onto certain things, and determine if you really need that giant foam finger in the back of your closet to be happy.

Transition. Start to downsize and properly dispose of the unnecessary things.

- Bring a reusable bag and water bottle with you everywhere!

- Get rid of the plastic. From storage containers to plastic grocery bags are toxic. For items that are lightly used, donate to your local Goodwill or Salvation Army. For products that are recyclable, do so.

- Replace these products with sustainable, long-lasting alternatives. Such as organic cotton, stainless steel, wood, and glass. Donate your crappy college plastic kitchenware for some nice glass, stainless steel, or cast iron. It is sexy.

- Be creative. Figure out what you can use in different ways. Organic cotton napkins can also be used as a drying mat, to store leafy greens in the fridge, or to bring lunch to work. Mason jars can be used for coffee, takeout, leftovers, toothbrush holders, lotion dispensers . . . and more.

- Make your home your sanctuary. For me, that means having a few things that are really important to me. Most of mine were either handed down to me or obtained on Craigslist. Secondhand!

- Minimize. Ask yourself, what do I not need? What do I wear every day? What did I buy last year that still has tags on it? Whatever it is, it most likely has a value of some sort. Whether donating to your local Goodwill or selling your products at a consignment store or on eBay, you can always get a return on your items.

- Think organic, think local, think sustainable, and *buy in bulk.*

She has also developed products to curb your reliance on single-use disposable items and has a bunch of helpful YouTube videos on her site www.trashisfortossers.com.

One other great way to start is to stop using straws. Americans use 500 million straws a day, many of which end up in the ocean. I stopped using disposable straws and joined actor and activist Adrian Grenier's campaign called #stopsucking. Adrien's PSA campaign has gathered support from Cameron Diaz, Dwayne the Rock Johnson, Justin Beiber, Elijah Wood, Lionel Messi, and Neil DeGrasse Tyson, amongst others. It's a simple first step and easy to remember—just stop sucking!

As far as the big picture, my man Jeff Orlowski, an environmental documentarian, put things in perspective. He says:

> Motivation and hope can swing like a pendulum at times, but in the broad scheme of things, I am very optimistic for a number of reasons. The pessimistic side of

me feels that if we continue down this path, things will get so bad at some point that people won't be able to deny it, and we will have to really put even more and more effort into stalling climate change. So, in my mind, we will solve this at some point, because we will just be faced with the brutal reality of it. But, the more immediate short-term optimism that I feel comes from the fact that the technologies that we need to solve this are growing so fast. These include advances in battery technology, the constantly declining crisis of solar and clean energy, and the constant movement to clean energy. If you're not on that bandwagon, you're going lose a lot of money. So, the questions remain: How long will it take for us to get there? How much natural disaster will there be between now and then? How much human suffering will there be between now and then? How many ecosystems are lost before we change? My analogy for our fight to stop climate change is imagine that you're driving your car on the highway. You look ahead, and see that there's a huge accident. You know that you're going hit the car in front of you. Is it worth stepping on the brakes or not? Of course, you would slam on the breaks, if not just to minimize the impact of a collision. But, when it comes to climate change, people are still debating whether or not we should step on the brakes. In reality, doing that can make things better in both the short term and the long term.

Some days, I wake up finding it difficult to believe both that the planet is in a state of emergency and that so many people still turn away from this harsh reality. In order to fully understand the connections that our oceans have to our climate, we have to remember our connection to the ocean. The sea has always been an essential component to human evolution, unless we evolve again soon, we may permanently destroy it. Our oceans are the lifeblood of the pale blue dot we call home. No matter how far inland we may reside, our existence is shaped by water. Never has there been a more critical time to defend that which gives us life. Forsake the oceans, and we forsake ourselves.

BUILDING AN ENTOURAGE OF EARTH GUARDIANS

An Interview with Adrian Grenier

Adrian is an actor, producer, director, and social good advocate. He is best known for playing the iconic role of A-list movie star Vincent Chase in eight seasons of the HBO smash hit *Entourage*. He cofounded the Lonely Whale Foundation in 2015.

ME: Talk a little bit about your sustainable brand, SHFT, about why you've taken on the task of introducing sustainable ideas and products into mainstream culture. How receptive has it been among people?

ADRIAN: Firstly, I think that everybody needs to ask themselves, "What do I want to do to create a society that helps to grow and evolve our people into a more conscious community?" Because if you're not part of the solution, well, then you're just absent from being a part of the solution! When I was younger, I was always trying to figure out how I could participate, what I could do as an individual. I gravitated toward content creation and communications. Over the years, as an actor and filmmaker, a lot happened in my environmental evolution. Ultimately, my experiences led me to cofound the Lonely Whale Foundation, which really is the result of a lot of growth and maturity.

I found a guy named Peter Glatzer. We started bonding over our ideas of sustainability and how some things about it inspired us, and certain things turned us off.

We came to agree that a lot of times this extreme environmental activism was a turnoff to us. It felt a little unrealistic and overwhelming. From that perspective, if you don't entirely sacrifice your entire life and lifestyle, to chain yourself to a bulldozer, than obviously you're not doing enough. I guess I fundamentally disagreed with that extremism. I thought things would be much better and easier if everybody came together and did a little bit, as opposed to a few doing too much or trying to take the weight of the world on their personal shoulders, telling everybody else what to do and how to do it. We went around pitching a show called *Alter Eco*, which was a moderate-lifestyle reality television show that demonstrated how you can live a conscientious lifestyle while still having fun and connecting with friends and community, showing a lot of aspirational, enjoyable lifestyle things that we thought were all too absent in the conventional tree-hugger extremism. At the time, we were way ahead of the curve. Nobody wanted to buy the show. We probably pitched it for a year, year and a half, until the tides finally turned. I guess it was just some time after *An Inconvenient Truth* that we started getting traction, and we finally sold the show.

That was a long story, but it's how it all came to pass. Ultimately, what happened was the show went to air. People really enjoyed it. It was great. The problem was that networks at the time—this is the early days of the Internet and people are just trying to figure out content on the Internet versus e-commerce—didn't know how to bridge the gap between conventional network and television media with the Internet. They really didn't do a great job in terms of capitalizing all of the positive feedback that we were getting. People were watching the show, they were getting excited about all the options and the products that we were sharing that they could embrace to become more conscientious, and yet they didn't know where to go get them or how to participate. People were hitting us up online saying, "Hey, where can I get that thing" or, "How do I get in touch with that person?"

Because we were sharing all that information, we realized that the wave of the future was the Internet. We wanted to go direct-to-consumer. Long story short, that's when we started shft.com, which was a lifestyle platform where we would share all of the best in sustainability with people. When they wanted to find options in the market to be more conscientious or more environmentally sensitive, they'd know where to go. That's pretty much how it was. Everything was very moderate and accessible, not extreme, but high aesthetic. It was all aspiration because we believe that it could be a market-based solution to the environment where we inspire people to make the right choices and vote with their dollars, instead of simply telling people how bad they are or how destructive they are as humans.

ME: Right. Yeah, man, it's a powerful story. I totally agree that the solution to the environment or the climate catastrophe we see isn't to stop living our lives, stop using our electricity and resources, and go live in the bush, but that there is that sense of humans want to be comfortable. That means finding ways to reach people where they're at. Platforms like yours can help reach people there. Do you think that changing our lifestyle is enough to change the direction of where the planet is headed right now, considering where our oceans are at, where our atmosphere is at, where the environment is at—the global state of the planet?

ADRIAN: Well, I think we have no choice but to be optimistic, because what's the alternative? When things seem dire or all seems lost, the only thing you really can do is be positive and optimistic about what's possible because the alternative is very depressing and bleak. What's the point in that? I don't know. I don't know if, as humans, our algorithms or our formulas are complex enough to know the future. I don't know. Just because we have some data that seems to point to really terrible, destructive things, I don't know if we have enough information to prove that all things will be lost or all things are bad. I think it's just important to commit to the change that you see or you feel in your heart. That's the lifestyle change. It's really a change of our vision as a society. What do we imagine the future to look like? Then go out and try and create that, or build that, or manifest it, or live it, and be in the ways that will allow that to exist. I really believe it's not about saving the world, being a hero for humanity or the planet. Those ideas are very grandiose and I find a lot of environmental instincts to be a little arrogant because we don't really know what we have in store as a humanity, as a species, as a climate.

All we can do is act humbly alone, within our own spiritual guideline.

That, for me, is living simply and trying to live for a positive vision of what is possible. For me, it's about living more connected, with more empathy and compassion for each other, and more sensitively to the world outside of ourselves. To me, that is a graduation from the capitalist ideal that has been, by default, made to be the end-all, be-all goal. I think as we graduate from that ideal, which tends to promote selfish consumption and exploitation of others and our resources, we will start to naturally fold into a lifestyle of purpose that is different and I think healthier and more balanced.

ME: Cool. Thank you, man. Thank you for sharing. Your organization, the Lonely Whale Foundation, from what I've read, that was created out of a documentary. My experience in activism was sparked by watching Leonardo DiCaprio's documentary, The 11th Hour. I think there is power within film and media. How do you see media help motivate people to act, and how have you used your own presence in Hollywood, in the movie industry, to influence the way that you engage in spreading your message and your voice?

ADRIAN: I think part of our human experience is to be able to learn from our memories, learn from our history, and then project potential futures, identify future dangers, and act accordingly. That's what consciousness is. We're unique to all other species in that we have the ability to remember and then to imagine. I think storytelling is an important way for us to inspire each other and share shared ideals and ideas. A film can do a lot in terms of bringing people together on something that we all can agree on and that maybe we can all work toward. But that's not all. A film is just ideas and information. It doesn't actually change anything. The real change starts with the individuals, the people who take that media experience, that intellectual cerebral experience, and then put it into action in the real world. I've been inspired by many films myself.

An Inconvenient Truth definitely changed everybody all at once. It was a big global revelation on some level. It was a tipping point, of sorts. A film that really inspired me was Encounters from the End of the World, a Herzog film. I come from 15 years of media, storytelling, communications, and ideas on the subject of environmentalism. At a certain point, I got frustrated because the information does exist. It's already all out there. How many different ways can we tell the same story? At the end of the day, what real change is that making? I'm actually working on that, personally; in fact, SHFT is transitioning from being a media company to trying to figure out how we can bring these ideas into tangible experience. How do we bring it offline outside of the media realm and into the action realm? That's what we've been trying to crack because I can only watch so many documentaries about the same topic, you know?

ME: Right, right, right. Yeah, and that's something that my organization,

Earth Guardians, is working with—how to help engage thousands of young people across the planet, particularly to use their passions to address really important issues by looking at the solutions. Specifically we are focused on what can we do, how can we actually address the problems of climate change and of these different environmental impacts? A lot of that is through creativity—the arts, music, poetry, storytelling. A lot of the work that you do is around activism to protect the oceans. I guess that is your passion, to defend our oceans? Why is it important for you to protect the oceans?

ADRIAN: Well, partly, I started focusing on the oceans just because I needed to focus my energy. I was getting involved in so many different environmental organizations and causes. Not only environmental, but also social, human, and otherwise. I'm only one man; I can only do so much. Each of us only has so much time in the day. So I decided that it would benefit me and my work to focus my energy. I decided on the oceans because I felt like the oceans were, and are, the underserved aspect of the environment. There's so much work to be done. It's such a big issue that goes grossly underappreciated and underresourced just because it is so abstract, vast, and outside of our everyday human experience. Not many of us experience the ocean daily, let alone yearly, let alone in any intimate way. It's this thing that is outside of our purview, out of sight, out of mind, and I think needs a lot of work to bring people closer to it so that they understand it. If they can't connect to it, they can't care. Given that the ocean is two-thirds of the planet, I think it has a huge, significant role in our environment at large. If we help it become the force of good that it can be, it could do a lot to actually reverse many of the environmental issues we're seeing, as well as feed many people, as well as provide a resource for relaxation, fun, and spiritual enlightenment—that sort of thing.

ME: What do you think has to happen to make the oceans more prominent in a conversation about protecting the environment?

ADRIAN: Well, I was saying before there's a lot of information out there, a lot of documentaries. I think partly it's a matter of being able to communicate and translate the language of the oceans—put what all of the whales and the marine wildlife are trying to communicate about their everyday experience in human terms, and make it aspirational, exciting, fun, and possible. Share the possibilities as opposed to the inevitability of destruction.

ME: What makes you optimistic for the future of our oceans?

ADRIAN: The oceans are extremely resilient, so I think if we can give them a break, they'll be able to bounce back.

CHAPTER 8

Future Food

Re-Envisioning Our Food Systems

"The time has come to reclaim the stolen harvest and celebrate the growing and giving of good food as the highest gift and the most revolutionary act."

—VANDANA SHIVA, SCHOLAR, ENVIRONMENTAL ACTIVIST, AND ANTIGLOBALIZATION AUTHOR

Just like anything else we do in life, the way we eat affects the world around us. My parents made sure I knew that from a young age. I was raised eating as much local and organic food as we could afford, and I've been vegetarian since day one. Mamma taught me how to pull my greens from the ground, and my dad showed me the significance of maintaining a strong connection to our food culture through cooking up traditional Mexican meals you probably can't pronounce the name of, and definitely won't find on the menu at Taco Bell.

Food doesn't only keep us alive and taste good but also it represents a direct connection we have to the Earth. I would definitely say that a love for food is a defining quality of my generation, myself included. One of the best things about traveling is experiencing how much incredible food there is in the world. The second I land in a new city, I grab my phone and

Xiuhtezcatl and Grandma Making Tamales

start reading reviews on Yelp to find the best food joints in town. I really enjoy the idea of learning about a culture or a part of the world through what they eat. Food offers you a glimpse into the traditions of a people and of the relationship with their land. Understanding our food system is critical in understanding the state of the planet and our effect on the world around us.

Both our diets and food choices have changed throughout time. We're in this crazy place in the history of the planet where much of how we produce and consume has absolutely nothing to do with a connection to the Earth. Our current industrialized food system has caused us to lose connection with where our food comes from. In that, we have lost part of what it means to be human. Food is what sustains us. When we take for granted what we put into our bodies, we neglect an important part of ourselves.

View from the Andes

My freshman year in high school, I spent 2 weeks in the Sacred Valley of Peru. This was one of the most incredible places I've ever been.

My school wanted to use Peru as a case study in understanding development and its impact on a country shaped by its deep and rich history. We visited the ruins of ancient cities, temples, and historic churches, soaking in a diverse array of perspectives on its past. Learning the history of Peru felt relatable, in that a great civilization of indigenous peoples had fallen to Spanish conquest. The genocide, colonization, and discrimination that the Quechua people faced seemed to run parallel to what my Mexica ancestors had endured.

After being in Cusco for 3 days and seeing how the whole industry there was commercial- and tourist-driven, we took a bus full of 12 students into the mountains. We were like 12,000 feet above sea level. We drove along a sketchy, windy, one-lane path overlooking this massive drop into the canyon to reach this little, secluded village called Amaru. This was a farming town, nestled along the steep slopes of the Andes. Amaru, meaning "snake" in Quechua, was one of the villages in Peru that has preserved the traditional life, language, and culture of the Quechua people. Spanish being my first language, I thought I'd have an upper hand in talking to my Peruvian relatives. When we left the cities, I realized that most of the families spoke more Quechua than Spanish.

Building an Adobe Greenhouse in Peru

As an indigenous person who has lost a lot of my heritage to colonization, it gave me hope to see that these ways of life were being protected.

Going into and living in these communities, we had opportunities every single day to go work on the land, cultivating potatoes, harvesting crops, and preparing the fields for planting. The crazy thing was that they were successfully growing food without machines, chemicals, or fertilizers on these steep mountainsides. Nothing was flat. Everything was at an angle, some of it nearly vertical at the very highest of these communities.

Back in Colorado, agriculture is a big industry. Although we have big mountains, the plains are where they're growing food. This place took my breath away, looking out over one of the most beautiful mountain ranges in the world. The diversity of the local food groups was unbelievable. For example, Peru grows more than 55 varieties of corn and thousands of different kinds of potatoes. I feel like potatoes are often seen as an Irish thing, but it's actually thanks to Peru that the world has hash browns and French fries. Even after harvesting for only an hour on one plot of land, we found over a dozen different kinds of potatoes in every color, every shape, and every size you could imagine. It was amazing to actually see and live that connection to my food.

Every family in Amaru has a plot of land that they work and live off of. Feeding their families and making money is dependent on their connection to their land. It's a direct symbiosis between them and nature. The father of the family that was hosting us led us on a walk to this beautiful point that overlooked the whole community and the valley below. As we walked past the purple fields of quinoa and pastures of freely roaming pigs and donkeys, he would point out and show us all the different kinds of plants that he used for medicinal purposes, to make teas, and to season their food. He talked about how the cycle of agriculture there is done in a way that is totally in balance with nature, not something that they just made up in the 21st century. It was a practice that has been carried on for generations, since before the Inca Empire.

Their lifestyle was in direct respect to preserving that land. Just enough so that they could feed and sustain themselves but also pass on the land to their children and their children's children. They would farm a piece of land with a more nutrient-intensive plant like corn, and, after they harvested it, they would let the land rest to allow the nutrients to be restored. The next time they cultivated that plot of land was with a different crop like quinoa or wheat. This deeply rooted understanding of agriculture is a stark contrast to how we are producing food in the industrialized world.

Part of what helps shape the actions of these communities are the principles passed on from their ancestors. The first is a commitment to help your neighbors. If someone needed extra help to prepare their entire field, all of the neighbors would show up to support them in good faith that, when they needed help, they would return the favor. This strengthened a sense of community and trust among the villages. The second principle was to work together for the greater good of the community, making decisions that helped everyone prosper. These values defined these communities, making it a living, breathing system based on the prosperity of all its people.

Toward the end of our trip, we stopped in another village called Mismanay to build a greenhouse out of adobe for one of the families there. My friends and I woke up with the sun almost every day, and we weren't even the first ones to rise. My friend Gabe and I would stumble out the door of the second floor of our host family's house, exhausted from the previous day's work to see the mother of the home already washing clothes, sorting potatoes, and feeding the chickens.

Walking along the dirt roads that connected the village, we passed kids that looked like they were 7 or 8 years old, herding sheep, pigs, and donkeys to their pastures along the mountainside. Every home on either side of the path was made of adobe and wood. Most days, we would stop to help elders in what looked to be their seventies carry heavy jugs full of water back to their homes. These towns lacked running water, plumbing, and electricity in some places. Not every family had a car, much less a Wi-Fi router. What the world saw as underdeveloped, I saw as a beautiful, simple way of living.

The most important lesson that I'd learned from this trip is that poverty isn't synonymous to suffering. These communities had a more sustainable method of agriculture than most of the world. They are almost entirely independent and have been able to preserve a way of life that maintains a sacred balance with the Earth that many of us have forgotten. Above all, these people are among the happiest I've ever met. These people are thriving, and the less they have in their lives, the less there is to stress over.

While our bodies are pumped with chemicals in our food, our water, our air, our medicine, and the products we use, they're among the healthiest I've met, even without easy access to modern health care. These two weeks in Peru were a snapshot of a lot of what my father taught me about life in Latin America. The things we value define how hard it is to be happy, and the value systems of the Quechua people, founded in a connection to the Earth, their culture, and their people, have a lot to teach us. These are practical things that don't need to be lost in history.

They are re-emerging for many nonindigenous people in the ideas of permaculture. The indigenous people of Peru, like modern permaculturists, found ways to irrigate without pumping water from aquifers, using the curvature of the ground and gravity-fed methods. It's why many of the principles within permaculture seem obvious to people who have been living this way for thousands of years. Principles like producing no waste and using and valuing diversity. These are the things that we've gotten away from and need to return to as quickly as possible to repair our broken food system.

LOSING OUR CONNECTION TO FOOD

Perhaps there is no more misleading title for a chapter in food history than what people call the Green Revolution. When we think of "green," we often think about sustainability or the environment. However, the "green" in the Green Revolution wasn't referring to that at all. In this case, "green" was meant to be the opposite of red, the color that symbolizes communism. The United States was concerned that poor peasant farmers would gravitate to socialism.

The idea of the Green Revolution was simple. By introducing industrial agricultural practices to include tractors and chemical fertilizers, farmers could increase their yield and the United States could keep them away from communism. Some have celebrated the Green Revolution as a success, because in some regions, it temporarily increased food production. One of the many downsides is that it made farmers reliant on a method of growing food that is both costly and resource-dependent. We can see the manifestation of the Green Revolution currently in the expansion of global Big Agribusiness.

Suicide Seeds and Suicide Culture

If there were a symbol for a lot of what is wrong with the food system, that image would be of a small tree branch in a brown rectangular box. This deceivingly friendly image is the logo of a company called Monsanto. The agribusiness giant specializes in GMO and hybrid seeds that either don't reproduce or are patented so you can't reuse them.

The seed monopoly they seek means that farmers have to buy seeds every year as well as high-priced fertilizers, pesticides and industrial agricultural equipment to continually farm and reproduce these seeds. This practice creates a tremendous amount of debt for poor rural farmers and takes a considerable toll on the land and the environment.

In places like India, Monsanto controls 95 percent of the cottonseed. They've patented it as Bt cotton. For the larger farms reliant on irrigation, the arrangement has worked out okay, as the farms can produce higher yields, allowing them to pay off their loans over time. However, this has been a deadly arrangement for the smaller farmer whose fields are rain-watered, which is 65 percent of India's farms. The debt these farms accumulate to grow GMO cotton puts them in a perilous situation, if anything were to go wrong. With climate change leading to more extreme weather events and drought, it is has become more common for India's farmers to see weather events wipe out their entire crops. This creates an impossible situation, with farmers going bankrupt and losing hope as their ability to support their family vanishes.

In India, it's estimated that a farmer commits suicide every 30 minutes. Recent studies have indicated that an increase in farmer suicide in rain-fed areas is directly related to an increased reliance on Monsanto's Bt GMO crop. The rate of farmer suicide has increased along with the increased use of Bt cotton. The Indian government says they are taking the new evidence seriously and re-evaluating dependency on GMO seed.

Monsanto has created a trap for farmers, making them reliant on their seeds and pesticides, while driving up costs over time. Indian scholar, and one of my personal heroes, Vandana Shiva notes that they have driven up the prices on patented seeds as much as 8,000 percent. According to the Indian government, 75 percent of rural debt is related to farming input purchases.

The suicide epidemic amongst farmers is not unique to India. In the United States, farmer suicide is double the national rate. We see a similar cycle of debt and dependency created by an increasing industrial agricultural system. The new agricultural model gives big farms a huge advantage over small farms and makes it harder for these small farms to sustain themselves.

We have also lost immense biodiversity because of a seed industry controlled by big business. *National Geographic* magazine estimates that 93 percent of the vegetable seeds available in 1903 have disappeared. Now, people are starting seed banks around the world to save seeds that might go extinct in an agricultural environment that is focused on "bigger is better" mentality.

Vandana Shiva and Earth Guardians at Uplift

SEEDS OF FREEDOM

An Interview with Vandana Shiva

Vandana Shiva is an Indian scholar, environmental activist, and antiglobalization author. She has authored more than 20 books and has worked to reinstate the tremendous wisdom in many traditional practices. She is a member of the Fundación IDEAS, Spain's Socialist Party's think tank, as well as an important part of the International Organization for a Participatory Society.

ME: For someone that doesn't know a whole lot, how do GMOs threaten our food security moving toward a sustainable planet?

VANDANA: It starts with the imposition of war chemicals into our agriculture. These war chemicals are made from fossil fuels, which drives 50 percent of the carbon emissions in our planet.

ME: So, how do GMOs affect the planet?

VANDANA: They don't exist separate from industrial farming. GMOs destroy 75 percent of the soil, 75 percent of the water, and more than 75 percent of the biodiversity. And, as I mentioned, it has contributed to 50 percent of the greenhouse gases. Corporations genetically modify corn, canola, and soya, which are in many of our foods, and even cotton. No one is leaping up in arms saying, "We want to eat GMO soya, we want to eat GMO corn," but 90 to 95 percent of the corn and soya of the United States is now GMO corn and soya.

My calculations are that the United States farmers are paying Monsanto 10 billion dollars annually just for the royalty part, besides the other costs of this kind of agriculture. So, you're further destroying what little biodiversity remains in farming. Corporations are increasing the use of pesticides. The claim was that this would be a substitute to chemicals, but it has actually increased the use of the chemicals that are harming our health. Seventy-five percent of the bees are gone. So, you know, the pollinators are going, and they're responsible for one-third of the food we eat. So, no matter which part of the ecological crisis you look at, the industrial system of the GMOs is really troubling farmers in India, as they recognize the health ramifications of this practice.

So, basically, it is agriculture that is wiping out farmers, and it's not as a side effect, it is by intention. They're now really talking about farming without farmers. Digital farming, where Monsanto is joining hands with Silicon Valley to own soil, have surveillance drones, and self-driving tractors; they have no idea about the Earth. They have no idea about the people or the food. But they want to make huge money on seeds.

In the early days, when I started my journey, there was talk of making a trillion dollars annually from seed royalties. They're talking about three trillion dollars from climate-related money making. So, this turned the problem they've created into their next market. I believe the biggest problem, for me, with GMOs, is that three corporations that created poison on this Earth want to control our food supply, and that kind of concentration of power is a major threat.

ME: What have you learned from past social movements, from historical movements, throughout time to understand the way to create movements today?

VANDANA: Well, you know, my activism began with this beautiful movement called Chipko. The original hug-the-tree movement. During this time, logging was impacting the people living in the mountains. The women understood that logging was leading to floods, droughts, and landslides. They were walking farther and farther to get water, and then they said, "No more logging." And, I think the most beautiful activism that I have experienced began with them saying, "We're going to hug these trees. And, you'll have to kill us before you kill the trees." It took 10 years of that kind of locate, of love, resisting. At that time, logging was the biggest industrial enterprise in our region, and they managed to stop it by showing the connections between the destruction of our rivers, the destruction of the soils along the area they'd walk to get water.

ME: Companies like Monsanto and Syngenta claim that GMOs are helping increase yield and feed people globally. How do you respond to that?

VANDANA: Well, I respond to it by basically doing the research myself and citing other people's research. There's a brilliant study out of the United States from the Union of Concerned Scientists. The title is "Failure to Yield." They've looked at every GMO release in America, and not in a single one is there an increase in yield. And, scientifically, one can predict that because, all you do with genetic engineering is shoot a gene into an existing plant material.

In India, the increase came from hybrid cotton. It created new pests and made the plant vulnerable to pests, and now you have a huge decline. Our scientific agencies have said it's a failure. So, our government is threatening to pull the licenses, and Monsanto is fighting that in court. So, all that anybody who wants to get this data should do is look at the government opinion data and look at the Cotton Researcher's Institute data. Remember, there are only four crops that they have commercialized in the landscape: corn, soya, cotton, and canola. You don't eat cotton. Canola, soya, and corn used to be food. Soya used to be in some Asian food. Corn came from Mexico and was the first nation's primary diet. Canola, original canola as mustard, came from India but has been distorted to take out the taste and the flavor to make it industrial oil. Ninety percent of these GMOs are going for biofuel and animal feed. So, it's time for them to stop lying and saying that they're feeding the world. They're starving the world.

ME: Why is it important for people to understand our food system?

VANDANA: Well, the first reason that is important to understand is that we are food. We are made of food. You don't eat, then your body doesn't get the nourishment it needs to replenish itself. But, the most important issue is when you eat toxic food, whether it be pesticides or pesticides plus GMOs, it's causing huge harm to our bodies.

We need to shift to putting organic matter back into the soil to do organic farming. It is not just to increase food production and reduce hunger. It's removing malnutrition and nutrient deficiencies because our research in Navania is showing that chemicals are depleting soil nutrients. Organic is actually increasing soil nutrients. As far as organic matter goes, we have increased organic matter by 99 percent in our soils.

ME: Do you have hope?

VANDANA: I have hope because I grow diversity. In society and in nature. There can be a happy ending. You give me hope for the future. Intelligent, bright minds like yours can be hope for adults in a world where we live among many adults that don't quite . . . aren't quite there yet.

POISONING PARADISE

While the economics of industrial agriculture hurts small farmers, the implementation of it hurts everyone. That's because the pesticides used by Big Ag like Monsanto are toxic and hard to control. On the island in Kauai, Hawaii, residents know the firsthand damage agribusiness creates. Kauai has become ground zero for tests of GMO crops, with five major chemical companies—Monsanto, Syngenta, Dupont, Dow, and BASF—occupying the Garden Island.

On two occasions, toxic chemicals from a Syngenta field next to Waimea Middle School caused teachers and students to go home ill, with some even being hospitalized. In a video taken by a schoolteacher, you can see a mist of herbicide being carried by the wind into the school facilities. These instances have the community deeply concerned. For good reason, the American Pediatric Society says that early exposure to chemical pesticides is associated with pediatric cancer, decreased cognitive function, and even behavioral problems.

The island residents weren't just exposed at their schools. Even their homes were not safe. Malia Chun, a schoolteacher and anti-GMO activist, describes the problem: "The only thing that stands between my home and these chemicals is a polluted irrigation ditch. We are surrounded by and exposed to pesticides on a daily basis." After the chemical companies moved nearby, Malia said both she and her family started experiencing shortness of breath, headaches, and bloody noses. When she asked her doctor what could be the cause of her adult-onset asthma, her doctor indicated that the environment probably caused it.

In response, Malia began to organize with her community to protect her native home. Together, with councilman Gary Hooser, they introduced House Bill 2491, which requires companies to disclose which pesticides they are spraying, and in what quantities they are doing so. In addition, HB 2491 requires a buffer between schools, hospitals, waterways, and other public spaces. Monsanto and others fought hard against the bill, but after years of organizing, the community was able to get it passed and signed by the mayor. It was yet another of the growing examples where a community defeated a giant. These companies, however, are refusing to adhere to the commonsense regulation, and responded by suing the town in federal court.

We've been told that GMOs, pesticides, and chemical fertilizers will increase yields and help feed people. Monsanto will tell you that they are curing world hunger one genetically modified seed at a time, but according to a study by the UN, small-scale organic family farming could double the world's food production in just 10 years, if we wholly committed to it. Fancy advertising can't gloss over the facts. These stories show us that what's in the best interest of the people often contradicts a corporate bottom-line approach.

GROW OUTSIDE THE LINES

In addition to being abundant, small-scale farming is healthier. Instead of products that contain GMOs and pesticides, you get a fresher, more-vibrant product. It tastes better, is better for you, and you gain something from having a relationship with your food and where it comes from. It's amazing to meet your local farmers and get your produce directly from the source.

Logically speaking, local or organic food should be less expensive. It costs money to send food across the planet and use expensive fertilizers and pesticides. To keep this costly food system in place, the United States government spends around $100 billion in subsidies every year, most of which goes to big factory-style food systems. This makes for an uneven playing field for small local farmers, who can't compete with an artificially cheap food market.

If we accounted for the true cost of the food we eat in terms of subsidies, health-care costs, and environmental impact, a fast-food hamburger would likely cost around five times as much. How many times have you heard someone say I would eat healthy, but it's too expensive? That's often true on the individual level, but when you look at the costs to society, it's a completely different story.

Despite a food system set up to benefit industrial agriculture, small-scale sustainable alternatives are on the rise. When we do have a choice, more of us are choosing organic and local options. Organic food sales are growing every year, and production will increase as demand does. Many farmers are learning that they can earn more by growing organic than through conventional means. The good thing about the food crisis is that we can literally eat our way out of it. If we don't support the industrial agricultural practices, they won't exist.

Local sustainable farming has the power to simultaneously address our connection to food and solve the climate crisis. The healthiest soil is living soil, full of good bacteria, fungi, and worms. This kind of soil absorbs the carbon and prevents it from entering our atmosphere and trapping heat. Industrial agriculture, drilling, and mining kill the soil. Estimates are that more than 50 percent of original soil carbon has now been released into the atmosphere. That's 320 billion tons of carbon. To put that number in perspective, it's the equivalent to 84,019 coal power plants or 67 billion passenger vehicles on the road for a year.

Ironically enough, Monsanto's web site recently started to include information tackling climate change and reducing our carbon footprint. Statistics show that agriculture accounts for between 19 and 29 percent of global greenhouse emissions. Regardless of what they say, their actions tell us that they are out for one thing, and one thing only: big profit. Reports indicate that the "faster, bigger, cheaper" approach to food is depleting the Earth's soil at more than 13 percent of the rate it can be replaced. Just as concerning, we've lost 75 percent of the world's crop varieties over the last century. Genetically engineered corn and soy are rapidly overtaking native grasslands and threatening indigenous land throughout the country.

Monsanto is the face of the problem, but if we really want to create serious change in the farming and agricultural industry, we have to start eating different and sourcing locally.

THE OG OF FOOD JUSTICE

Every now and then, you meet people that have methods of resistance so creative and unique that it changes your perspective on the world. Using the elements of hip-hop, my homie Ietef Vita a.k.a. DJ Cavem is changing the conversation of the food justice movement. He is a wicked MC, a DJ, a B-boy, and an organic gardener. People also know him as the OG (organic gardener) and the founder of the eco hip-hop movement. Mixing the cultures of hip-hop and food through performing and giving presentations and workshops that educate about healthy living,

DJ Cavem is bringing sustainable food practices to the hood and beyond.

In 2015, he was invited to the White House with his inspiring wife, Alkemia, as part of Michelle Obama's Let's Move celebration, with top chefs like Bobby Flay. The two of them are an incredible team that has traveled nationally to teach others about the power of plant-based food through culinary concerts. During these shows, DJ Cavem spins records and spits bars, while Alkemia teaches delicious vegan recipes, so you get your beats however you like—shredded, juiced, or amplified.

It's important to know food injustice doesn't affect everyone the same. People of color are often forced into situations where the only easily available food is toxic. They are largely left out of the conversation of food justice. DJ Cavem has been a pioneer in bridging this gap. One of the reasons he has been so effective in working with inner-city youth is that he can relate to them. DJ Cavem grew up in the low-income neighborhood of Five Points in Denver. He says, "Right down the block from the house that I grew up in was a youth penitentiary. Two blocks away from the youth penitentiary was a liquor store. Across the street from the liquor store was the high school that I went to. Three blocks away from there was another fast-food joint that's been causing high blood pressure and diabetes in my community. The freshest thing you could get on my block was a lemon at a liquor store."

Many people refer to these urban areas without access to good food as food deserts. Seeing little opportunity in his neighborhood, DJ Cavem began rolling with a gang. But my man turned it around. Now, he says that real Gs have hoes, and turn soil with them. He's been educating youth about how diet and exercise affects our health, our happiness, and the well-being of our community.

DJ Cavem says, "We started thinking about how we flip what we brought into our community, and a lot of times it takes beets—fresh juiced beets, you know? They need to have that vitality in their hand that they can taste and listen to at the same time. So, when I do these workshops, we're always packed and over capacity because of the fact that they know we're bringing something that they won't be able to get the rest of the week."

Using art to create change is one of the most powerful ways to reach people, especially youth. The true roots of hip-hop culture lie in

DJ Cavem Going Green, Living Bling

empowering and bringing communities together. DJ Cavem has brought his story to the world through the art he creates and his vision for using food to build solutions to our climate crisis, and empower the voiceless.

From writing beats in the studio together, to making vegan nachos in the kitchen, DJ Cavem has always had my back, teaching me to see food as a crucial part of a healthy climate, planet, and people.

To Change Our Diets, We Need to Change the Conversation

Even in the activist community, veganism is an issue that can be nearly as divisive as climate change. Meeting Ietef helped me see veganism in a different way. I've never eaten meat in my life, but, until recently, I never thought about how the dairy industry is also a big part of our environmental and climate crisis. It's estimated that it takes about 1,000 gallons of water to produce 1 gallon of cow's milk, with most of that going into growing the corn to feed the cows. Dairy, like the beef industry, is a huge contributor to greenhouse gases, because cows are ruminants who burp and fart methane as part of their digestive systems. Methane is one of the worst greenhouse gases, far worse than carbon dioxide, and recent studies show that just methane from cows contributes about 4 percent of humanrelated climate emissions.

After understanding the immense impact, I cut cow dairy almost entirely out of my diet. I still eat some goat dairy from mostly local farms, which has a smaller environmental impact, and my family gets our eggs from 10 free-roaming chickens in my backyard. I'm not perfect with my eating choices, but I'm willing to engage and learn. Having conversations about our food is essential to addressing our climate and environmental problems. Like many people, I've personally experienced a lot of hate and judgment around what I choose to eat. I've been attacked by people saying, things like, "If he really cared about the environment, he would go vegan," ignoring the rest of what I do for the planet. Many vegans are committed to nonviolent ways of living but some of them are starting more "beef" than a factory farm.

For many indigenous people, eating meat is a part of their culture. It has been for hundreds of years. The way many indigenous people consume meat is through a more connected and spiritual approach, where they honor and give thanks to the animals for the life they've given. Yet they can feel vilified for doing what their ancestors have done by people who lack cultural understanding. Even if you're not indigenous, being shamed for your lifestyle choices isn't the way to start a conversation or shift consciousness. The most successful way that I see the vegan community reaching all people is to meet them where they are and show compassion to the different situations people face.

Part of what's broken about our food system is that unhealthy, processed fast food (which is rarely vegan) is cheap. Not everyone has the same level of privilege when it comes to our food choices. A lot of people can't prioritize animal rights and climate stability when they're struggling to feed their families.

Rather than pointing fingers, let's work with people to help make better food choices. My approach when talking about this super important issue is to invite people to take small steps they can commit to. For people who eat fast food on a regular basis, the first step could be to cut back on the amount of fast-food meat that they consume, and try and turn toward locally sourced meat with less of a carbon impact. If you're heavily dependent on meat, you could start trying "meatless Mondays" or picking a couple days a week where you can cut back on your meat consumption. The most important thing is to have a sense of awareness, and to feel empowered to do what you can. From the first small steps, you can continue to eventually cut meat and dairy out of your diet entirely

Just as important as being vegan is being aware of where your food comes from. For instance, many vegan products can contain palm oil, such as butter substitutes. As I discussed in Chapter 6, palm oil is a big contributor to climate change, while destroying the habitat of many endangered species. Many milk substitutes come from far way and are also resource intensive. It's important to have an open mind when it comes to these things, and to recognize that everything has an impact.

I love having these kinds of conversations with Ietef. Whenever we travel together or I'm at his home, I'm always eating delicious, vibrant vegan food he and his wife prepare or from one of the many dope vegan restaurants across the country. Even though we're at different places with how we eat, the positive dialogue and supportive approach I share with Ietef has empowered me to reach further to live a more sustainable life through my diet. From super-dedicated vegans to traditionally heavy meat-eaters, changing the way we have this conversation is critical in bridging the gap between all of us and the way that we eat.

GROW FOOD, NOT LAWNS

As DJ Cavem is building a connection between inner-city youth and the food they consume, a similar movement is turning lawns into farms. The movement is called Fleet Farming and is led by the Orlando based nonprofit IDEAS for Us, founded by my friend Chris Castro. They were able to connect these uncultivated front lawns with an appetite for local food. They began to organize swarm rides, where a group of mostly young people would ride bikes to a home that had donated its front lawn for food growth. The only prerequisite was that the homeowners hadn't sprayed their lawn with chemicals for at least 2 years. Ideas for Us would till the soil and bring in 12 inches of organic mushroom compost to put on top.

From Lawns to Gardens

The homeowner got 5 to 10 percent of the fresh organic vegetables, with the rest sold as shares via community supported agriculture (CSA), at the farmers' market and to local restaurants. The organizers then used the money to pay community members to maintain the small farms (called farmlettes). The idea has taken off, with more than 300 people signing up to donate their front lawns, even though they currently only have the capacity to run 20 farmlettes in Orlando. The model has spread from Florida to California, and all the way to Uganda. Together, they've engaged more than 1,000 people in urban gardening and have produced more than 4,000 pounds of produce.

"Our goal is to replicate this model to food insecure neighborhoods and communities around the country and use food as the medium for community development, empowerment, and prosperity," says Chris Castro. "We are working to redefine how we produce and distribute food by converting lawns and underutilized land into a distributed network of mini organic farms (a.k.a. farmlettes) and empower communities to reconnect with the natural world through an edible education experience."

There is ample room to grow with fleet farming, as more than 40 million acres of lawn space could be used to supply abundant fresh produce for the community. Unfarmed lawns end up sucking water and energy, with 30 to 60 percent of fresh water in the US cities used to water lawns and 580 million gallons of gasoline used annually to mow them. In addition, the average plate of food in the United States travels up to 1,800 miles to reach your table.

This type of community farming not only drastically reduces the carbon footprint of agriculture but also it helps store carbon in the soil. We have already surpassed 400 parts per million of carbon dioxide in the atmosphere, but former NASA atmospheric scientist James Hansen says that the safe level of carbon in the atmosphere is below 350 parts per million. To get there, we need to take carbon out of the atmosphere. The safest and best way to do that and reverse this trend is to store carbon in the soil.

The fleet-farming movement is growing fast, and you can join at www.fleetfarming.org. It's the type of solution that you can implement in almost any community. It turns an environmental liability, like water-hungry lawns into an incredible resource. Start a fleet-farming project in your own community or join an existing one. This is just one possible way you can get involved with building soil and growing food. Below are some other ways I love.

Build food forests. The idea of edible forests is a part of the permaculture movement. These food forests mimic forests that occur in nature. They are designed to be rich in biodiversity and productivity. Not only do food forests feed us but also they can produce food for beneficial insects, pollinators, chickens, goats, songbirds, and other important wildlife. Choosing the right plants will also reinvigorate the soil, as many edible plants are known to reintroduce carbon into the ground. Cities such as Seattle have introduced edible forests. This is another great way to store carbon in the soil. You can push your city to start one, and you can build a food "forest" in your own backyard. You can find out more at www.foodforestfarm.com.

Take composting to another level. Composting is a dope tool for sustainably disposing of organic waste and creating healthy soil ecosystems, rebuilding even the most depleted soils. Simply put, compost is a mixture of organic materials, such as leaves, manure, and food waste that decomposes into nutrient-rich plant fertilizer. Besides adding nutrients, compost can help soil maintain moisture, stabilize its pH, and degrade harmful compounds. You don't need a ton of space to set up a compost bin and your yard waste, extra food, and coffee grounds can all be used to create incredibly healthy soil.

Support our pollinators. No pollinators, no food. Pollinators like bees, butterflies, hummingbirds, and bats are essential for healthy ecosystems. They are responsible for the success of one-third of all produce grown in the United States, supporting and increasing biodiversity within the food system. In order to support our pollinators, make sure to use plants that are native to your area, are free of neonicotinoid pesticides (neonics for short), and bloom at different times of the year to provide a consistent food source. You can also follow in the footsteps of Earth Guardians in Boulder and work to get pesticides banned in public parks.

Add nitrogen for the perfect soil recipe. Nitrogen is incredibly important for the health of soil, thanks to the symbiotic relationship between many plants and bacteria. Certain bacteria can aid plants in converting atmospheric nitrogen into a form that can be stored in the soil and used by the plant. Legumes, including peas, beans, favas, and lentils, are some of the best nitrogen-fixing plants and can be grown easily in home gardens. Other nitrogen-fixers include lupins, mesquite trees, alder trees, the honeybush, and even licorice. These plants are also ideal for dry climates, as nitrogen-fixing plants will help repair the soil to better retain moisture and allow you to garden with less water.

Always buy local. We are lucky to live during a time when a growing number of farmers are offering their produce directly to consumers. In recent years, the Farmers Market Coalition has reported more than 8,600 registered farmers' markets in the US, four times the amount registered in the mid-1990s. Buying our food from local farmers helps build local resilience, while cutting the carbon footprint of our food transportation. We have the power to change this by buying locally.

Right to know. As a society, we also need to work for transparency in what foods we buy. In 2016, the US Senate approved legislation that would require food to carry labels listing GMO ingredients. Despite this law, consumers must still do their research to determine which products contain GMOs. One downside to the law is that, rather than direct and on-the-package labeling, companies can choose to slap a QR Code on the package, requiring the consumer to scan it to determine which GMO ingredients are included in the food. Even though it is not the best version of the bill that could've passed, it is still a step in the right direction. As it stands today, we are still years away from true transparency. The good news is that when you buy USDA certified organic foods, you don't need to read the label because they are guaranteed to not contain GMOs.

Next time you take a bite of a piece of fruit or dive into a sandwich, think about everything that went into the journey of that piece of food. Be aware of where your money is going and what type of agriculture you are supporting. Food should be a source of joy and community, not just profits for businesses that are threatening our planet.

ORGANIZING FOR A NEW FOOD SYSTEM

It's not enough to change our personal habits alone, we need to make sure that the old oppressive systems are dismantled so the new just food system will have room to flourish and grow. This will not be easy, because the agricultural giants have a lot of money and influence, but we can start on a local level. One way to do this is by organizing schools. The National Farm to School Network now estimates that more than 42,000 schools are participating in local food sourcing that has mobilized $789 million to be spent in regional agriculture. Many of these local food programs are also teaching young people about where their food comes from and how important that connection is. Find more at www.farmtoschool.org

College students are also organizing on their campuses with the Real Food Challenge (RFC) to get their schools to commit to replacing industrial farmed food with locally sourced community-based agriculture. So far, more than 70 campuses have committed to increasing the amount of what they call "real food" by at least 20 percent. The students and young organizers with RFC are also working with the supply chain to make sure that workers are paid and treated fairly. Their organizing goes beyond just food into food justice, and while they are organizing so students eat healthier and have a smaller environmental impact, they are also breaking down the systems of oppression that limit access to food.

Part of this means taking their work into the broader community. They are a part of a coalition called HEAL (Health Environment Agriculture and Labor), which includes the Union of Concerned Scientists, Friends of the Earth, The Foodchain Worker Alliance, and many other labor, agricultural, health, and environmental groups. They are working together to expose how damaging and unjust our current food system is, while working to transform it. West Coast Director for Real Food Challenge Estefania Narvaez explains their strategy: "The solutions already exist at a local level, so what we need to do is expose the bad and block it to allow for these systems to change."

The phasing out of industrial agriculture and implementing the solutions need to happen simultaneously. Our food is what sustains us, it gives us life and connects us, but it can also be our undoing if we let big corporate interests control what's on our plates. We've had the solutions all along, we just need to implement them and wipe away this chapter of producing food from factories. Resistance is fertile.

FOOD FOR THOUGHT
An Interview with Suzy Amis Cameron

A noted environmental advocate, founder, and mother of five, Suzy Amis Cameron is committed to the principles of sustainability in all aspects of our lives. In particular, she is focused on reducing our ecological footprint through plant-based eating. Ten years ago, she cofounded MUSE School to prepare young people to live consciously with themselves, one another, and the planet. In 2015, MUSE became the first school in the country with a 100 percent organic, plant-based lunch program. With her husband, director James Cameron, Suzy founded and is executive director of Plant Power Task Force, with a mission is to show the impact of animal agriculture on climate change and the environment. She is also a founder of Food Forest Organics, a marketplace and café to taste, learn about, and purchase plant-based food in New Zealand, and Red Carpet Green Dress, an organization that showcases socially and environmentally responsible fashions. As an actor, she has featured in more than 25 films, including *The Usual Suspects* and *Titanic*.

ME: Before you worked in environmental advocacy, you were engaged as a Hollywood actress. How did you find a voice and what kind of advice do you have for other people who are looking to pursue their passion and have a positive impact by using that passion?

SUZY: The one word that pops out is "opportunities." I think all of us across the world have opportunities that are presented to us. The opportunities look different for everyone, but if people would take the time to actually take advantage of opportunities, sometimes they can lead to all kinds of different great adventures that end up changing their pathway. I grew up in Oklahoma and was outside an enormous amount. We had a farm, so I grew up riding horses, and I was always exposed to the outdoors. I had an opportunity to go off and be a model when I was 17 years old, which allowed me to travel the world. It was in those years that I started seeing devastation that was already starting to happen in the world—littering and waterways that were filthy and places where I couldn't drink the water in some of the locations where I went on these magazine shoots.

That led to an opportunity to become an actress, and I took that opportunity. From there, interestingly enough, I learned to be able to get up in front of people and speak and have an actual platform. I think there are a lot of us who could be using their platforms for great things, even though they might be using them to take selfies and post whatever the last restaurant they went to or whatever. I realize the platform that we have is able to make a difference in the world. I take it very seriously, and it's a huge responsibility for us to be able to go out and make speeches, write books, make films, start schools, start organizations, whatever it might be. We realize that we have opportunity sitting right in front of us to be able to have meetings and phone calls and collaborations with people like you and other people in the world, and we use that very carefully and certainly don't want to abuse it in any way. We want to use it only for trying to make the world a better place for our children to grow up in.

ME: It's so inspiring hearing your stories and just thinking about waking up. You founded Muse School, an independent school based in Los Angeles, focused on sustainability and living consciously with the planet and each other, largely, I think, because of the frustration with the lack of environmental awareness as standard school curriculums. How does education play a role in the way we talk about climate change and in the way we address our climate crisis?

SUZY: Jim and I met 21 years ago. It was very clear that both of us were on a path of becoming aware of environmental impact. I would say that at the time mine was certainly more close to home in terms of how we were recycling, if we were using or not using plastics and cleaning products—that sort of thing. He was looking a lot at renewable energy, the energy sector, and that sort of thing. We sort of melded our interests together. Starting Muse actually was a very selfish endeavor, because I was looking around for schools for our three young children, and I couldn't find anything that would teach them about the environment, feed them beautiful food, or teach them in a way that celebrated who they are and allowed them to learn in their own way, at their own pace, and really dive into their passions and their interests.

In fall of 2015, we went 100 percent plant-based. There are certainly health reasons for that, but the main reason we did it was for environmental reasons. I'm sure this happens to you all the time. You get up and give a speech, and at the end of the speech, people raise their hands and say like, "What can we do?" It can be demoralizing to hear all of the information about climate change and the state of the world and all of that, and people just get paralyzed. They don't even know where to start.

I used to say things like, "Oh, well, you can change your light bulbs and drive an electric car or a hybrid and put in solar panels," and things like that, which are all great to do, but not everybody can afford that. Especially if you're talking to young people, they might not even be driving yet, but they want to be able to do something that makes a change. There's one simple, elegant thing that everyone can do, is look at what you're putting on your plate.

The more fruits and vegetables you eat, the more plant-based, the more you're making an impact. Every time you eat plant-based you cut your carbon footprint and your water footprint in half. People's jaws drop when I tell them that one of the top three contributors to climate change is animal agriculture. It doesn't matter if you're 5 or 95, you can decide what you put on your plate. You can make a difference every time you eat.

ME: You and your husband, James, have instituted some pretty large campaigns, including an effort to make fashion more sustainable. You're also committed to helping the environment in your personal lives, adopting a plant-based diet, which we covered. How can people make changes in their everyday lives to lessen the impact?

SUZY: I started a campaign of Red Carpet, Green Dress around sustainable fashion. It was focusing on creating a sustainable dress to walk the red carpet at the Oscars. I think we're in year 8 now. Starting in the first year, I realized how difficult it was just to find beautiful fabric that was dyed in a conscious way and milled in a conscious way and wasn't creating waste or polluting waterways. I was planning on just doing it for one year, but of course it opened up a can of worms—I couldn't let it go. In year two, I thought this is kind of silly because creating one dress for the red carpet didn't make sense. How sustainable is that?

So I started talking about the fact that we all wear clothes every single day. From the moment you're born until the day you die you're wearing clothes—unless you're running around having fun being naked. Starting with that point of view, Jim and I have started Cameron Friendly Farms, where we are growing a lot of hemp. One of the things that will come out of it is that I will have my own sustainable clothing line, hopefully within a year. We'll be able to follow it all the way from the seed, because we grow our own seed. In terms of things that you can do every single day, you can seek out clothes that are plant-dyed and don't have pesticides in them. People think of organic cotton, but cotton takes an enormous amount of water to grow, so we switched to rain-fed organic cotton.

Then I go back to the one thing that you can do every day is pay attention to what's on your plate, even if it's one meal a day. Just think of it as one meal a day for the planet.

ME: Talk to me about the Plant Power Task Force, which sounds to me like the creation of this attitude that we should look toward a plant based diet, right?

SUZY: I think part of the problem, at least from my perspective, is that we don't have a lot of transparency in regards to the foods that contain animal products that we wouldn't expect. We just don't realize it. If I eat something that comes from an animal, obviously, it's animal-based. If I eat something that comes from the ground and it's green and leafy, it's obviously plant-based. The problem is the hidden stuff that we really don't know about.

ME: What advice would you give to the young generation that's trying to figure out what we should be avoiding, what we shouldn't be avoiding, that maybe aren't as obvious as we think?

SUZY: I was on an airplane with my son, and beforehand we had stopped at a magazine place and grabbed a bunch of little snacky things. I grabbed some chips because I love chippies. I was just getting ready to open mine, and my son goes, "Mom, don't eat those." I'm like, "Why?" He says, "Because they've got milk products in them." It was a bag of chips. Anyway, so the advice would be to really read labels. A lot of time now they have written in bold, at the bottom of the ingredients, "contains milk, contains gluten," and so on. I know when I first was learning about everything, I spent an enormous amount of time in the health food stores looking at labels. The cool thing is it's almost five years since Jim and I went plant-based, and the amount of products with cheese alternatives and meat alternatives has probably quadrupled since then. When you're in a restaurant now, people really understand when you can ask for dishes without dairy. We end up ordering a lot of sides because they are mostly vegetables and beans. And you can always get salads without cheese or meat.

Sometimes I'll look at the body of the entreés and notice the vegetables that they serve with the meats. I would say 9 times out of 10, the chef is perfectly happy to create something that just has veggies in it. Just put them on a plate and steam them or whatever. Make sure that there's no butter on them, and give me a side of marinara sauce, a little dish of soy sauce, or something to dip them in such as vinaigrette.

It would be great if you can go organic or reduce your meat and dairy consumption. If you can't, you're still making a huge difference not only for the environment, but also for your body if you just reduce your meat intake. And those cute little fuzzy animals will appreciate that. It doesn't matter why you go plant-based—whether you're doing it for ethical reasons, for the animals, for your health, or for the environment—everybody wins. It's a win-win-win situation all the way around.

CHAPTER 9

The True Cost of Fossil Fuels

The Future of Energy Is Not Down a Hole

*"We pull out of the ground death. We burn death
in our power plants. Why do we get shocked
when we get death in our sky in the form of global
warming, death in our oceans as oil spills, death in
our children's lungs as asthma and cancer?"*

—VAN JONES

uman beings have done an incredible job of constantly evolving, developing, and progressing as a species. Just look at the major technological advances and discoveries that we've made over the course of our existence. We've explored space, cured disease, created democracy, and, in 2012, we even brought 2Pac back to the stage in the form of a hologram. Even so, our greatest challenges lie ahead.

The resources from the fossil-fuel industry have led to amazing technological innovations, while becoming one of the most profitable industries in the history of the world. However, the next steps we take as a species cannot be fueled by a finite resource. Fossil fuels are the

People's Climate March

remains of dead animal and plant matter, dating back to the time of the dinosaurs. They cannot be replenished once they are gone.

While coal, oil, and natural gas still supply most of the world with energy, we know that there is a ticking clock on the fossil-fuel economy. Our dependency could be our downfall. Unless we start to transition away from carbon-based energy sources, we'll pay the price of having our food, transportation, and heating tied into the price of oil.

This is especially concerning, because the price you see on the gas pump isn't actually what it costs to produce the oil. Like Big Ag, fossil fuels are heavily subsidized. A 2013 report by the Global Subsidies Initiative found that fossil fuels receive an estimated $548 billion dollars in direct subsidies and tax breaks combined, at least five times that of renewable energy. Some of these subsidies are for production and help companies cover the cost of extraction and processing, while others are exploration subsidies that help companies look for more fossil fuels to mine and burn. The study also showed how these subsidies are specifically designed to undercut the competitiveness of renewable energy.

Those, however, are not the only subsidies we pay. Taxpayers have been forced to pay the toll for nonrenewable energy sources that damage our environment, health, and public infrastructure. The International Monetary Fund (IMF) estimates that we pay around $5.3 trillion annually for the costs the industry leaves behind. That is more than $10 million a minute that we are spending to prop up an industry that's harming our health and our environment and our economy.

A Harvard study estimated that, if we accounted for the true cost of coal, it would be double or triple the price, because of environmental, health, and climate impacts. This is considered an indirect subsidy. Without these subsidies, it would no longer be economical for coal companies to mine and burn coal. By making these corporations pay for their damages instead of the people it most impacts, we could keep greenhouse gas emissions in the ground and begin to heal the Earth.

CANARY IN THE COAL MINE

Coal mining has largely shifted from underground mines to surface mines, also known as strip mining. Mountaintop removal is one method of strip mining, which has been used by coal companies along the Appalachian mountain range and around the world. The practice destroys wildlife, as explosives blow the tops off mountains leading to tremendous debris burying valley and river habitats. We are so desperate for fossil fuels that we are literally blowing up mountains to get at it. That's messed up.

The emissions from burning coal not only contribute to climate change, but they cause acid rain, smog, and respiratory illness, severely impacting both global and local communities. A study from the Clean Air Task Force found that particulate matter coming from burning coal in power plants leads to 7,500 deaths annually in the US. In places like India and China, the problem is even worse, with an estimated 670,000 premature deaths in China and 115,000 in India due to coal emissions. I've seen videos of what's going on in China, and people have to check an app on their phones just to see if the air is clean enough to go outside. It's insane, but that's their reality.

Coal is still cheap in much of the world, but the costs to society are enormous. Those costs often fall on the poor and the historically oppressed. In the United States, people of color and those earning less money are more likely to live within 3 miles of a coal power plant. A Report by the National Association for the Advancement of Colored People (NAACP), Indigenous Environmental Network (IEN), and Little Village Environmental Justice Organization (LVEJO) found that power plants that disproportionately affect communities of color emit higher rates of sulfur oxide and nitrous oxide, two of the worst pollutants to human health. This is a clear example of environmental racism.

In my home town, there is a coal power plant called Valmont Station. We began educating the public with creative tactics like a "coal ash" lemonade stand. The creativity and continued public pressure eventually paid off, and the EPA arranged for a public hearing in Denver. At the hearing, I testified along with other Earth Guardians, ranchers, ministers, doctors, and members of Native American tribes affected by coal ash on their tribal lands. We all urged the EPA to adopt the strongest possible regulations for coal ash. Several months after the hearing, the EPA announced the first-ever national regulations for the safe disposal of ash from coal-fired power plants.

This was one example of a successful fight against coal happening around the country. The good news is that we've made a lot of progress over the past decade. Coal is down 53 percent over that time, and it's estimated that this shift is saving thousands of lives a year. Trump has threatened to turn back the clock on this progress by abandoning clean-energy laws passed during the Obama years. But, just like we can never go back to the days before the Internet, we can't return to a toxic and dangerous industry like coal. Our health and our future are too important.

HELL ON EARTH

We can't just stop the impacts of coal; we also have to work to stop the harm done by oil and gas drilling. The cost of oil extraction continues to increase, because as the easy-to-get fossil fuels are becoming harder to find, we are moving to more extreme ways to get at underground reserves. These new methods of extraction are more expensive and more resource intensive than ever and include tar sands mining, deep-sea oil drilling, and fracking.

Tar Sands in Alberta, Hell on Earth

The tar sands have about a 15 percent larger carbon footprint than conventional oil. For every gallon of gas produced by the tar sands, it uses about 6 gallons of fresh water. Almost all the water that is uses becomes so toxic that it can't be returned to the hydrologic cycle, so they hold the water in giant open-air pits. These toxic lakes cover approximately 176 kilometers in Northern Alberta and are considered some of the largest human-made structures on Earth. The lakes are so large that they can be seen from space. Eleven million liters of this toxic fluid leak into the Athabasca River and watershed on a daily basis, which is enough to fill up the Toronto hockey stadium 2.5 times over every day.

Looking at the photos above, it doesn't even look like planet Earth.

The transportation of tar sands crude oil also poses a massive threat. There are more than 2.5 million miles of oil pipelines that crisscross the country, many of which are extremely hazardous to valuable water reserves. In 2015 alone, there were more than 40 major pipeline spills, resulting in personal injury and/or mass contamination. Pipelines containing tar sands oil from Canada are both more likely to spill and more hazardous when they do.

Tar sands pipelines spill up to 3.6 times more oil per mile than conventional oil pipelines. This is because the chemistry of the oil and the heat that they need to transport tar sands leads to corrosion of the pipes. Once it spills, the tar sands is more toxic and difficult to clean up. Because it's heavier, it sinks down to the bottom of the riverbed and coats it. For instance, the Kalamazoo River tar sands spill in Michigan took years and more than a billion dollars to clean up.

Once the oil industry extracts the black tar, they then have to export it overseas, because the cost of mining for tar sands is so high, it's only profitable in foreign markets. This means that pipelines have to traverse long distances from landlocked Alberta to coastal cities in the United States and Canada. These pipelines have become major battlegrounds in the movement to protect climate and water with the most high profile being the movements to stop the Keystone XL Pipeline and the Dakota Access Pipeline.

FIGHTING KXL

In 2008, The US Department of State issued a presidential permit for a $5.2 billion Keystone pipeline to transport crude oil. Shortly thereafter, TransCanada, the manufacturer of the pipeline, filed paperwork to expand the existing pipeline to include a new Keystone XL route. It would extend from Canada through Montana, South Dakota, and Nebraska. This expansion would enable the pipeline to carry more than 800,000 barrels of Canadian tar sands a day to refineries.

In 2010, the southern leg of the Keystone pipeline began construction, as public resistance to the northern portion grew. A group of native climate activists who had been working on the pipeline for years joined organizations like 350.org and Tar Sands Action to form a massive protest. Over 10 days in the summer of 2011, more than 1,000 people were arrested at the White House, demanding that Obama reject the pipeline. It was the first of three major actions at the White House where people were arrested while opposing Keystone. It ignited a nationwide movement that would help define an era of fossil-fuel resistance.

Over the next 4 years, the pipeline struggle would go through a variety of bumps, twists, and turns. Congress tried to force President

Obama's hand by passing legislation requiring approval of the Keystone XL pipeline within 60 days unless the president determined the project does not serve the national interest.

On November 7, 2011, just 1 year before the election, climate activists reminded Obama in part why they voted for him. They surrounded the White House with 10,000 people calling for the president to reject the pipeline. They held signs with quotes from Obama's campaign, literally surrounding him with his own words. One sign used an Obama quote from election night: "We want our children to live in an America . . . that isn't threatened by the destructive power of a warming planet."

The momentum continued to build. By February of 2013, the movement returned to the National Mall in D.C., this time with 40,000 people in attendance. In addition, actions happened in 19 other cities, including in Denver, where my brother and I performed before a crowd of protestors. Everyone came wearing black, and afterward, laid down to mimic a human oil spill. Back in D.C., Van Jones spoke to the importance of this moment: "This is the last minute of the last quarter of the biggest, most important game humanity has ever played."

People continued to act with that kind of urgency, with 20 groups delivering more than a million comments to the White House, calling on the president to reject the pipeline. Then, in 2014, the youth movement stepped up with an action called XL dissent, where 400 young people were arrested by chaining themselves to the White House fence.

Before the action, I addressed the young people and said: "When I come to protests like this, when I see the youth arising, when I see the youth taking the lead in these movements, when I see the youth putting aside everything that society has told us, that we can't, we're not good enough, we're too young, we cannot make a difference, we are proving them wrong, right here right now, because we have the power."

It wasn't just young people and environmental activists involved. There were ranchers and farmers who had formed a group called Bold Nebraska to help stop the pipeline. They began working closely with the Indigenous Environmental Network in what was called the cowboy and indian alliance, and in April 2014, they took to D.C. again. This time, they formed a camp surrounding the Washington Monument in another action that made international news. Later in 2014, Bold Nebraska won a lawsuit preventing the pipeline from going through their land, further delaying the process.

The legal battle continued, with mounting pressure from the oil and gas industry. In 2015, Congress tried again to push a bill that would force Obama to make a quick decision on the pipeline, but days after it passed, he vetoed it. Then, on November 6, 2015, Obama rejected the permit for the pipeline, saying, "America is now a global leader when it comes to taking serious action to fight climate change. And frankly, approving this project would have undercut that global leadership."

This incredible victory stemmed from the power we have as people. They told us that the pipeline was a done deal, but we refused to accept this as an answer. In my lifetime, this was the first time I saw people all over the country uniting to fight a single fossil-fuel project. Don't underestimate what we can accomplish when we focus our minds on a crucial task. It was powerful for everyone who cares about climate justice, indigenous rights and clean water.

Fighting for Climate Justice

Unfortunately, the celebration was short-lived. On January 24, 2017, the climate denier in charge of the United States had the audacity to sign an executive action to fast-track the approval of the Keystone XL pipeline. Two months later, he approved the pipeline permit allowing it to cross international borders into Canada. The pipeline still faces significant hurdles, including a state permit from Nebraska, a process that will likely take longer than a year. It feels like this is a zombie pipeline that just won't die. Days before the pipeline was approved, a North Dakota pipeline spilled more than a half-million gallons, offering a warning of what is to come if Keystone XL is built.

People are still rising up to stop the pipeline, but the threat continues, now stronger and more apparent than ever. This time around, we do not have allies in the White House, so it's going to be up to us to shut this monster down for good and fight for a clean energy revolution.

LOOKING TO THE SKY FOR ENERGY

As we look to the resistance against in the Keystone XL pipeline, and the dangerous transportation of oil and gas, there is hope. There is more than enough renewable energy to power our entire world, with great benefits for our environment, our economy, and our health. The Solutions Project headed by Stanford scientist Mark Jacobson, has mapped out how every state and country could run off clean, renewable energy, while creating jobs, saving money, and saving lives.

The Solutions Project estimates that the switch from fossil fuels to renewables would create more than four million jobs in the US over 40 years. In addition, the transition would save more than 45,000 lives annually that would otherwise be lost to air pollution, and save the country $602 billion. In the year 2050, consumers would save an average of $300 a year from energy costs alone, but combine that with the projected savings from health and climate expenses, and you would be saving the average person $8,316 annually. Taking action on climate is not only the right thing to do but also it's the smart thing to do.

The oil and gas industry wants us to believe that there are no other reasonable options available to us. The truth is that the fossil-fuel industry knows that they have an expiration date that's approaching fast, but we can't wait until all the fossil fuel are gone to make the switch toward renewables. The Stone Age didn't end because we ran out of stones. We have all the tools and all the technology we need. Now, we just need the political will to leave fossil fuels behind, only to be remembered in history books. Imagine our great grandchildren reading about the time we almost wiped out life on Earth, because of burning dead stuff we dug out of the ground. We are at a point in time when we are writing the end of this chapter. What will your role be in writing our legacy?

Here are some ways to lessen our reliance on fossil fuels.

Divest. Money is power in our society. So, you give big fossil-fuel companies power when you send your money to them. The fossil-fuel divestment movement emerged from university students and was modeled after the movement to boycott companies involved with South African apartheid, which helped lead to the toppling of the apartheid regime. Since 2012, the fossil-fuel divestment movement has shifted more than five trillion dollars from fossil-fuel holdings. Students have created divestment groups at their schools, and some have convinced their administrations to divest their endowments of fossil-fuel holdings. The Divestment Student Network helps to train and mentor students and is a great way to get involved with activism and lessen our financial reliance on fossil fuels. You can make a huge difference by helping to get fossil-fuel money out of your school, your place of worship, and your community.

Lobby to put a price on carbon. One solution that makes a lot of sense is putting a price on the carbon burned. The way it works is that the funds would be pooled for greenhouse gases emitted, then everything collected would go back to the people equally. It would make big polluters pay for the harm they cause. The idea is called a carbon fee and dividend. Citizens' Climate Lobby estimates that, if implemented, this could get greenhouse gas emissions to 52 percent below 1990 levels within 20 years. It would also stimulate the economy, creating jobs and saving lives. You can find out how to lobby your representatives at www. citizensclimatelobby.org.

Localize your energy. In 2011, my hometown of Boulder started the process to own our electricity and utilities and get off of Xcel Energy. Xcel provides Boulder with about 90 percent fossil-fuel energy, and it's estimated that, if we ran our own utility, we could run on 40 percent renewable energy with a 60-percent reduction in greenhouse gas emissions. Boulder localizing its energy to combat climate change can be a model for other cities looking to shift the electric grid to renewables.

Participate. Nonviolent direct action (NVDA) has played a critical role in helping communities stop fossil fuels, from Shell Arctic drilling to Keystone XL, and many more. This is often a last resort for communities who have exhausted all other options and need to put their bodies on the line. I highly recommend that, if you want to participate in NVDA, you are trained by people who know what they are doing and go in with a solid plan. Make sure that the action you are engaging in has a narrative that helps your cause and that all roles are taken care of to ensure the safety of everyone involved. Ruckus Society is one of many excellent organizations that provide NVDA trainings to help you prepare. You can request training at www.ruckus.org.

Above all else, we all have to shift the way that we see the world. Be aware of how much energy you use in your life, and conserve, whether it's turning the lights off when you leave a room or unplugging electronics when you're not using them. All these little things add up to make a real difference in mitigating climate change. But, perhaps the most important thing we can do to reduce our reliance on fossil fuels is to change the way we think about energy. The oil and gas industry spends billions of dollars to program us to think that looking to the alternatives is not in our best interest. The renewable energy technology is here, and it's becoming cheaper. The hidden costs that come from our addiction to fossil fuels is becoming more apparent every day, but so, too, is the resistance.

CHAPTER 10

Fracking for Fool's Gas

The Crisis of a False Solution

*"It's like giving the Earth an Alka-Seltzer,
if the Alka-Seltzer shattered your internal organs
so that oil companies could harvest your juices."*

—STEPHEN COLBERT

Nowadays, "fracking" has become something of a buzzword. When you hear it, you might see the image of a flaming water faucet or an earthquake. But that hasn't always been the case. This relatively new method for drilling for shale gas has exploded over the past 10 years. According to the *Wall Street Journal*, more than 15 million Americans live within a ½ mile from a fracking well. Fracking is a method of extracting oil and gas that's trapped in shale by shooting water and chemicals deep into the earth. It's an extremely toxic industrial activity, and the impact on our communities has been tremendous, poisoning water, air, the climate, and our democracy.

To get a sense of how we got here, you have to go back to when I was just 5, when vice-president and former Halliburton CEO Dick Cheney

A Fracking Wastewater Holding Pond

convened the infamous Energy Task Force, made up almost entirely of fossil-fuel executives. They produced the Energy Policy Act of 2005, which exempted fracking from the Safe Drinking Water Act. This allowed for the oil and gas companies to blast toxic chemicals into the earth without revealing what they are using. Guess which company patented this chemical mix used in fracking? Halliburton. Coincidence? I call bullshit. This ridiculous exemption is commonly referred to as the Halliburton loophole.

However, we can't just blame Cheney and the Republicans for the widespread damage the fracking industry creates. Environmentalists and democrats embraced fracking for "natural gas" as a solution to the coal and climate problems. In 2007, Sierra Club's Beyond Coal campaign began accepting more than $26 million from oil and gas billionaires like Chesapeake CEO Aubrey McClendon. McClendon actually went on a tour with Sierra Club President Carl Pope, promoting natural gas as a clean, green transition fuel. Sometimes, when you want to stop something so bad, it can blind you to the big picture. In the haste to beat back coal, another toxic monster was created.

The process of fracking for natural gas is, of course, anything but clean, but at the time, not a lot of people knew that. Then, in 2010, *Gasland* happened. The documentary begins with filmmaker Josh Fox opening a letter from a company who offers him $100,000 to frack underneath 19.5 acres of his property. Instead of signing the lease, Josh begins to go on an investigation about the impact of fracking. The trip first lead him to Dimock, where he saw an entire community living with poisoned water from fracking, including one family who can actually light their well water on fire. He would later go out West to places like my home state of Colorado, Texas, and Wyoming, only to see the same story everywhere; people with toxic water, poisoned air, and a number of health impacts that came when fracking started in their communities. The film swept the country, winning an Emmy Award and being nominated for an Oscar.

Another person nominated for an Oscar in that same year was also ahead of the curve on fracking awareness. Most of you know him as the Incredible Hulk, Mark Ruffalo. He originally thought natural gas was a good thing, perhaps slowing the climate impact of fossil fuels. However, after traveling to Dimock, Pennsylvania, he visited families with water so contaminated they had to have all their water trucked in, even for showering. When they showered with the water contaminated by fracking, they would get hives and sometimes pass out from the gases coming from the showerheads.

In May 2011, Mark joined folk legend Pete Seeger and grassroots organizations like Catskill Mountainkeeper and Frack Action at a press conference at the capitol in Albany, New York. The moment generated buzz, and a day later, the legislature passed a moratorium (temporary halt) on fracking in New York State. The movement continued to grow. It wasn't just Mark Ruffalo and Josh Fox. Over the next several years, more than 100 grassroots organizations, a thousand businesses, and a host of influential scientists would join the movement. Over that same time, more than 100 cities and towns in New York passed local bans on fracking.

(continued on page 149)

SHINING A LIGHT ON SOLUTIONS

An Interview with Mark Ruffalo

Mark Ruffalo is an actor, humanitarian, social activist, and film producer.

ME: In the late 2000s many people working on climate issues hadn't woken up to the dangers of fracking. You were one of the first public figures to speak out on the issue. What opened your eyes and motivated you to speak out before others?

MARK: At that time, many people in the environmental movement saw natural gas as the remedy to the horrors of coal. Most of the big green NGOs saw the transition to methane as a way for us to combat climate change and pollution. My family and I had moved to upstate New York around that time and little did we know, we had landed right smack dab into the Gaslands that Josh Fox's excellent documentary *Gasland* portrays. At first, like many environmentally conscious people, I thought that methane was a reasonable transition fuel because it burned clean. I was not aware of the devastating impacts methane has as a heat-trapping gas or how destructive the process of fracking is on the environment. I would have felt differently had I known how much pollution it produces and how damaging it is to air, water, and land. I started to study it, and what I came to learn was a very different picture from the one that its supporters were painting. What really moved me was my visit to Dimock Township, Pennsylvania. Ramsay Adams, executive director of Catskill Mountain Keeper, invited me to visit a fracked community. What I saw and heard on my visit broke my heart and drove me into action. I saw a community that in most ways could have been living in a banana republic. It was like a gold rush. The rule of law had become a single industry falling over itself to turn profits as quickly as possible.

What was the outcome? A community devastated by an industry that had all but bought off the local and state government. The Pennsylvania Department of Environmental Protection was in charge of promoting drilling in the state, which put it at odds with its own reason for existence. You had neighbor hating neighbor and an influx of money into the hands of a few while property values plummeted, trucks tore down single lane country roads, and people's drinking wells became contaminated by methane gas and fracking chemicals. The general mood of the place was utter despair and desperation. The federal EPA was also at that point a somewhat captured agency with the false belief that methane was the lesser of two necessary evils. They too were falling all over themselves to accommodate and accelerate the transition from coal to methane. During my visit to Dimock, 30 people came together to testify to me and others about how this out-of-control freight train had ruined their lives. It was in the pleas of the good, decent, blue collar and working class people in Dimock that I found my calling to fight against this monstrosity that was already deeply established and heartily welcomed from Wall Street to the big greens NGOs...from devastated farmers to the president of the USA.

ME: You are a cofounder of the Solutions Project, a nonprofit that has mapped out the way the entire world can go 100 percent renewable, while creating jobs and saving lives. What do you think is keeping us from making this transition as quickly as possible?

MARK: The two "I"s: inertia and ignorance—some of it accidental, but much of it willful. We have to remember that much of America's supremacy in the world hinges on the fact that we have cheap fossil fuels and that we have built an entire economic hegemony on that basis. This gives the fossil fuel industry and the utility and transportation industries an outdated and unprecedented amount of influence over our political and economic system. We can't forget this didn't come about overnight and for the most part the entire growth of our nation over the last hundred years is wound up and bound tightly to the fossil-political industrial complex. Even with the emergence of clean energy that every day becomes cheaper, and even when all of the hidden costs in the fossil fuel paradigm are factored in—pollution, remediation, health effects, wars fought over resources, infrastructure, and the damage of climate change—most of our politicians and many of our business leaders are doing as much as they possibly can to stand in the way of the inevitable transition to clean and renewable energy sources.

Why? Well, what makes a human being do thoughtless, senseless things that hurt their communities, harm their neighbors, cause them to go to war, bury their humanity and become deaf to the voice of common morality that lives in the minds and hearts of all healthy people? The answer is money and power. Political and business leaders don't want to lose out on the money and they don't want to cede their power. A transition to 100 percent renewable energy will give an enormous amount of power to the consumer. It will ensure that money circulates inside communities instead of going to a single corporation like Exxon or a monolithic utility company that will take money out of the community and send it to coal companies or share holders. The 100 percent distributed energy system simply harvests what is falling down out of the sky, blowing across our lands, and moving through our waters. It puts power and money into the hands of the many instead of the few. Unfortunately, there are some very cynical forces that will do anything they can to stop the current system from being disrupted. It is in their best interest to pretend that climate change is a "hoax" and that renewable energy is unaffordable. Of course, climate change is a very real threat, and renewable energy is abundant and accessible to all. There is no turning back now. We must address the ignorance of society at large, perpetuated by the media and our politicians, and spread the word that renewable energies are ready to go now and will give people a better life and world.

ME: You went out to Flint, Michigan, and put a spotlight on a community whose basic human right to clean water has been neglected. What did you learn from your trip to Flint?

MARK: The one thing that I constantly see is that when a community comes together and fights for what is right, and the world is given a chance to hear their concerns and experiences, over time, they will eventually win out. We all share some basic understandings unless our minds and hearts have been poisoned in some way. We have an innate decency and compassion in us and even if we don't agree with another person's point of view, we can usually agree that person has a right to life, liberty, and happiness. Most sane people can agree that when a community is poisoned and children's lives are altered forever, and when the government is complicit in that injustice, there is a serious problem at hand. Where things get particularly ugly is when folks start lying to protect themselves or are on the take in one way or another. That seems to be a huge part of the problem in Flint and in most places where there are contaminations. There is often money passed around from industry figures into the hands of local politicians. In Flint, just as in Dimock and Standing Rock, the strength lies in the community uniting and fighting together. When alone, most folks are generally fearful and feel powerless. When you get a group of people standing together under a common banner of righteous morality and decency, their fear, fatigue, and fragility fall away and you get the emergence of a decency movement. That is what I have taken from all of my travels. My job has been to draw the cameras to me so that the people who need to be heard can step into the field of the American viewers' sight.

ME: We are living with a president who denies climate change and is reversing a lot of the progress we've made on climate change over the last 8 years. Do we need to change our approach to match the reality of a Trump administration? Are there lessons we can learn from the 2016 election?

MARK: We need to resist and renew. With every action there is an equal reaction. The Trump presidency will not only be marked by the tragedy of a regressive and reactive political shift that feeds off our baser, intolerant, and fear-driving tendencies, but also by the amount of people it has awakened to the fact that we must engage in our lives. Donald Trump is the ugly part of America that has taken precedent. Greed, power, fear, ignorance, intolerance, white supremacy, and hatred are the shadow side of the character of this nation. It has always been there. It was concealed and played out in dog whistles and double-speak, winking at those who share the same darkness but who would normally be unwilling to show themselves from under their hoods in the light of decency. Those darker shadow tendencies have been made manifest in the Trump ascendancy. The shadow nature of our country is now given the full expression of its being. We get to see now the exact nature of our shadow selves. We can no longer claim ignorance to this part of ourselves and now must make a conscious choice about who we are and how we intend to live in the world. So what do we do in the face of this? What every civilized nation has done in the face of tyrannical rule. We resist. To quote Mario Savio,

"There comes a time when the operation of the machine becomes so odious, makes you so sick at heart, that you can't take part, you can't even passively take part, and you've got to put your bodies upon the gears and upon the wheels, upon all the apparatus, and you've got to make it stop. And you've got to indicate to the people who run it, the people who own it, that unless you're free, the machine will be prevented from working at all."

Climate change is like gravity. It cannot be denied for too long. Sure, you can deny it for a while, like jumping from a building into the air. As you go up, you can say, "See, there is no such thing as gravity. I fly!" But very soon, you will plummet, because that is the reality here on Earth. Climate change and man's hand in it are another undeniable reality. We can only hold off the outcomes of our ignorance for so long before we are bitten or beaten by the truth. Climate change will continue to get worse and as this happens, people will become more emboldened to join those putting themselves "upon the gears and upon the wheels, upon all the apparatus" to make it stop. That is the resistance. Anyone who is serious about fighting climate change should also learn the techniques of nonviolent action laid out and taught by groups such as Beautiful Trouble. As for renewal, we should first help front-line communities transition equitably to renewable energy and unite the great movements of native rights, civil rights, and climate justice to ensure that we imagine, create, and talk about what kind of abundance will exist for us when we leave the fossil fuel paradigm behind. It is a paradigm that extracts without reciprocating in kind. It is inherently unjust, unfair, and unsustainable. We must renew our commitments to the idea of decency toward each other and decency toward the world around us.

ME: You're constantly in films, you're on Broadway, you're a spokesperson for a movement, you have two nonprofits, and you have a family. As a family man and the father of three beautiful children, how do you feel about the future your children will inherit?

MARK: Oddly enough, despite all of the chaos that has moved into the public realm, along with the promise of much more, I am gaining in my sense of calm and hopefulness. My resolve for a better and more just world remains ardent. Not because I see some easy way of getting there or that I have some inexhaustible source of energy and time, but because so many people are becoming aware of so much. Our knowledge grows as our ignorance diminishes. We are able to speak directly to each other instead of through centralized and easily manipulated systems, and young people like you and my children are becoming more engaged, aware, and empowered. I'm not going to lie, however: We are really up against it. Things will probably get worse before they get better, but what is clear and what I have witnessed is that together we can do extraordinary things. There is reason to celebrate. I am also reminded of a great Hopi elder's quote at this moment: ". . . At this time in history, we are to take nothing personally, least of all ourselves. For the moment that we do, our spiritual growth and journey comes to a halt. The time for the lone wolf is over. Gather yourselves! Banish the word struggle from your attitude and your vocabulary. All that we do now must be done in a sacred manner and in celebration. We are the ones we've been waiting for."

The grassroots movement was fueled by some cutting-edge science coming from the college town of Ithaca in New York. Cornell University is home to college professors who finally dispelled the myth that fracking was good for the climate. The argument for fracking was originally based on the notion that natural gas emits about half the carbon dioxide of coal when burned. What scientists Robert Howarth, PhD, and Anthony Ingraffea, PhD, found was that because of methane leakage, in many cases, fracking was worse for the climate than the continuous burning of coal. Methane is the primary component of natural gas. When it escapes unburned, it is an 86 times more potent heat-trapping gas than carbon over 20 years and 34 times as bad over 100 years. A recent Harvard study found a more than 30 percent increase in US methane emissions over the past decade, likely related to an increase in fracking in the US, wiping out any climate benefit of switching from coal to gas.

While Dr. Howarth and Dr. Ingraffea were providing crucial data, another scientist from Ithaca was helping lead the movement. Sandra Steingraber, PhD, is a biologist and highly acclaimed author. She is a cancer survivor, and evidence shows that her cancer, along with that of her family and friends, was possibly related to chemical exposure from the pesticide industry. Her story was documented in the amazing film and book *Living Downstream,* in which she helps expose the links between cancer and industrial toxins in the environment. She is a cancer survivor herself and grew up in a town where industrial agriculture contaminated her drinking water. She has won many awards for her work, including the prestigious Heinz award for leadership in the New York antifracking movement. She donated much of the $100,000 prize as seed money to help form the powerful grassroots coalition New Yorkers Against Fracking (NYAF), which pushed New York Governor Cuomo for a ban.

Dr. Steingraber's engagement went far beyond financial contributions though. In August of 2012, she and NYAF's David Braun led 1,500 people at the Albany capitol in the Pledge of Resistance to Fracking. They called for activists to show their commitment to clean water and air by pledging to engage in nonviolent direct action NVDA. Before reciting the pledge, Dr. Steingraber gave a powerful speech talking about her duties as a mom, "I don't want anyone to get hurt. I don't want to fill jail cells with good people. I don't even like confrontation. But if we do have to activate this pledge, and if it turns out that I can be a better parent inside of jail than outside, I will be that parent. If we have to lay our bodies down, I promise I will be there with you."

Although horizontal fracking would not come to New York State, Dr. Steingraber would make good on her pledge when she was arrested defending her home region from a gas-storage facility underneath Seneca Lake. After hundreds more were arrested to stop the dangerous project, it was finally abandoned by the company Crestwood. The pledge would also make its way to my home state of Colorado, when Dr. Steingraber joined the Frack Free Colorado rally at the capitol in Denver later that year. In addition to Sandra, performers Jakob Dylan, Daryl Hannah, and Elephant Revival headlined the show. I also performed that day, playing a fairly new track called "What the Frack?" I was still learning to compose hip-hop. Let's just say this wasn't some Kendrick Lamar level flow, but, cut me some slack, I was 12 and had just built my first dope hip-hop beat. People seemed to like the track though, and it created some social media buzz that led the organizers to invite me and my bro to perform. Being cute and conscious will get you far in this world.

I remember seeing the people with their fists raised to the sky while reciting the Pledge of Resistance as my mom's good friend Diana Caile, who had helped form the Mothers Project, read it from the stage. Around 6 months later, I joined in with the Earth Guardians to help put the pledge into action. The Boulder county commissioners were meeting to discuss regulations for 1,800 fracking wells in my home county of Boulder. We interrupted the meeting with the people's mic (call and response occupy style). The commissioners left the room because they couldn't silence us.

Seizing the opportunity, my homies and I grabbed the open seats left by the commissioners at the front of the room. My friend Dakota was wearing a sick furry tiger hat with earflaps that turned into mittens. I started out by saying, "We are the future, but we are also the present, we are here now, we are here today and we are fighting for our future." At that point, I took a poll of who wanted to ban fracking. "Alright . . . everyone who wants

Taking Over the County Commissioners' Meeting

fracking banned put your hands up in the air," I said. Everyone in the crowd who wasn't a paid oil and gas attorney put their hands sky-high.

The county commissioners claimed that there was nothing that could be done, but that didn't stop us. We joined groups like Frack Free Colorado and East Boulder County United in an emergency meeting, with over 500 people and again we recited the pledge of resistance and broke out into groups for nonviolent direct action. The commissioners eventually got word of the meeting and seemed more willing to listen afterward. Then, the county staff made a unanimous recommendation to extend the moratorium and the commissioners completely flipped their positions, passing an 18-month moratorium.

Five months later, in the fall of 2013, four cities in Colorado voted to put temporary bans on fracking during the election, joining Longmont and voting for a full ban during the year before. Despite being massively outspent by the oil and gas industry during the campaigns, these grassroots operations were successful at the ballot. The signature campaign in Broomfield was led by Laura Fronckiwiecz who was 9 months pregnant. Just a day after they collected enough signatures to reach the ballot, she gave birth and ran the campaign office out of her home with a newborn and a toddler. What a legend. The campaign in Broomfield was too close to call on election day, and 2 weeks later, they ended up winning by just 17 votes.

Instead of honoring the choice of the people, Governor Hicken-looper joined the oil and gas industry and straight up sued us. While this may seem ridiculous for a Democratic governor, Hickenlooper was an oil and gas puppet from the very beginning. A former geologist for the industry, Hickenlooper became the choice of wealthy oil and gas funders when former Democratic Governor Bill Ritter started to tick off the industry by installing some small regulations. Ritter, the previous choice of the Democratic oil and gas-funding machine, mysteriously decided not to run for a second term.

Hickenlooper soon earned the nickname Frackenlooper, for his willingness to do anything and everything to please his corporate funders.

My Little Sister Taking to the Streets

Long before the day when Donald Trump was describing chocolate cake as he was forgetting which country he bombed, Hickenlooper was bragging about drinking fracking fluid. "You can drink it," he said in front of a Senate committee. "We did drink it around the table, almost ritual like, in a funny way." It's unclear whether Hickenlooper was in on the joke, or if this was just another slick publicity stunt from Halliburton. The truth was that he drank a "prototype" with food grade ingredients that has never been used to frack a well. Hickenlooper actually had to write an e-mail to his supporters telling them not to drink fracking fluid because real fracking fluid will definitely mess you up.

Fracking fluid is a patented formula, kept secret by the industry. According to Theo Colborn of the Endocrine Disruption Exchange, about 30 percent of the chemicals used are suspected carcinogens, 30 percent are developmental toxins, and 60 percent can harm the brain and nervous system. Imagine an Olympic-size swimming pool filled with chemicals. That's how much they use in every well.

To let people know about this danger, we followed Hickenlooper to Aspen for the Democratic Governors Conference he hosted. We held a rally called "Good Governors Don't Frack Their People" with Food and Water Watch, Frack Free Colorado, 350 Colorado, and others. The Earth Guardians youth set up a fracking fluid stand, and performed a skit, which showed just why you'd never want to drink real fracking fluid. After the rally, my boy Russell, and his friend Suzanne from Frack Free Colorado, found Hickenlooper and asked him some questions with the cameras rolling. At first Hickenlooper denied all damage due to fracking. But Russell pointed out that Dr. Ingraffea used industry data to show that 5 percent of new fracking wells leak, and up to 50 percent leak over time. Hickenlooper said "yeah, but you're talking about hydrocarbons like benzene, look oil and gas is a highly industrial activity that none of us wants in our backyards." Then, he looked at the man holding the camera and said, "Is that on? Turn that off. . . . " Busted.

While Hickenlooper was ignoring science and actively working to overturn the will of the people in Colorado, Governor Cuomo was taking a much different approach. Cuomo's administration was applying the precautionary principle before allowing high volume horizontal fracking in New York. After reviewing hundreds of studies to determine fracking's safety, Department of Health Commissioner Howard Zucker asked himself the question: "'Would I allow my family to live in a community with frack-ing?' The answer is no," he said. "I therefore cannot recommend that any-one else's family to live in such a community either." Afterward, Cuomo would say that it was the people who got him to listen to science.

Many of the same studies Cuomo based his fracking ban on were studies that came out of Colorado. Lisa Mckenzie, PhD, of the Colorado School of Public Health released a study showing that within a ½ mile of a fracking well, risk for many health impacts increased. In another study, she showed that there was a 30 percent increase in birth defects like congenital heart disease for babies born within ½ mile of a fracking well. This wasn't a surprise to the many people who know about volatile organic compounds (VOCs) like benzene, toluene, and xylene. All these toxic chemicals are released during the fracking process and are known to have harmful health implications when inhaled. VOCs were shown to be significantly higher in heavily fracked regions.

Infant mortality rates skyrocketed in regions with a large number of fracking wells and VOCs in the air. Weld County is 30 minutes from my home and one of the most densely fracked places in the country. Infant mortality rate spiked around the time fracking started there. The same happened in the Uintah Basin of Utah with one of the highest leakage rates in the country. A midwife there was harassed and threatened for making the connection between the fracking boom and all the miscar-riages. She was so scared of the backlash for exposing this that she had to sleep with a gun at night and eventually fled town.

VOCs don't just cause disease by the wellhead. It also causes ground-level ozone, or smog when mixed with sunlight and nitrous oxide from car exhaust. Because fracking wells and infrastructure leak VOCs, and there are around a 1,000 truck trips over the life of a well, fracking is a huge cause of ozone. The National Oceanic and Atmospheric Administration (NOAA) estimated that fracking along the front range of Colorado accounted for 55 percent of ground-level ozone. In rural parts of Wyoming, where there is only one person per square mile, ozone levels reached levels higher than downtown Los Angeles. While ozone is known to be a leading cause of asthma and lung disease, Hickenlooper said suspending ozone regulations "would be a great idea." Fracking has destroyed Colorado's once-pristine mountain air. Now, we face ozone violations every year from the impact of fracking. Some days, it's hard to see the mountains because of the smog hanging over it. In its 2016 report card, the American Lung Association graded every Front Range county (which are the counties on the eastern edge of the Colorado Rockies) an "F" for air quality.

Education is the first step to bringing an end to this pollution. It will also help to unravel an industry based on lies. That's why I created such a huge controversy when I started doing presentations on the facts of fracking at schools across Colorado. One school was Evergreen Middle School, west of Denver. A teacher had reached out to me and my brother to present and perform for her class. We rolled up to this school thinking we were going to talk to just a couple classes of students and were surprised when the library started to fill in with every kid in that grade, including the head of the school and a bunch of teachers. We gave a presentation about fracking and performed our track "What the Frack?" getting the whole audience to sing with us.

Many of the kids went home that night and told their parents about what they learned from our presentation, and some of the parents got very heated. They worked for the fracking industry, and they started posting the video of us performing on all sorts of right-wing message boards. All of the sudden, I had people hurling obscene insults all over my Facebook and YouTube pages. I even got some death threats. They claimed that I was brainwashing kids. But, I knew what was up, they were going after me and my bro because we were exposing the truth— the greatest enemy of the fracking industry.

I wrote an article, called "Why Would People from the Oil and Gas Industry Bully 10- and 13-Year-Old Kids?" I pointed out all the propaganda that the industry uses to influence young people, including producing coloring books for kids, like "Talisman Terry the Friendly Fracosaurus." In Colorado, this industry spent more than $75 million on public relations in a 3-year period, flooding television and the Internet with advertisements trying to persuade people that fracking is safe. Yet, despite the fact that they've spent so much to confuse the public about what's happening, they were absolutely terrified of two kids with a couple mics and some slides. The parents pushed to have the teacher fired and made the school district distribute oil and gas propaganda to all the teachers and parents.

We weren't about to let them stop us, so later that year, we brought a petition to the Colorado Oil and Gas Conservation Commission (COGCC), with the support of Our Children's Trust, asking them to place a moratorium on fracking in Colorado until it could be proved safe for human health and the environment. I testified in front of the commission and pointed out the ways in which they failed in their own mission statement. I told them, "The children of this state are being endangered because of your lack of responsibility to do your job."

The COGCC denied our petition, so we appealed to the Colorado District Court in Denver. The COGCC won in the trial court, but we appealed to the Colorado Court of Appeals to get our petition reheard. We held a massive rally on the State Capitol steps the day before the appellate court was to hear our appeal. We included lawyers from Our Childrens' Trust, youth, and indigenous speakers. We marched past the courthouse, and DJ Cavem and I rocked the crowd afterward with a couple of tracks. We ended as we began, with a ceremony given by the Aztec dancers, calling in the four directions. After we finished the ceremony, we gathered on the Capitol steps for a photo, and a hawk flew overhead in all four directions before flying off. You could feel something powerful was about to happen.

Then on March 23, 2017, while I was writing this book, the court sided with us (the plaintiffs), saying that protecting public health, safety, and the environment is a "condition that has to be met" before oil and gas drilling can be done. This was a huge victory and allows communities a legal tool to help protect themselves from the harms of fracking. One example is Bella Romero Academy, a middle school that has 24 wells permitted within 500 feet of the school soccer field. Families and youth who attend the school or live nearby are suing to protect their health and safety, and with the new ruling, they have strong legal ground to stand on.

The appellate court decision became even more important after a home in Firestone exploded from gas migration coming off a nearby oil and gas well. The explosion killed two and critically injured another, Erin Martinez, a high school chemistry and physics teacher. After the explosion, Anadarko shut off 3,000 vertical wells in the region. They are now being sued along with Noble Energy, for their negligence in protecting health and safety of nearby homes.

The Colorado Attorney General has requested that the Colorado Supreme Court hear an appeal of our victory from the Colorado Court of Appeals. We'll see if the Supreme Court accepts their appeal, but this is just another example of how oil and gas money compromises our elected officials. How can you argue that health and safety should not prioritized when it comes to an industry that is literally killing people?

Meanwhile, other places are looking at Colorado and choosing a different direction. In 2017, Republican Governor Larry Hogan signed a bill to ban fracking in Maryland, because of strong statewide movement. The so-called bridge to renewables has been revealed as a fraud. Fracking isn't helping to combat climate change. It threatens the health of our communities just like coal, and it's only kept us from transitioning to renewables.

From 2000 to 2014, coal went from 52 percent of the energy we use to 42 percent. Meanwhile, natural gas went up from 16 percent to 26 percent over the same time period. That 10 percent difference in coal could've been renewables instead. Except Democrats and big environmental groups didn't want to piss off the big fossil-fuel lobby, so they compromised. They endorsed fracking because they feared that, if they didn't, all the fossil-fuel money would par into the hands of Republicans, and they would lose elections. This is what I mean when I say fracking hasn't just polluted our air, water, and climate, but it's also polluted our democracy.

Other countries have realized that going the direction of renewables is not just best for health, safety, and the climate, it's also the best thing for their economies. In Germany, the country decided to get rid of nuclear energy for health and safety reasons. Some feared that coal would take its place. But, between the years 2000 and 2014, solar production tripled as both nuclear and coal declined. Germany, like other European countries, has learned from our mistakes in the United States and chosen not to exploit its shale gas reserves. As of 2017, they were also the fastest growing large economy in the world, with the highest budget surplus since 1990, and rising employment. This didn't happen by accident, though. It is the result of Germans organizing, taking over the electrical grid, and taking on the corporations to create a better environment for themselves.

They have literally taken the power into their own hands. In 2004, four utility companies generated 95 percent of electricity, but now, they own just 59 percent of generation, as people are taking over the grid and producing renewables. The model has taken off and now the country is over one-third renewable, and nearing its 2020 target of decreasing carbon emissions to 40 percent below 1990 levels.

TAKING THE POWER BACK

In my hometown of Boulder, we are trying something similar to the German model. We have been working to transition our energy supplier from the Xcel Energy to a city-run model. The city would then take aggressive steps to help address climate change and move entirely off of fossil fuels. We've voted at the ballot box multiple times to make this change. We aren't going away. Xcel is making it as difficult as possible for us, because they know Boulder could just be the first straw. When other cities see how we can save money, increase reliability, and fight climate change, we can expect a whole lot of other cities to follow. Youth led organizations like New Era Colorado fueled the campaign. They were able to overcome Xcel Energy's big spending at the ballot.

A big reason it's taken solar so long to take off in the United States is because the utility companies like Xcel fight to keep solar down. These big corporations can make more money generating energy from coal and gas because they own the power plants, while solar is often sourced from rooftops. Under that model, it would be your neighbors and not the corporations making the money. This is the democratization of energy and taking the power back to the people where it belongs.

The Sunlight Revolution

Even with big corporations fighting progress and many politicians still asleep at the wheel, the energy has shifted toward renewables, specifically solar. A recent Department of Energy report says that solar power employed almost double that of coal, oil and gas combined in 2016. Meanwhile, renewable energy is creating jobs at a rate 12 times faster than the rest of the economy. This is all with solar as just 1 percent of electricity generation in the United States. Imagine how many jobs we could create if we just started collecting all the sun that hits our communities every day.

Donald Trump may be trying to block the sun and crawl into a hole for energy, but you don't have to. We have ambitious and intelligent vision for our energy. Here are some ways you can get involved with the sunlight revolution: You can put solar on your roof, and actually sell electricity to the grid. The price of solar has come way down over the past 10 years, so if you have a roof that's angled right you can actually make money off switching to solar. If you don't have a roof or yard to put panels on, you can join a community solar program or solar garden. This means that you can share a solar project with your neighbors that provides energy to the grid, and helps everyone. In some places, like Colorado, you can sign up to get your energy from roofless solar providers like the Clean Energy Collective. You can find more information at www.earthguardians.org/action.

Keep It in the Ground

While we work to build the solutions, we also have to stop the destruction from fracking. Donald Trump's administration wants to open up millions of acres of public land and parks to fracking during his time in office. In order to stop climate change and protect water and wildlife, we must stop this plan from moving forward. A powerful coalition has come together to keep these fossil fuels in the ground, which includes Greenpeace, 350.org, Food and Water Watch, Rainforest Action Network, and luminaries like Mark Ruffalo, Shailene Woodley, and Bill McKibben. You can find more at www.keepitintheground.org.

Education is the key to move us in the right direction. So, take what you've learned about fracking and share it with your community. Show a documentary film about fracking or offer a presentation to your local school. We are at the tipping point when renewables can overtake fossil fuels as the main source of new energy, but to get there, it's going to take knowledge, power, and our collective will. We may have been fooled into fracking, but we don't have to be foolish about where we go from here. We are running out of coal, oil, and gas, but the sun and wind are abundant resources that will never run out. We must look to the skies for the future of our planet, our energy, and our economy. It's up to us.

CHAPTER 11

From Protestors to Protectors

What Standing Rock Taught the World

"Someone needs to explain to me why wanting clean drinking water makes you an activist, and why proposing to destroy water with chemical warfare doesn't make a corporation a terrorist."

—WINONA LADUKE

I think it's easy to be cynical about the human race. I've found that, in doing this work for the planet and fighting for something bigger, you can't help but question what's happened to humanity. Zooming out on the world, things can look pretty dark. This planet has survived and thrived for millions of years in near perfect balance. Of course, it's always gone through death and rebirth, but all of the sudden, humans come into the picture and, for the first time ever, we are facing an unnatural collapse of life on Earth. The greed of man is pushing our world closer and closer to a point of no return. I don't think we've lost our humanity, we've simply forgotten it.

#nodapl Protectors at Standing Rock

My father taught me that, as indigenous people, we have a responsibility to give back to the Earth for all that it's given to us and for all we've taken. We celebrate nature and the gifts of the Earth that give us life through prayer, song, and dance. It's our responsibility to be stewards of this planet and protectors of our land. I've realized that my connection to the Earth is part of what defines my identity as an indigenous person. It's not just a connection to our culture, our language, our ancestry, our ceremonies; part of what makes us indigenous is a deep respect and understanding that we are a small part of a very fragile world, and maintaining that connection is crucial to our survival.

In today's modern world, no matter how big your city is, no matter how far from your food or water source you live, or how invisible the connection is to you, you're still just as dependent on the planet and the land as indigenous peoples. We have ignored this critical piece of our humanity. I believe that indigenous or not, part of what makes us human is a connection to our Earth.

An example of that wisdom came recently with my personal experience at Standing Rock, a place that inspired millions around the world, as tens of thousands indigenous led water protectors held an encampment along the Missouri River, blocking off a section of the Dakota Access Pipeline.

The Energy Transfer Partners–sponsored project ran through native territory and threatened the water of Standing Rock Reservation and 18 million people living downriver on the Missouri. This is not the first time we've seen native lives threatened by fossil-fuel development. Originally, the pipeline was set to go through the City of Bismarck, which has mainly a white population, but because people in the city complained, they re-routed the pipeline to go past the Standing Rock Sioux Reservation. This threatened their water source and was a clear example of environmental racism.

I spent 2 days at Standing Rock in solidarity with all the freedom-fighters, front-liners, and tribal residents. Honor the Earth invited me there to perform alongside Immortal Technique, Nahko Bear, and other indigenous MCs. I remember arriving at Standing Rock and seeing hundreds of tents scattered throughout the encampment. I could smell burning sage and campfires as I watched native youth riding by on horseback. As I pulled into the camp, I saw hundreds of flags from different indigenous nations on either side of the road, resting on tall flagpoles. They symbolized the unity of Standing Rock, as thousands of indigenous people came together to support a singular cause. This was the most significant gathering of these tribes in recent memory. They

Standing in Solidarity

came together to fight a common threat and raise their voices so the world would have no choice but to listen.

One thing that was incredibly powerful, not only to me but to the entire world, was the way those front-liners identified themselves as water protectors. How long have we let others label us in ways that draw away from our core message? By being called water protectors and not protestors, leaders showed that we should be defined by what we love and seek to defend, not by what we oppose.

Protestors demand change from someone else, while protectors enact change themselves. We are actively protecting water, the source of all life. We are standing up for the rights of all indigenous people, our way of life, and our connection to our sacred land.

I want people to know that before the demonstrations became massive, before thousands of people traveled to remote North Dakota to stand for water and indigenous rights, before people saw images on their Facebook feeds, this started with young people. The youth who planted the seeds for all the power and ceremony that was to come did so as a means of survival. I think it's important to tell the story of how Standing Rock came to be.

Jasilyn Charger is a young native woman from the Cheyenne River Reservation just south of Standing Rock in South Dakota. When she was 17, she left the reservation for Portland to get away from the drugs and hopelessness on the reservation. When she was 19 years old, her

Riding Through Standing Rock

closest friend committed suicide. She flew home for the funeral. Just 2 days later, while she was still there, another friend took their own life. She was shocked and saddened by the death of her friends. There were 30 teen suicide attempts that summer on the reservation. This is a problem that a lot of reservations are facing. Teen suicide is 1.5 times more likely among native youth than the national teen suicide average.

I witnessed the challenges facing native youth personally during my trip to the Black Hills Unity Concert in South Dakota. The concert was organized for the purpose of returning the sacred Black Hills to the Great Sioux Nation. Just before this powerful concert, three native girls on the Pine Ridge Reservation killed themselves. I performed the following day with my brother and sister, and afterward, we hung out with the local kids from the reservation. They told us about everything they were facing from depression to alcoholism to lack of access to healthy food. Talking to these young girls who were the same ages as my brother, 11 or 12, and hearing what they had been through was really intense. It helped me to understand the toll of poverty and 500 years of oppression on native youth. After the concert, we did workshops with young people from the reservation. They sang, played games, and showed us their connection to their ancestors. You could see that this and the positivity of that concert gave them hope and made them come alive.

Jasilyn would later say the suicides "really woke us up." Her cousin Joseph White Eyes also felt a need to bring positivity and a purpose to the youth of their community to combat all they were up against. Along with their friend Trenton Casillas-Bakeberg, they started a youth group on the reservation. They fundraised for a youth basketball tournament, and they traveled to a native film festival to get young people off the reservation and expose them to different experiences. Mostly, they counseled youth in their communities to help provide them with a sense of belonging and meaning, along with important alternatives to drugs and alcohol.

As they were able to curb the wave of suicides on the reservation, the newly named One Mind Youth Movement began to turn political. They joined the fight against the Keystone XL Pipeline (KXL), which threatened to contaminate the Cheyenne River near their reservation. At that time, Indigenous Environmental Network (IEN) had set a "Spirit Camp" around the Cheyenne River Reservation. Jasilyn and other One

Mind members had been trained there, learning the skills of nonviolent direct action (NVDA). After the Obama administration rejected the permit, they began to focus on the Dakota Access Pipeline (DAPL), which was to go underneath the Missouri River and carry a half million barrels of oil a day through this area.

DAPL was not only a direct threat to their cousin reservation of the Standing Rock Sioux but also it was an example of the greater threat of the fossil-fuel industry toward people everywhere. In April of 2016, the youth answered a call from Standing Rock Sioux tribal members to help stop DAPL. The youth formed a small prayer camp along the Dakota Access route. There was still snow on the ground at that point. With few available resources, they mostly lived off bologna sandwiches, potato chips, and water. It was a spiritual retreat of sorts, with alcohol and drugs strictly forbidden. The small, tightly knit group of young people, mostly under age 25, had gone from fighting to prevent youth suicide to trying to prevent society from killing itself by poisoning the water, air, and climate. They brought other youth in, passing along their skills and training them in NVDA.

After weeks at the camp, the youth knew that they needed more support. They decided to embark on a bold and powerful action. Along with the young indigenous mother and long distance runner Bobbi Jean Three Legs, they devised a relay run from Sacred Stone camp to the Omaha, Nebraska, Army Corps of Engineers office, a distance of 500 miles. IEN supported the run with a social media campaign, phone calls, and letters to gain the support of other tribal members. Within just days, the Army Corps of Engineers representative agreed to meet with the youth leaders.

Even though they got the meeting, they decided to carry out the run in hopes that it would continue to raise awareness and connect youth from the surrounding reservations. The Sioux people are made up of seven bands of people organized into seven council fires, known together as Oceti Sakowin. The runners thought that by running through as many reservations as possible during their run, they could begin to unite the youth of Oceti Sakowin, fulfilling a long-foretold prophecy. There was a sense that there was something bigger here than just one pipeline. This was a fight for justice and equality.

INDIGENOUS RESISTANCE

An Interview with Dallas Goldtooth

Dallas Goldtooth is the Keystone XL campaign organizer for the Indigenous Environmental Network. He cofounded the Indigenous comedy group, the 1491s, and is a Dakota culture and language teacher. He is also a poet, traditional artist, powwow emcee, comedian, and proud father.

ME: Let's get it. You were a leader in two of the most important climate justice campaigns of our time. What do you think it was about Keystone XL Pipeline (KXL) and Dakota Access Pipeline (DAPL) that resonated with people and helped wake them up?

DALLAS: Oh, man. Shit, that's a heavy question. There was a stark difference between KXL and DAPL. I think of KXL as round one, like an appetizer. It triggered a lot of folks to really start thinking about not only climate change overall, but also really how there's different ways to attack and address climate change. It's not just a matter of stopping it at the pump of wherever it's being extracted from, but also it's how you can address the issues of transportation of fossil fuels and how you can address the refinement of fossil fuels. Also, I think it continued that conversation of how do you stop it at the consumption of fossil fuels. That fight, I think, really triggered a lot of people and kind of got things moving, even though construction didn't even start. We stopped it before it even started. Now compare that to Dakota Access— that's where construction was happening at the doorstep.

I think that the entire time, whether it's KXL or Dakota Access, our narrative as native people never changed, and it still hasn't changed. For the benefit of Mother Earth, and for the sacred integrity of the land and water in ourselves, our own bodies, we have to keep fossil fuels in the ground. We have to stop it at the source. Actually, it's kind of crazy. Native folks have been saying that for generations now. It's just now where the mainstream of society are catching on to what we as native people have been seeing since the beginning, that we have to be in balance with Mother Earth or else we're going to get fucked off this sucker. It's imperative for us to see the necessity for us to just do the best we can to protect Mother Earth for the benefit of all life. I still carry, like a lot of us do, some PTSD from the Dakota Access fight. A lot of us carry some trauma. It's real legit, you know? We have to stop this from even going any further.

I think that when you see that an individual, let alone an entire people, has such strong core values and is willing to walk the talk of those values, that's inspiring. I think that's what we saw. I think that we saw a moment in time, right now, where we needed to see people put into action what we've been saying to protect Mother Earth. Win or lose, we have to do that. Win or lose, we can't sacrifice those values. I think that's what it was. People were just inspired to see this movement, this action taken, just backing up what we've been saying all along.

ME: Do you think part of what defines us as indigenous people is the connection to the Earth, more than just cultural, cultural ancestry? Do you actually see a connection to our Earth as part of what defines us as indigenous people?

DALLAS: I think so, wholeheartedly. We always have to be careful about the royal "we," because we always have to acknowledge the immense diversity of indigenous peoples. I think that from just general experience and observation, it is apparent that our languages, our philosophies, our way of life, and our science are based off the land. As indigenous peoples, as native peoples, we are a mere reflection of the land in which we were born into and created and formed from, and that it is the land that defines us. That's why, for me, as a language activist, it's essential for us to remember those terms because the terminology of the language was a critical part of our vision, and a lot of our languages are threatened right now. Everything we are as indigenous peoples is born on that relationship to the land itself.

ME: How can we take steps to decolonize the climate justice movement?

DALLAS: I think for most folks it's obvious. There are different levels. There are different points of intersection of decolonization. You interact with decolonization on a very personal individual level. There's the interaction of decolonization on the community level, and then there's the interaction with decolonization on a nation level, society level. Honestly, that fancy word, that intersection now, that's what it really speaks to. We freaking stress out trying to provide healthy food for our community, when around the back of your mind, you're like, "Shit. We've got to find proper housing for our community. We've got to find a better economy for our community." You go into a tailspin.

I think that, as long as we continue to advocate for people working in this environmental justice movement, that decolonization isn't just about the systemic apparatus that's continuing our dependency on fossil fuels. It's also on a very personal level of, "How do we interact with each other?" In that effort, we must try our damn freaking hardest to continue to have empathy for our relatives out there who are on the same path as us. That's why like ... one big part of the work that we do as native people is because sometimes, man, we come across some crazy-ass white people. We come across a lot of folks who are like...I like to use the term cultural vampires or cultural raccoons who basically go and they pillage and they find the little things that they like and they amalgamate it together to find some cultural relationship to Mother Earth. In the process of doing so, they're appropriating cultures and actually hurting the communities that they want to respect.

That is an issue. That is a problem. That is something that we have to continue to be mindful of and encourage our allies and ourselves not to take. We have to be mindful of our steps on the stairs of cultural appropriation. We also have to have the empathy to say, "Look, who are we? What are we demanding? "It's choppy waters. It's difficult. A lot of our nonnative relatives are on that journey as well. They're trying to find a better way to return to Mother Earth. As native people, as people of color, we don't have the answers for everything. We don't even have the answers for ourselves at times, but we have to have the empathy to understand that the only way change is going to happen is if we do it all together.

ME: What is the biggest change you've seen in the greater climate justice movement in your lifetime?

I'm seeing Big Green businesses more attuned to the necessity of showing respect to frontline grassroots leaders, of incorporating the principles of environmental justice into their practice and saying, "Look, we can't go from a top-down approach in environmental justice. We have to do it bottom up." That is much credit to the years and years of work of EJ organizers to get Big Greens to get to that place or to continue down that path. We're seeing Big Green NGOs having frontline budgets and having frontline organizers are supporting that effort. That's key. I think that's something I'm really seeing as really something positive.

The other one, I guess, is straightforward, the keep-it-in-the-ground campaign. The keep-it-in-the-ground fight is to keep fossil fuels in the ground. The first, that call to action came from native brothers and sisters. You go back 15 years. At the very earliest you have native brothers and sisters from the Amazon to Alaska who are demanding to keep fossil fuels in the ground as the only proper resolution or solution to address climate change, or as I guess one of the most direct ways to address climate change. That was for the benefit and protection of their own communities and the land that they live in.

If you go back 10 years ago, native people and our organization were on the streets of all these UN gatherings and saying, "Moratoriums, keep fossil fuels in the ground. We cannot, we have to see moratoriums on extraction." You would have Big Greens on this side, who were literally saying, "That's not realistic. Come on, now. We can't say that. We can't demand that. Let's be pragmatic about this." Fast-forward to where we're at now, and that's the buzzword that we're all enveloped in. That's beautiful, but we have to remember where that comes from. Definitely.

ME: You used to put humor both in your activism and your comedies, your 1491s, yeah?

DALLAS: Yeah.

ME: What do you see as the role of comedy within organizing and not taking yourself too seriously?

DALLAS: Oh, man. Shit, I think in the world of organizing our greatest weakness is our own egos. It's quite easy. It's any type of community leadership, any type of community organizing. It's quite easy to slip into the frickin' savior complex, right? A lot of us get it out of college, man. Shit, I went to Berkeley, and everyone there was like, "I'm going to go home to save my people!" You get home and you're fucking hit with the realities of like, it's not about you. It's about us. It's about your people.

For me, comedy is a way to balance the playing field or help me keep humble. You know what I mean, not being afraid to make fun of myself or make fun of the people I roll with, or make fun of or tease at the roles that we assume—whether it's the hardcore activists or the down-as-F rapper. I think that's comedy abundant. Making light of that situation not only keeps us centered, but it also introduces humor and laughter, which were our greatest survival tools as people of color in the Americas. The ability to make light of your situation got people through the darkness of times. We have to cherish that, feed it, adapt it, make it work for us in this current time of challenges.

ME: Hell, yeah. Last question. After DAPL, where are we headed from here, as far as the next steps of mass organizations of people?

DALLAS: I mean, we're seeing right now with the Resist 45, this under-standing that the White House administration and Trump represent something more than just a fight against the pipeline or this entire systemic attack upon our ability for self-determination. It's difficult because I think that people are really connecting the dots. The buzz-word *intersectionality* is a word I had never heard until about 2 years ago. It was like the hot topic, but the concept is nothing new to us. I think that is the greater beast in the room that we can't forget.

It's the same in the Dakota Access, in the fight against these pipelines. The fight against the pipelines only goes so much until we start having a conversation about stopping that source. There's a fight in British Columbia against Kinder Morgen Pipeline. That's going to be big. I'm already seeing it. I'm predicting that because folks are organized and people are steadfast in resisting that project. The same one goes for all the Enbridge pipelines out east, but you can only go down that path of resistance until you start realizing we're going to keep fighting ten-tacles of this octopus until we start actually looking at the heart of it and stopping it at the source. I think that ideology of organizing in the heart of these extraction points is going to be something major and needed and actually the hardest part of the work yet. These are places where the local economies are entirely dependent on the fossil fuel industry, where people are forced into a situation where they have to depend on those jobs. I think that's it. I'm trying to stay positive. I also know it's changing fast. I'm more, because of my trips to like the UN COPs, the Conference of Parties, because of the trips to these interna-tional spaces and hearing the stories of our relatives in the forest-dependent nations in the equator, in the jungles, and our relatives in the Arctic, I'm worried for them. I'm like, man, it's happening so quick that I know there's some stuff that's not going to be changed and some people are going to suffer. I'm focused on saying, "What can we do in this moment and in this time to help mitigate that as much as possible?"

ME: Yes. Dang, bro, yeah, got to keep that positivity, got to stay optimistic and hopeful. Bro, truly appreciate your time. You're a legend. Truly appreciate your contribution.

THE PROPHECIES OF THE BLACK SNAKE AND THE SEVENTH GENERATION

There are several ancient prophecies that have converged into the current moment of youth leadership against DAPL and KXL. One story from the Sioux leader Black Elk dating back to the 1890s foretells that, in seven generations, the great nations of Turtle Island will unite to protect the Earth. Around the same time, the Mohawk to the east had a similar prophecy of the Seventh Generation coming to restore the Earth from destruction. Yet another Sioux legend from that era foretold of a black snake that would threaten the world. The Hopi to the south similarly said that one of the signs that an era was ending would be the land crossed by snakes of iron.

The youth runners felt a sacred duty as the Seventh Generation to not only defeat the "black snake' symbolized by KXL and DAPL, but to unite indigenous people across Turtle Island (what many native people call the North American continent). Their run would serve as a catalyst, or a wake-up call. They pulled in youth from every band of Oceti Sakowin water protectors along on the run.

After returning from Omaha, where they met the Army Corps representative, Bobbi Three Legs and the group began to make even more ambitious plans. In the mid-July heat, 30 runners took off from Standing Rock to make the 2,000-mile journey to Washington, D.C. But just 11 days into their run, the Army Corps announced that they had approved the pipeline. Undeterred, the runners decided to complete their journey to D.C. The significance of their action inspired an increasing amount of support from the native community.

Allies like IEN began calling on tribes from all around to rise up like these incredible youth runners had and help build out the camp at Sacred Stone. The camp began to grow and grow, until it swelled to more than 10,000. The issue became of international importance and, what started as a small group of youths working to overcome the ill-effects of teen poverty, led to one of the most inspiring movements of my lifetime. More than 300 tribes from New Zealand to South America gathered in support of Standing Rock.

On Labor Day weekend, the movement was out in full force as the

pipeline construction began to approach the camp. In an attempt to protect their ancient burial grounds from the bulldozers, the tribe produced
evidence that the pipeline route went through these sacred sites. The very
next morning, Energy Transfer Partners bulldozed the entire area where
the burial ground had been shown in court documents. Water protectors
broke down the barriers to the area they were bulldozing and were met by
a militarized police force that sprayed mace in their faces and unleashed
attack dogs that bit protectors. Democracy Now caught the whole scene
on video, and it went viral with more than a million views. Suddenly,
mainstream media began to give coverage to the issue, showing video clips
of the police attack. Social media began to blow up with #WaterIsLife. It's
mind-blowing that the youth were able to give birth to such a powerful
moment with just prayer and the strength of their will.

The standoff continued to escalate, and, on Thanksgiving weekend,
as police fired water cannons and rubber bullets at protestors in sub-
freezing temperatures. At least 17 protectors were hospitalized with
hypothermia and more with rubber bullet wounds. One young woman
nearly needed her arm amputated from a concussion grenade blast the

Xiuhtezcatl and Chief Raoni from the Amazon

police deployed. People watched in horror as images of peaceful protectors contrasted with the brutality from a militia-style police force. I wasn't at the camp at that time, but every day, I would wake up and check social media to keep up with all that was happening. I was on edge knowing what my brothers and sisters were going through up there.

On December 4, 2016, after months of resistance and protectors continuing to endure violence from the Morton County Police Department, President Obama announced that the pipeline permit would be halted, pending an Environmental Impact Assessment. It was a huge victory for native people and a huge win for people everywhere who seek to protect water and the planet, but it was short-lived. Donald Trump would take over the Oval Office in just 6 weeks' time. He had invested in Energy Transfer Partners, the company building the pipeline, and their CEO was a hefty contributor to his campaign. One of his first acts in office was to issue an executive order approving the pipeline. According to a report by EarthJustice in June 2017, "A federal judge would later rule that the Trump administration's quick approval of permits to go under the Missouri River violated the law. Judge Boasberg, who was presiding over the case wrote, 'the Court agrees that [the Army Corps of Engineers] did not adequately consider the impacts of an oil spill on fishing rights, hunting rights, or environmental justice.'"

The pipeline is now pumping crude oil, from the North Dakota Bakken. The first pipeline spill occurred soon after it became operational. While it was a relatively small spill of 84 gallons, it might be a sign of things to come, as crude oil pipelines frequently leak. Just weeks before the Dakota Access spill, another pipeline run by Energy Transfer Partners spilled five million gallons. The spill zone included a sensitive wetland, and the contaminants killed just about all of the wildlife in the area. These are the types of events that the water protectors are fighting hard to avoid.

Still the mark of my generation had been made. During the encampment, the International Indigenous Youth Council (IIYC) was formed with leadership from Jasilyn Charger. My spiritual elder, Arvol Looking Horse, the man who gave me my name, bestowed upon the youth a ceremonial pipe, called a *chanupa*. It is a sacred element of the Sioux people, a symbol of the coming together of community. It was an act that seemed like a passing of the torch, to this the Seventh Generation, set to reawaken the world. IIYC continues to organize runs, lead actions, and raise awareness.

They had laid the groundwork for the movement of our lifetimes. Standing Rock was not just about one pipeline, it symbolized a struggle for justice of all kinds—racial justice, economic justice, treaty justice, gender justice, and climate justice. Those fights were all alive at Standing Rock. It is the latest in a long line of brave actions that cause us to pause and re-examine the true meaning of the word "justice". Like the lunch counter sit-ins of the Civil Rights Movement, Standing Rock made it impossible to ignore the historic and present oppression of indigenous peoples.

Racial justice. It is unfathomable to think about what's happened to the indigenous people of this continent over the past 500 years. Standing Rock taught us to deconstruct colonization and understand the ways that native people are still colonized. The treaties signed by the United States government, which gave indigenous nations sovereign rights and territory, have been almost completely ignored by our court system. Federal judges have ruled that treaty law does not apply to oil and gas pipelines, because colonizers created the court system. They stacked the deck against indigenous people, and they loaded their bank accounts as they continue to exploit sovereign territory for corporate profit. As you can see with DAPL and KXL, the fossil-fuel industry is an existing expression of colonization. Our society has been corrupted by a mindset greed, which teaches us to continually take without ever giving back. We've forgotten that we are all indigenous to this earth, and our home is sacred beyond measure.

Economic justice. Impoverished by an economic system that doesn't recognize the value of wisdom, native peoples have struggled to survive after being pushed to the least-desirable lands. Poverty has ripped apart native communities, giving rise to alcoholism and teen suicide, as kids look out at their world and see little opportunity for themselves. Breaking the cycle of poverty starts with offering these youth the chance to recognize a better quality of life. One of the only ways out of this is through a college education, but even then, student loans saddle too many young people with a crippling debt. It is time that we reconstruct our economic system to fit with indigenous wisdom, so that giving back is balanced with taking.

Gender justice. A mindset that the Earth is a resource to be exploited is the type of thinking that can only come from a society that doesn't recognize the importance of balancing masculine and feminine energy. As native people, we see the Earth as living; we understand that abusing that which made you is the definition of insanity. No matter what you do, it's this planet that sustains you, the air you breathe, the water you drink, and the food you eat. Without a planet, you'd be shit out of luck. Showing respect for creation should be as natural as showing respect for your mother. We cannot overlook that many of the leaders of the Standing Rock encampment are women, like Jasilyn Charger, Bobbi Three Legs, Ladonna Allard, Winona Laduke, Kandi Mosset and many, many more. Women are the cornerstones of our society. They are the creators of life and are regularly fighting to secure gender equality and equal protection in a sometimes chauvinistic and egocentric world. A movement that doesn't recognize the importance of balance between masculine and feminine energy cannot reach its full potential.

Climate justice. The cycles of nature, which native people have relied on for millennia face severe changes due to man-made climate change. Climate change is a problem that affects everyone. However, for people who are more reliant on the land, the impacts of floods, draughts, tornadoes, melting ice caps, and other disasters are even worse. The wealthy can pick up and leave or create physical barriers and safeguards to protect against these growing threats, while people without means are forced to reconcile with life as a refugee. For native people, who have a spiritual connection with the land, leaving home can represent an enormous loss of ancestral history. Indigenous rights means climate justice.

Shifting the paradigm. Direct action has the power to make injustice a felt experience. It contrasts those standing up for what is just and right with those imposing an oppressive system. The emotional response we have to this kind of juxtaposition is a powerful thing. It's where we begin to see hearts shift and beliefs change worldwide, even those of the oppressor.

One of the most shocking things I learned about the Civil Rights Movement was that George Wallace, former Governor of Alabama and one of the main bad guys in the film *Selma*, later renounced his positions and asked for forgiveness. At one time, he was a symbol of segregation, famously saying, "segregation now, segregation tomorrow, and segregation forever." This was a man who once ordered his state troopers to use billy clubs and tear gas to stop the famous march from Selma to Montgomery. Thirty years later, he came to the commemoration of that same march, saluting those who bravely stood against his own oppressive state. At the memorial of 50 years since the march, his daughters marched with Martin Luther King, Jr.'s, daughter.

One of Wallace's daughters, Peggy Wallace Kennedy, now considers John Lewis a personal friend, even though he was a man her father had ordered beaten on the bridge in Selma. She spoke to him during a speech at the Alabama State Archives, "Fifty years ago, you stood here in front of your state capitol and sought an opportunity as a citizen of Alabama to be recognized and heard by your governor. And he refused. But, today, as his daughter and as a person of my own, I want to do for you what my father should have done and recognize you for your humanity and for your dignity as a child of God, as a person of goodwill and character, and as a fellow Alabamian and say, 'Welcome home.'"

This is one of many examples of the power of nonviolent movements to not only create change but also to bring about an evolution of consciousness. We dream that someday Governor Jack Dalrymple of North Dakota, who ordered violent acts on protestors and the desecration of sacred sites, will also ask for forgiveness, and that his children will march with the descendants of water protectors. It took a great many steps to bring about the end of segregation and give black people voting rights. It took sustained, committed, and direct action that would eventually cause that system of oppression to crumble. I believe that someday we will look at Standing Rock the way we look at Selma, or the Children's March in Birmingham. This was a time when people began to wake up and see the incredible injustice toward native peoples. A time when they began to see treaty rights ignored, sacred land and water desecrated, and 500 years of genocide and oppression.

Standing Rock helped to plant the seed of reconciliation. In early

December, around the time Obama sent the pipeline back for review, 4,000 veterans showed up at the camp. They were led by Army Lt. Wesley Clark, Jr., son of former Supreme Allied Commander of NATO Gen Wesley Clark. The veterans engaged in a powerful forgiveness ceremony. General Clark kneeled before native elders like Chief Leonard Crow Dog and spoke these words:

> Many of us, me particularly, are from the units that have hurt you over many years. We came. We fought you. We took your land. We signed treaties that we broke. We stole minerals from your sacred hills. We blasted the faces of our presidents onto your sacred mountain. Then, we took still more land, and then, we took your children, and . . . we tried to eliminate your language that God gave you, and the Creator gave you. We didn't respect you, we polluted your Earth, we've hurt you in so many ways, but we've come to say that we are sorry. We are at your service, and we beg for your forgiveness.

This was an important step, but to make the full dream come to fruition, we cannot stop now. We must continue to amplify and support those on the frontlines of indigenous struggles to keep fossil fuels in the ground and shift a broken paradigm. We must educate our community about what's happened to native peoples of this land, the genocide, the forced migration, and the ignoring of treaties. For allies who choose to show solidarity, it's important to come first from a place of listening and humility, just like General Clark.

Here are some ways you can get engaged.

Help provide legal aid. Let's first support those who have been on the front lines, like the courageous water protectors who put their bodies on the line in an attempt to stop DAPL. This work was not only critical to temporarily halting the pipeline, it also changed the landscape of what it means to protect our water, land, and Earth. Many people were arrested for this peaceful protection and are now facing a battle in court with Energy Transfer Partners, who have selected some of the top law firms to represent them. One of the primary legal defense funds is the

Lakota People's Law Project, who is doing a fantastic job delivering their expertise to serve and support convicted water protectors. The charges given to water protectors have been harsh; activist and Lakota People's Law Project Attorney Chase Iron Eyes was accused of a felony, while trying to establish the Last Child camp.

Chase Iron Eyes and Red Fawn are just some of the water protectors currently facing legal charges. There were 141 people also arrested the same day that Red Fawn was brought to jail, including One Mind Youth Movement cofounder Trenton Casillas-Bakeberg. He was pouring water at a sweat lodge ceremony in the frontline camp when police surrounded the camp. Before they had finished the ceremony, a gloved hand reached in and pulled him out in his underwear. He asked the officers multiple times to bring him his clothes, but they refused despite the cold weather. Trenton compared it to "police breaking into a church and arresting people while they are praying, then destroying their alter." He and everyone who was arrested that day received felony charges for conspiracy.

Support and recognize indigenous youth leadership. The indigenous youth who planted the seeds for Standing Rock face many of the same problems today that they did before Standing Rock started. The leaders of One Mind Youth Movement are still doing powerful work to support young people on the reservation. They are organizing to build a safehouse that will help homeless youth avoid potentially dangerous situations, and a supportive place to overcome drug and alcohol addiction. On their web site www.omym.org, you can find out more about their work to build the safehouse and upcoming projects.

William Brownotter, Jr., is another young leader who rose out of the run to Nebraska, and, at age 16, he is working to make a difference for youth on the reservation. As the International Indigenous Youth Council was forming, William was beginning to see the struggle for the Boys and Girls Club of the Standing Rock Tribe. They were losing staff, and the threat of closing was imminent. He took action along with a couple of other youth and raised a little over 20 thousand dollars to keep the club running through the winter. Now, William is working to keep the club open on a longer-term basis.

The Boys and Girls Club provides two meals and is open 5 days a week. This program is like a second home, and what the club provides may be the first meal of the day for some of the 50 kids who come regularly. Some youth leaders, like William, credit the Boys and Girls Club with empowering them to take leadership on stopping the pipeline. Without their dedication, the Standing Rock movement would not have become a worldwide phenomenon, and it's crucial that we continue to support their work. "People say they are here for the youth. But many people just use that headline to look good. We are working hard, and our voices deserve to be heard." You can support the Standing Rock Youth Council's work to save the Boys and Girls Club at www.standingrock-bngclub.wordpress.com

Move your money. Banks are funding the climate crisis by pouring millions of dollars into pipeline projects such as the Dakota Access Pipeline. It's not just DAPL that these banks are funneling millions of dollars into; many of the same large banks such as Wells Fargo and Citibank fund multiple pipeline infrastructure projects. As customers, we have the power to put pressure on these banks to stop financing the destruction of the planet. If we aren't on the ground fighting pipelines and oil and gas infrastructure in our communities, we can still show up in solidarity with people on the front lines. Bank divestment not only helps to stigmatize the oil and gas industry but also gives you power as a customer to pressure these massive institutions to stand on the right side of history. A critical part of a just transition away from fossil fuels is moving our money into just and sustainable solutions. This fight is far from over, and we need to be exercising and leveraging the different places we hold power, if we're ever going to win. Additionally, we encourage you to send a letter to your bank notifying them of your action. Many Defund DAPL groups have sprung up, and you can join an existing divestment campaign or organize a Defund DAPL action in your community. You can learn more by going to www.defunddapl.org to get more information.

Find your front line. The Dakota Access Pipeline is a perfect example of how the oil and gas industry is destroying communities, and how the government and a militarized police force prop it up and protect it. Many of the patterns of exploitation and putting money before the health and safety of people are not unique to the Dakota Access Pipeline. There are pipelines, fracking, mountaintop removal projects, and tar sand fights happening in local communities across the country. And everyday people, who are struggling to maintain their dignity and rights to a clean environment, are fighting back. By strengthening local power in one community, we contribute to the larger fight against the oil and gas industry. To start, you can do research on what oil and gas projects are being proposed or are already happening in your community. Find organizations and see if they are taking action on the issue. It's important to do your research before taking action so that we don't reinvent the wheel. We also should work to understand that protecting the environment is a collective responsibility, and we can all play a critical role in the fight against climate injustice and fossil-fuel exploitation. While we need to be building the new, it's equally important to stop the destruction in our own communities.

We are protecting water, the source of all life. We were protecting my generation's right to a just, sustainable planet. It's up to each of us to continue what the youth runners started, so that seven generations from now, the youth of that day will be able to enjoy a planet at least as vibrant and full of life as the one we now live on.

ACTIVISM ROOTED IN PRAYER

An Interview with Shailene Woodley

Shailene Woodley is an actress and activist. She is best known for her starring roles in the *Divergent* series and *Snowden*.

ME: So many people know you from your role in the Divergent films and other incredible acting roles and movies like Snowden, but you're recently becoming recognized more and more as a voice for indigenous rights, climate justice, and different social justice movements. How have you been able to find your voice as an activist?

SHAILENE: For me, it's never been about finding a voice or even figuring out my role. It's been more about listening to the guidance and really standing strong and striving for something, or standing up for something, because my heart tells me to, not because my mind tells me to. I think, in activism, there is a misconception or a disconnection between what we are being asked to do and what we actually get done. Our hearts and our intuition might guide us to perform certain actions, while our minds spin us in other directions.

It's a hard concept to explain, but for me, the only way I can articulate it is, if my mind wants to do something because it sees that something's wrong, I have to make sure that my heart and my mind are in alignment. If they aren't, it probably means that I'm not the best person or I'm not the right person to perform that kind of an action. Then, when I am called to do something, it's because I have a certain tool, or I have a piece of a puzzle that needs to be lent to a particular movement or a particular cause. Everything sort of seamlessly falls into place.

I think another thing about finding your voice in activism is that there are so many things to fight for. There are so many things that are wrong in our world right now—that are unjust, unfair, incredibly traumatic, and sad—that if we force a particular type of activism instead of really connecting with something that we're meant to do, then it's easy to get lost in the chaos. The last thing we need in this world right now is activists lost in chaos. We need people who are grounded and centered, and in prayer.

That was one of the things about Standing Rock that I think was one of the biggest reasons why I was guided to stand in solidarity with the youth from the very beginning of the movement. It was because it was so prayerful and so grounded in ceremony, especially at the beginning. That's something that needs to infiltrate into the activist world, and so, for me, when I'm grounded, when I'm centered, when I'm in my prayer, and we meditate, I can see the bigger picture instead of the immediate now. Then, I feel like that voice, that activist voice, naturally weaves itself into my story and guides me to particular places that I'm meant to be.

ME: Kind of jumping off the back of your talking about Standing Rock, what are some important things you learned from Standing Rock, and what are your thoughts on recommendations and guidance for nonindigenous allies to support the struggle of native communities to protect their land and water? What did Standing Rock teach you about that?

SHAILENE: Standing Rock has taught me so much. It taught me that you can operate with forgiveness and with communication and with prayer. That's why that movement, especially in the beginning, was able to accomplish and do what it did. It was because of the ability to be vulnerable in a traumatic situation and to acknowledge historical trauma and current trauma in a way that invited people to learn.

When it comes down to nonnative allies, understanding why it's so important to stand with indigenous communities, like you said, to protect clean water or to protect human rights, really, at the end of the day, and our sacred Earth, we must learn to seek to understand. What that means is, whether you go into a Native American community, whether you go into an African-American community, a Latino community, any community that's outside of the community that you know and the community that you associate with and exist within, it's important to ask questions, and it's important to humble yourself and to listen.

Especially in the activist world, we have so many good-hearted people who want to do amazing things, and who want to change the world in a positive way. The issue sometimes is ego, and one great thing that I learned at Standing Rock, which I learned in other situations as well, but I'm saying that because it was such a mass movement, and because there were so many different communities involved, learning about Native Americans for the first time. The moment that you think that you're doing something right, someone points out to you, "Hey, there may be another way to do this," or, "Hey, I understand that your perspective is stemming from this story, but there's also this narrative that perhaps you've never heard before." It's important to remain humble and to remove ego from the situation, so that we might actually listen.

I believe that a reason we have these divisions amongst our communities is our inability to listen, to receive that information, and to learn how to work together to create a common goal, a common solution. At Standing Rock, they were able to do that.

I think, toward the end, there were a lot of nonnatives who were going to Standing Rock and felt very confused. They didn't know where their place was. They didn't know how to interact. They didn't know how to help. They went to Standing Rock with good intentions and pure hearts, totally, but because they didn't know how to help indigenous communities in North America, they couldn't make a difference. We know very little about how their communities exist today, but also all of the history that we've been told from a different lens throughout the last 200 to 300 years.

It's really important for us to start removing those narratives and understand that we really know nothing, and the only way to learn the truth is to ask the source. I invite people, specifically if we're talking about Standing Rock, to just ask questions and to admit that they may be wrong, and to admit that they might not know, and to change the course of history by doing something that most of our white ancestors didn't do, which was listen.

At the end of the day, you take labels aside, you take politics aside, you take divisions aside, we're all human beings just trying to survive and do the best that we possibly can. When you look at environmental crises around the world, most indigenous communities are at the forefront of them, because they have a direct connection with Mother Earth, and because they have a direct connection with understanding that all things function synergistically, and without one piece of the puzzle, this whole world will fail. It's important for us to recognize science. Science has its place. It's important for us to look at the graphs, look at the sketches, and look at all of the different guidebooks that are published, but the most important thing we can do is listen to stories and listen to experience, and indigenous communities hold these stories and these experiences in a way that I haven't witnessed in most other communities.

ME: You were arrested at Standing Rock, strip searched, and put in an orange jumpsuit for asserting a right to clean water, essentially. Can you tell us something about that experience and how it affected you, and the effect that it had on the world when they saw what had happened?

SHAILENE: Yeah. Oftentimes, activists choose to be arrested because it brings attention to a situation. I didn't choose to be arrested. I was picked out of 200 people because I was Facebook livestreaming. It's the same story that happened with Amy Goodman and many other journalists that had been there. The whole thing caught me off guard. I wasn't prepared for it. I didn't choose it. It was scary. The criminal justice system in this country is so fucked up. It's one thing to know it, and it's one thing to fight for it, and against it, or fight against it from the outside, but when you're actually in that orange jumpsuit, you realize things on a level that you can't without that experience, or at least I couldn't without that experience. It was incredibly humbling to be in a room where all the doors were shut, and there were no handles from the inside. Had there been a fire, or an earthquake, I would have had no chance in this jail. These are what prisons are. They're cages.

Too often, activists get locked up in cages when we need them on the ground, we need them fighting, but they get locked up because they're trying to change the criminal justice system from the inside out, or the criminal justice system has attacked them, and cornered them, and stuffed them away. So many of these people now who are up against these judges and up against these juries in North Dakota, they're all getting found guilty. Me, personally, I was criminally trespassing. I can't fight that. That's the truth. I was on land that I shouldn't have been on, and even though I was the only person arrested out of 200 people, I still was criminally trespassing.

I was there standing in solidarity with all of these other brothers and sisters who were at the forefront of this movement, and so if my piece of the puzzle could have been getting arrested and blasting it out, and sort of bringing attention on another level to this movement. I wouldn't ever see it as a sacrifice. I saw it sort of as a blessing and a gift. I think that there was that component of it, and then there was a lot of strangeness for me, and I talked about this a lot. It took a white female "celebrity" for people to start caring about Standing Rock.

I think on a mass level and on an insular, independent, heart-based level, we really need to start recognizing that most often in our world, we remain apathetic and numb to situations until they directly affect us. For some reason, when a celebrity's seen, people feel very connected and very close to people that they don't know, which is why, when my sister got arrested, a few people knew about her arrest, and when I got arrested, millions of people knew about it, and not only knew about it, but then immediately took action, immediately came to Standing Rock, or immediately started throwing around the hashtag #freeshailene, or donating to a fight that I didn't create, that somebody else created.

There's a lack of care until it's on your front doorstep, and I think that what we need to start recognizing in activism, in general, is that, yes, it was a beautiful thing that I got arrested, because it did mean more people found out, but why did it take my getting arrested for people to find out? Why didn't CNN show up before? Why didn't MSNBC show up before? Why didn't all of these mainstream news media outlets cover it? These are major questions that we have to start looking at.

I didn't choose it. I think it was definitely a guided protocol, a guided situation, but I think it's bigger than just: "Shailene Woodley got arrested for protecting clean water." I think it's an invitation for all of us to meditate on, "What does it really take for us to begin to care about something that doesn't perhaps directly affect us, and yet, in the bigger picture, does?" Which, everyone needs clean water, but if you don't live along the Missouri, or if you're not Native American, or if you don't have any connection to Native Americans, why would you care about this subject? Ultimately, you need water to survive, too.

Looking at it from that perspective, I think that it offered us a lot if we are able, as people, to address our apathy and address our attachment to fame, and to celebrity and to "cool." That was another thing that I witnessed with my getting arrested that, all of a sudden, Standing Rock became cool. It became kind of cool to talk about it. It became kind of cool to put something together, and I think that's wonderful, it's beautiful that so many petitions were started after that, and so many fundraisers were started after that. But why did it take my arrest, and sort of the coolness of a situation to invite people to begin caring about a situation that actually wasn't cool at all? It became hip. It became a cultural, social community-builder, which is wonderful. There's other things to meditate on. There's no right or wrong or good or bad. There are just things to think about.

ME: It seems like your activism is very prayerfully rooted and just very wise. I just wonder if there have been any teachers in your life that have helped bring about this perspective, that have helped bring that awareness into your life?

SHAILENE: No one that I can think of, apart from trees and this earth. I said apart from trees and this earth. I always find using nature as a metaphor and animals as a metaphor and as an example for how we should perform action and take action in this world is incredibly. . . . I receive a lot of guidance and I receive a lot of wisdom from them, from the patience that nature has, from the fierce force that nature has, and from the ability to stand strong despite the injustice that is occurring around this Earth. As far as human examples, I have a few elders, but they didn't really come into my life until later on in my life, as far as exchanging knowledge and wisdom, and just listening to their stories about when they were young in the 1950s and 1960s and 1970s, fighting the Vietnam War and standing up against injustices that were performed then.

I would have to say that nature has been my steadfast guide, because when you're in nature, and you're there for longer than a quick, few-hour hike, and you really take the time to connect to this source, to this mother, this planet, what you're actually doing is you're taking the time to connect to yourself and connect to all things. When you are in that space and connected to all things, I find it pretty difficult for ego to dominate. I find it pretty simple for innate love, for unconditional love to take over, and at the root of activism, at the root of humanity, at the root of existence, is love. That's all we're doing, really. We can call it social injustice. We can call it environmental injustice, environmentalism. We have all these different labels, but it's just love. It's unconditional love, and nature provides that, if we're able to listen, and provides the guidance as to how we can further spread and exist, in and with that love. Relatable.

ME: As a young person with big ideas, do people see your perspective as being too idealistic? Do you see a need for greater respect toward the views of youth in our world today?

SHAILENE: Constantly. I feel like I have received more comments about being an idealist than I have about being someone who can actually create change, which, honestly, you can't really give two fucks about. . . . You can't really care on too deep a level. For me, it kind of just adds fuel to my fire, in a way. Last year, just as an example, after Bernie Sanders lost the California primary, I had this idea to organize a caravan across the country to the DNC, because I wanted people to stay politically involved, and many young people felt disenfranchised by the Democratic party, and so we wanted to do a caravan for Bernie supporters, for Hillary supporters, even for Trump supporters. Really, anyone in America who was interested in democracy, and helpful debate, and the political system.

Now, I wake up each morning, and I say, "Trump is our president. You know what? There's a lot of hope in this, because it means people get to start talking to each other. It gives us an opportunity to create change in a way that we couldn't have if Hillary Clinton or Bernie Sanders had been president." As a people, we have more power now than we've ever had before. We just have to learn how to harness it. Obviously, I would never choose Trump to be president, but it's where we're at, and I often get looked at in funny ways for that. I get called an idealist, or a ridiculous optimist, but I also sort of feel like the idea and the concept of idealism, in general, is a very adult way of looking at an imaginative, wonder-filled, creative situation. There's no right or wrong way to do anything. We're all here to learn, and we're all here to witness, and we're all here to serve, and hopefully, we serve with love. That's the goal.

One thing that we lose as we become adults is our sense of imagination, and our sense of creation—creation from anything. If you look at activism as an art form, and you look at idealism as sort of the paintbrush for whatever creation you're about to manifest, then you can use idealism as a tool to be as imaginative, as creative, and as uninhibited as possible, as long as you're doing it with compassion and love. That's what our children do.

Our kids have so much ability to recognize where shifts can occur and how they can play, and how they can show up unconditionally with love, day after day after day, because they don't have ego developed yet. Our elders have developed ego and let go of their egos, because they've seen where it's gotten them, and where it hasn't gotten them. In that idealism, we are able, for a second, a millisecond, to remove our egos and just pray, and allow ourselves as adults, or allow ourselves even as teenagers, as youth, to strip away all rules, all restrictions, all the things we've been told that are black-and-white and find the gray again, find the rainbow again, find the colors again, and infuse that into a world that desperately needs some cushion and some relaxation and some reprieve from the black-and-white nature of right and wrong, and rules, and laws.

PART III

———— ✕ ————

THE GAME PLAN

"When we stand together there is nothing
we cannot accomplish. But when we're divided,
the big money interests will always win."

-BERNIE SANDERS

CHAPTER 12

Justice, Not Just Us

Growing Intersectional Movements
for Lasting Change

*"Never forget that justice is what
love looks like in public."*

—CORNELL WEST

The perfect balance of nature exists within the interconnectedness of every species in an ecosystem. Every one of them plays an important role, no matter how big or how small. The strength of a forest isn't found solely in the composition of its trees. Diversity is what supports prolific, thriving, and resilient systems. In nature, monocultures have proven to be weak, unsustainable, and vulnerable. The same is true in monoculture movements. Biodiversity is the genius of evolution, and it makes sense that the most successful movements to protect this are those that follow in nature's footsteps and embrace the power of diversity.

When I first started working in the climate movement in 2006, a lot of people saw the environment as a privileged thing to care about. Climate change and nature conservancy have been seen as primarily white issues. Part of this was a reflection of people empowered in leadership roles. I saw that marginalized communities were more likely to face income inequality and struggle to thrive in a system historically stacked against them. Issues like climate change didn't seem as important as the immediate challenges many of these communities faced.

Climate change and fossil-fuel extraction disproportionately affect communities of color. We have traditionally viewed climate change as an issue separate from us. Images and videos of melting ice caps and polar bears weren't as relatable for inner-city communities prioritizing immediate safety and survival. Many people of color were excluded from the traditional environmental movement.

Not only did the climate conversation lack racial diversity, but me and my crew were nearly always the only youth at most of the events and conferences I attended in the first few years of my activism. For a long time, the climate movement was fractured and incomplete, leaving some of the most important stories on the sideline and unheard. When I got involved, the environmental movement was using many of the same tactics that they had used since the 1960s. In a world where the crisis we are opposing is becoming exponentially more disastrous and serious, we need to rise up to meet the urgency of the crisis we face.

I've always known that young people were going to play a very important leadership role in fighting for the future of the planet, and I began to see it surface when I attended the United Nations Conference on Sustainable Development (Rio+20) in Brazil. Youth from more than 100 countries showed up in Rio to send a message to the world leaders that we weren't going to allow our voices to be excluded from these critical conversations. There were dozens of delegations and organizations coming together to pressure the UN to remember that we will feel the consequences of whatever decisions they make. Ultimately, their decisions need to represent the generations that will feel the greatest impacts of our climate crisis.

We stayed in a community at the edge of the city, right in the outskirts of the jungles. I've never gotten more mosquito bites in my life. This community had several houses on either side of the small cobbled road that wound through the jungle, housing many of the youth that had come to the Rio summit. Sitting down for meals with everyone felt like a movement jam session, sharing stories, ideas, and perspectives with so

Lighting the Flame at the Rio+20 UN Summit

many incredible young people. It felt like the passion of each individual was exponentially amplified by coming together and knowing our fight was bigger than just us. My brother and I were invited to join Indigenous leaders from the different tribes of Brazil, deep in the jungle before the Rio+20 UN Summit. There I was invited to help light the sacred fire that would hold the prayers of the indigenous peoples from those lands. I cried as I offered my prayer during the ceremony. Myself and another indigenous youth from that land carried the flame to their sacred place. The Elders kept the flame lit for the duration of the summit.

We organized marches in the streets and did ceremony with dozens of indigenous tribes that came to represent the indigenous nations from all over Brazil. We threw parties and concerts, and organized events and dialogues of our own to run parallel to the summit. The youth brought life to a conversation that hadn't made progress since the first Rio summit in 1992. What defined that moment wasn't the failure of the leaders to agree on binding climate action, but how the younger genera-tion showed the world that we refused to have our voices left out of the most important issues of our time. This was the first glimpse I got of a global grassroots movement led by the generation with the most to lose.

I think it takes an understanding of the absolute urgency of our climate crisis to be motivated to get engaged. Many people fail to act when they don't see it as a problem that is directly connected to them. The devastation and displacement of people we've seen from climate change in the last 5 years alone has been enough to change the climate conversation toward seeing this as a human rights issue that will continue to affect us all. In the same way that the voices of marginalized communities have been disempowered from taking leadership, the younger generation has been pushed away from believing that we can make a difference. The effects of climate change disproportionately threaten the security of the world my generation will inherit long after the fossil-fuel CEOs and corrupt politicians are gone. We're finding ourselves in a place where our futures depend on the action that we take today, and in response, youth are rising up across the globe. From Standing Rock to the movement to fight Keystone XL to student divestment and Earth guardians, the world is beginning to see the most historically diverse generation take the lead in creating a more sustainable future.

CHANGING TIMES

In 2014, the People's Climate March in New York City was the biggest mobilization on climate in history. I was invited to march at the front holding the banner alongside a group other frontline indigenous youth that were there to lead. Overall, the climate march had empowered frontline communities and people of color to march at the front and act as spokespeople. On that day, 400,000 people from every walk of life marched through the streets demanding bold and urgent action for the global climate crisis.

We did something I'd never seen before when the march reached Times Square. The message started with the marshals, and then spread to everyone. We were going to hold 2 minutes of silence for the communities worldwide who had been impacted by climate change and the fossil-fuel industry. In what I'd always seen as the most chaotic and loud city, there was complete silence for 120 seconds. For every home washed away by storms and floods, for every family's water well contaminated by fracking, for every kid that got asthma from living near a power plant, and for every child born in these crazy times. At 1:00 p.m. on September 21, 2014, 400,000 people broke our silence into a ruckus of celebration and cheering in hope of the future we will create.

It was a powerful moment that helped launch us into a new era of climate leadership. That march laid the foundation for the growth of the People's Climate Movement. Since the first march in New York City, they have organized more than 200 actions in 48 locations. On the 100th day of Donald Trump's term in office, hundreds of people around the nation marched in the streets to oppose his anticlimate agenda and take a stand for real solutions. Their platform they launched before the march shows just how far we've come as a movement.

- Directly and rapidly reduce greenhouse gas and toxic pollution to successfully combat climate change and improve public health.

- Mandate a transition to an equitable and sustainable new energy and economic future that limits the temperature increase to 1.5° Celsius above pre-industrial levels.

- Provide a just transition for communities and workers negatively impacted by the shift to a new energy and economic future that includes targeted economic opportunity and provides stable income, health care, and education.

- Demand that every job pays a wage of at least $15 an hour, protects workers, and provides a good standard of living, pathways out of poverty, and a right to organize.

- Ensure that in the new energy and economic future, investments are targeted to create pathways for low-income people and people of color to access good jobs and improve the lives of communities of color, indigenous peoples, low-income people, small farmers, women, and workers.

- Make bold investments in the resilience of states, cities, tribes, and communities that are threatened by climate change, including massive investments in infrastructure systems from water, transportation, and solid waste to the electrical grid and safe, green building and increasing energy efficiency that will also create millions of jobs in the public and private sector.

- Reinvest in a domestic industrial base that drives us toward an equitable and sustainable new energy and economic future, and fight back against the corporate trade-induced global race to the bottom.

- Market- and policy-based mechanisms must protect human rights and critical, native ecosystems and reduce pollution at the source.

Each of these significant steps better positions each of us and the world in which we interact to mitigate climate change and protect our very fragile Earth. Mother Nature needs allies in the battle, and we can all join in and become part of a very substantial solution.

BUILDING INTERSECTIONAL MOVEMENTS

The People's Climate Movement is a model of how we can take steps toward more intersectional climate work. We are at a really important moment in history. With a Trump administration representing an opposition to progressive values, there is an opportunity to come together and form a movement of movements. There is now a majority of people who want a more just and sustainable planet, built for the people. In the past, a variety of circumstances prevented us from coming together and taking up each other's causes in a meaningful way. The primary reason is the "otherization" and "tokenization" of traditionally marginalized communities. Building strong intersectional movements requires hard work and education.

The Jemez Principles for Democratic Organizing have been an incredible resource that many organizations and big events like the climate marches have relied upon. They were developed in December of 1996 when 40 people of color and European-American representatives met. I've thought a lot about these principles and tried to integrate them into my own understanding of movement building. Based on Jemez and my own experiences, here are three steps to building intersectional movements.

Step 1: Recognize privilege and history. It's essential when working in multiracial groups to understand the ways in which history and privilege play a role in society and our interactions. For people with privilege, it's easy to ignore. But for people on the other side of the equation, not so much. For many white people, it's not easy to imagine what it would feel like to be racially profiled or to be followed by security in a grocery store because of your skin color. It's also not easy for heterosexual people to understand what it's like to have to hide your sexuality to feel safe. Understanding the history of oppression that some communities have gone through and listening to their experiences with a willingness to learn is crucial.

Some people may be less likely to speak up at meetings than others because of historic oppression or a school system that seems not to value certain voices. These people may have something brilliant to add but may never say it unless space is made for them to express their opinions. Remember, we live in a system where the most dominant voices are those of white males. To combat this at our strategy meetings, we often use "step up, step back," asking people who tend to speak a lot to allow space for others to speak and inviting those who typically don't speak as much to express themselves.

Part of understanding privilege is recognizing that there are basic inequities in our society. In the United States, women earn 79 cents on the dollar, while black women earn 60 cents on the dollar and Latino women earn 55 cents on the dollar. White young people are more than twice as likely to receive a college education than black and Latino young people. Some people simply have a higher mountain to climb, because the decks were stacked against them since birth due to their race, class, gender, sexual orientation, religion, or birthplace.

When planning direct action, where some people may risk arrest, it's important to be aware of privilege when it comes to the law. Police are often more violent toward people of color, and some people have an immigration status that could be risked by participating in escalated action. This is why, many times, people with privilege are asked to assume higher risk levels on the front lines.

We have been programmed to believe that our identities divide us, but the more we understand each other, the more it actually brings us together. This was made so clear to me when I was talking with Deirdre Smith of the BlackOUT Collective and program director of the Wildfire Project. She said, "Unity is our power and the very thing these systems have been designed to destroy. When we're trying to do intersectional work and we're trying to be powerful together, it requires remembering our history and our ancestry. Trying to think outside of the parameters that society has set about how we solve problems and who gets to lead is actually required for us to find the root and the connection of our issues."

Step 2: Take steps for genuine inclusion and prioritize frontline leadership. Who are the first spokespeople you think about when you think of the climate movement?

For me, it used to be Al Gore, James Hansen, Bill McKibben, Richard Branson, Leonardo DiCaprio, or even the Pope. All white, all male, and mostly older. That's not to say these voices aren't important, as they've done a remarkable job of communicating the issue in a way that's engaged people around the world. We need more than just their perspectives to solve this problem, we need people with different backgrounds and life experiences. It's hard to speak to people about climate change in the inner cities of America unless you understand where they're coming from.

This is changing. Over the past 10 years, we've seen new and powerful voices emerge into the forefront of climate activism like Van Jones, Reverend Lennox Yearwood of the Hip Hop Caucus, and Winona Laduke of Honor the Earth to name a few. Seeing new faces in the media talking about climate activism is important, because it allows all people to see their potential for leadership in this time of great need. I hope that the attention my activism has gotten will inspire other youth to realize, no matter how young you are, no matter where you come from, or how difficult your name is to pronounce, you can make a difference in this world.

We have to elevate the frontline leaders like Dallas Goldtooth, Jasilyn Charger, Kathy Jentil-Jenner, and more. They have crucial stories to tell the world that can change the way we look at climate change. It's not enough just to recognize frontline spokespeople, though. Groups and organizations on the front lines must be prioritized and must be at the table from the very beginning. Too often, organizations of color are reached out to at the last minute when an organizing coalition realizes that they are not diverse enough. This can be tokenizing and doesn't allow the communities to have a say until a strategy has already been created. We can do a better job of including more types of voices at all levels from the initial strategy meetings to staffing to coordination.

In August 2014, when Deirdre was an organizer for 350.org, she wrote an incredible piece entitled, "Why the Climate Justice Movement Must Stand with Ferguson." This came at a time when the nation's eyes were on the city just north of St. Louis. Protests had grown enormous in size after an 18-year-old unarmed black man named Michael Brown was shot six times and killed by a Ferguson police officer. "Black Lives Matter" became a rallying cry as people began to expose racial inequities like the fact that black teens are 21 times more likely to be killed by a police officer than white teens.

In the article, Deirdre describes the connection between the way black people were treated in the wake of a climate disaster like Katrina and police violence in Ferguson. She spoke about the dehumanization of black people that led to whole communities left stranded in New Orleans, and to police killing an unarmed black man once every 28 hours in the United States.

In the article she said, "The events in Ferguson offer an important moment, if you're a climate organizer, looking around the room, wondering where the "people of color" are. It's a time to dig deep and ask yourself if you really care why—and if you are committed to the deep work, solidarity, and learning what it will take to bring more "diversity" to our movement. Personally, I think the climate movement is up to this necessary challenge. . . . I can't stress enough how important it is for me, as a black climate justice advocate, as well as for my people, to see the climate movement show solidarity right now with the people of Ferguson and with black communities around the country striving for justice. Other movements are stepping up to the plate: labor, GLBTQ, and immigrant rights groups have all taken a firm stand that they have the backs of the black community. Threats to civil dissent are a threat to us all."

Some in the climate movement are beginning to hear that call. May Boeve, the executive director of 350.org, later sent out an e-mail telling climate activists to show solidarity for Ferguson. She said, "We believe unequivocally that working for racial justice is a crucial part of fighting climate change." This progress was reflected at the 2017 climate march where protectors of justice—indigenous, frontline environmental and climate justice communities—marched at the front.

This is just one of the ways that people are coming together to stand for justice against systems of oppression. Many representatives of the Black Lives Matter movement came from across North America to Standing Rock to deliver supplies and stand in solidarity with the water protectors. In an interview with Fusion, Kim Ortiz, BLM activist and organizer of NYC Shut It Down said, "We decided that we really need to stand in solidarity with the tribes out in Standing Rock, because we know very well that all of our struggles are connected, and until we unite, we're never going to win."

The fossil-fuel industry's attack on clean water, clean air, and our communities stretch from Standing Rock to tar sands in Canada to power plants in black communities that lead to some of the highest cancer, miscarriage, and asthma rates. This corrupt, greed-driven system connects black and indigenous communities to defend the lives and rights of both.

Black Lives Matter says: "We are clear that there is no black liberation without indigenous sovereignty." Their official statement of solidarity: "Our liberation is only realized when all people are free, free to access clean water, free from institutional racism, free to live whole and healthy lives not subjected to state-sanctioned violence." These connections are a representation of what successful movements will look like in the future, recognizing the things that tie all of us together in our struggles for justice.

FINDING SOLIDARITY IN UNEXPECTED PLACES

It is crucial to show up in a real way for communities who are oppressed because of race, religion, or sexual orientation. But, we should also show up for those across the political spectrum. This is what real compassion looks like. Van Jones has embodied this with his campaign Love Army. Rather than continuing to vilify Trump voters and blame them for the terrible position our country is in, he is changing the conversation and now he is fighting for them.

At the end of 2016, health insurance and pensions were set to expire for tens of thousands of former coal miners. Many of these workers come from impoverished areas of Appalachia and have bared the health effects of treacherous working conditions, often times developing black lung disease or industrial bronchitis from breathing in coal dust. Even though coal miners often vote Republican, and many supported Trump during the election, Van Jones saw their humanity and decided to support their human rights. It's the hope that this kind of compassionate leadership will help bridge the divide between working-class liberals and working-class conservatives, who, when they vote Republican, are voting against their own best interests. Having a black environmental leader rally support for the health of people with opposing views could be a kind of medicine to a country paralyzed by partisan politics.

The Idle No More SF Bay chapter is also finding unusual allies in their work. Idle No More is a movement that was launched by indigenous women in Saskatchewan and whose powerful actions in resistance to a bill to erode native rights in Canada spread worldwide. Chapters started up in other ZIP codes like the one in the East Bay that stemmed from a grandmother's prayer group. My friend and fellow RYSE Youth Council member Isabella joined the group in 2014, and they began planning powerful actions called refinery-healing walks.

On the healing walks, they go from polluted site to polluted site, telling the story of the area and praying for healing. One of the refineries they often go to is the Chevron refinery in Richmond, California. This is the location where Isabella lived—just six blocks away. While there, and in 2012, there was a huge explosion. The sky was filled with a giant cloud of toxic black smoke that traveled a very long distance. She worried about how the chemicals and toxins might affect her health later on in life. She shared with me that being an organizer on the healing walks helps her to feel empowered and supported in talking about her experience.

Indigenous movement leaders like Dallas Goldtooth, Kandi Mossett, and Idle No More cofounder, Nina Wilson, often join walks, but they also invite people throughout the community to walk with them. In April of 2017, while the walkers were in front of the Tesoro refinery in Martinez, California, they prayed for the workers, and during that time, someone who worked at the refinery and their family stepped forward to tell their story. Penny Opal Flame of SF Bay Area Idle No More, who is the visionary behind the walks, told me about the experience, "We had a long conversation about just transition and healthy jobs for refinery workers . . . It was a dream come true for me," she said.

Building Just Solutions

Good solutions solve multiple problems at once. One of the first people who showed me how this could be done was my homie Van Jones. In his book *The Green Collar Economy*, he outlines what he calls the Green New Deal, where we invest in communities that need jobs to build the infrastructure we need to solve the climate crisis. It's an extraordinary idea for extraordinary times. Imagine all the problems this could address at once. We can:

- Solve issues relating to climate change by transitioning to renewables and sustainable local agriculture.
- Solve poverty by employing low-income inner-city youth.
- Solve prison-industrial complex by providing inner-city youth with good jobs so they are less likely to get involved with drugs and gangs.
- Solve foreign policy with sustainable locally sourced energy so leaders will be less likely to invade foreign countries for oil.

According to Van, the idea stemmed from a panel discussion at the Omega Institute in upstate New York with activist Julia Butterfly Hill, who is famous for sitting in a Redwood tree for nearly 2 years to raise awareness about the destruction of our old-growth forests. "I remember coming to Omega and having my eyes opened. There was a girl named Julia Butterfly Hill here. This girl was crazy. She climbed up in a tree and didn't come down. We bonded over the myth of disposability. The whole green jobs thing was born on Omega's stage with me and Julia Butterfly Hill trying to understand each other," he said.

As a civil rights attorney and community organizer with the Ella Baker Center for Human Rights in Oakland, Van helped plant the seeds for what would become a nationwide movement. He started a Green

Jobs Corps in Oakland to help employ at-risk youth with good jobs, retrofitting houses and putting up solar panels. The program started with $125,000 in 2005, but after initial success, Van helped fight for the Green Jobs Act of 2007, which funded the program with $125 million. In 2008, he founded the organization Green For All, which would continue to take the movement for green jobs forward. They helped launch the Clean Energy Corps, which would create 600,000 jobs retrofitting and upgrading more than 15 million American homes.

Among Van's many admirers was a young Senator from the state of Illinois, named Barack Obama. After he was elected as the 44th President of the United States, he reached out to Van to join his transition team and eventually appointed him to be a member of his administration as the White House Council on Environmental Quality. He was only in the White House for about a year, but, in that time, he was able to steer nearly a half-billion dollars into green-collar jobs programs like the Green Jobs Act.

Running parallel to the Green Jobs movement is the Just Transition movement, which involves a number of local community stakeholders to ensure that the transition to a low-carbon economy works for everyone. This includes inner-city youth and even employees of the fossil-fuel industry. The idea is to build a new economy that supports communities rather than one that continually takes from them. Many of these just transition models focus on social justice and worker-owned cooperatives. Much of what created climate change is an economic model where only a few have power and resources, so the just transition seeks to use a model where wealth and power are shared in an equitable way. This involves the workers who are employed in industries like fossil fuels and industrial agriculture, which are destroying the planet and must be phased out. We can't forget these workers in our transition toward a clean-energy economy. Everybody will be included in the movement to build the future we are striving for.

Projects like the Our Power Campaign are perfect examples of this kind of transition in action. This is a campaign out of the Climate Justice Alliance that's leading the fight, with a network of organizations who are moving local and state governments to create millions of climate jobs. They are building a new regenerative economy that works for all of us, rather than an extractive one that works for only a few. Through their network, they are creating regional food systems and helping to provide clean, community-owned energy.

You can see this with the Black Mesa Water Coalition (BMWC) within the Our Power Campaign network. It's an intergenerational group on the Dine Reservation in Arizona who are working to build a transition from a coal-based economy to a Navajo Green Economy. They focus on addressing issues of extraction, water depletion, and health within Navajo and Hopi communities.

The Our Power Campaign is also at the forefront of supporting and helping connect renewable energy-worker cooperatives and other projects with a focus on localized, worker-owned production. Cooperatives give those most impacted by climate change the chance to have direct ownership of energy, while moving toward a just transition. This is what true energy democracy looks like. At the same time, this model can support marginalized communities and those who have not historically been able to benefit from the renewable energy industry. Get involved at www.ourpowercampaign.org.

Reinvest in Real Solutions

Like I've talked about in previous chapters, moving the money is crucial to bringing about the changes we want to see. It's not enough to just take money out of what we don't want. We need to move it into systems that give the power back to the people and save ourselves from climate disaster. This means organizing our campuses, churches, pension funds, and other institutions to taking their money out of fossil-fuel corporations and invest in new economy solutions like renewable energy cooperatives and energy efficiency efforts.

An example of this is happening in Cleveland. There, a group of institutions like Case Western Reserve University, the Cleveland Clinic, and the Cleveland Foundation have pooled their endowments to support something called the Evergreen Cooperative. Evergreen is a collective of worker-owned businesses, including an energy-efficient laundry company, hydroponic farm, and solar installation company. In addition to investing in these cooperatives, the fund helps provide start-up funds for similar solution-oriented businesses.

Another great place for institutions and especially universities to reinvest is in Climate Action Plans to reduce greenhouse gas emissions. This is actually proven to make schools more money over the long haul than just investing money in the stock market. A 2012 study found that investing in "green revolving funds" in which campuses reinvest in their own efficiency gave schools a median annual return of 32 percent— much better than the average of 7 to 12 percent return on investment from university endowments.

It's Going to Take All of Us

There are more people who want a just transition than there are people who want to keep going with the same extractive economy that's been killing our planet. If we can use our differences to bring us together, rather than allowing them to divide us, we amplify our power. It's going to take hard work to get there, and it will take all of us. Whether you're a student, a teacher, or a fossil-fuel industry worker, everyone has a role to play.

Donald Trump and the fossil-fuel execs controlling our country are threatened by the powerful potential of our movement. Seeing people of all races, genders, and religions united in a movement for just climate solutions scares them. Why? Because together, we are unstoppable. Our movement is growing daily not only in size but also in knowledge and wisdom. Close your eyes and envision it. See the people taking back the power, with our own energy, our own food, and our own creative solutions. When we let the walls and barriers fall down, nothing will stand in our way. This will be the future of movements around the world fighting for justice.

BOLD COMPASSION IN THE ERA OF TRUMP
An Interview with Van Jones

Van Jones is an activist and commentator and served as former president Barack Obama's environmental adviser. He is regularly on CNN and hosts *The Messy Truth with Van Jones*. He prides himself on the many social enterprises and environmental justice projects he has worked on and is the author of two *New York Times* bestselling books, *The Green Collar Economy* and *Rebuild the Dream*. Today, he spends his time inspiring and motivating the youth of this world to step up and become the foremost leaders for change and justice.

ME: As an architect of the Green New Deal, what do you make of the Just Transition movement, and what can we do to speed up the transition while making sure the opportunities come to those who need it the most?

VAN: This is a part of a serious moral challenge for the environmental movement. In some ways, the environmental movement faces two decision points. One is how to deal with the people of mostly color who are getting hit first and worst with the consequences of our pollution-based economy and the climate crisis. Are we going to fully empower the voices on the front lines with money and access and all the things that are needed to mount a serious fight for their lives? Or are we going to continue to have white environmental organizations, so-called mainstream environmental organizations meaning white organizations, that have 120- or 130-million-dollar-a-year annual budgets while grassroots environmental organizations are lucky to raise two hundred thousand? That's the real question. It's not about making big rich groups more diverse. It's about making the diverse groups bigger and richer, and until the environmental movement steps up to that challenge, we're gonna have a big problem.

The other dilemma is, how do we deal with the people that, right now, at least from a paycheck point of view, are benefiting from the pollution-based economy? The oil workers, the coal miners, the frackers? All of those people are human beings with families and dreams and part of the transition to a clean and green economy would be taking away some of their livelihood and opportunities. Are we gonna continue to use the words "just transition" and hope that nobody notices that we have no plan for just transition? Or, are we actually gonna sit down knee-to-knee and elbow-to-elbow with the present energy workers and have a real, honest dialogue and attempt to truly understand what the need is, what the fear is, and what the opportunity might be? Both the mainstream environmentalists and the environmental justice people have been giving more lip service to the idea of a just transition than actually walking side-by-side with the coal miners and others to come to an answer.

ME: Right. Cool. Thank you, man. I remember last time when we chatted, it was in upstate New York. During your presentation, you talked about your program Yes We Code. That program works to help train youth from underrepresented communities the skills to succeed in the tech world, particularly. I just wanted to know about the progress of that plan? What's the importance of that initiative, particularly empowering underrepresented young people?

VAN: The future used to be written in law in Washington, D.C. Today, the future is written in code in Silicon Valley. Civil rights activists fought for a very long time to open up the political system so that black people could go from being property under slavery to being president in the 21st century. We fought to open up the political system so that women could go from not being able to vote to being the decisive vote in almost every election, from soccer moms to security moms and all the way to Hillary Clinton winning the nomination and Sarah Palin the VP nod.

However, the fight is just beginning to open up Silicon Valley to participation from African-Americans, Latinos, underrepresented Asians, and other folks who are usually left out of that whole conversation. Women are woefully underrepresented in Silicon Valley, so the Yes We Code movement is working very hard to expand who even gets a chance to participate in designing and building the future for the human species. We have now announced this year a 46-million-dollar scholarship fund that will help people from low-opportunity neighborhoods have access to computer science training, both at the college level and at the boot-camp level, which is a more accelerated program.

ME: Definitely. Awesome. So, you're one of the few people that warned us to take Donald Trump seriously. From your point of view, how did we get here? How can we avoid a similar situation to this one in the future?

VAN: Mm-hmm (affirmative). Three-step process. Everybody's to blame. Number one, both political parties at the elite, very top level signed off over the past 30 years on a terrible agenda for middle-class and working-class Americans. Both political parties said that we should deregulate the banks, sign on to these global free trade deals, build prisons everywhere, and get involved in these stupid wars overseas. It wasn't just Republicans, it wasn't just the Democrats. Both parties sold America on these bad ideas, and now the neoliberal economic policy has wrecked big parts of the middle class across the country, and we've essentially imported Third-World conditions into the United States.

So, when you have that level of leadership failure at the top, you're gonna have real problems, and so, then, that opened the door to all these rebellions. Some rebellions I like. Occupy Wall Street and Black Lives Matter and Bernie Sanders, I like. Some rebellions I don't like. The Tea Party and the Trump movement, I don't like. But, all these rebellions are in some ways justifiable because of the crime against the country committed by the bipartisan elite.

Number two, the Republican Party was established to stop slavery, but it has been totally corrupted by racial bias. That party today has neo-Nazis running around in it, and they won't do anything about it. And so, that has allowed for the Republican Party to be open for business for straight bigots to get in there like Donald Trump and say the most atrocious things about Muslims and Mexicans and African-Americans and women and find an audience.

And then number three, the Democrats and Progressives, who have done a better job on race and gender, have not done as good a job at keeping class and working-class issues at the forefront. So, some of the working-class white guys who might have at one time felt at home in the Democratic Party have frankly felt offended and left out by the constant drumbeat from the left that basically straight white males are the problem. And, when you put that whole mix together, you have a big crisis. You have a right-wing party that could nominate a Trump because you already have the conditions for racial demagoguery growing inside of it, and you have a left-wing party that can't do anything about it because we've drawn our circle too small, and there are too many people who haven't felt loved or listened to outside of that circle.

ME: So, do you think that the Democratic Party dropped the ball by dismissing Bernie Sanders's candidacy? If so, what is the best way that the party can engage the voices of young voters moving forward?

VAN: I love Bernie Sanders, but he didn't lose because the Democratic Party didn't like him. He lost because he couldn't get black votes in the South during the primaries. That was his problem. Look, the Democratic Party is a disproportionately black party. Ninety-plus percent of black people vote for Democrats, so we have an outsized influence on that party, and the Clintons have spent a lot of time, at least with the older black generation, building relationships, making common cause, and showing up. Bernie, as much as I love him, really stopped doing that in the 1960s and 1970s. He spent most of the last 20 or 30 years being in Vermont and being in D.C. So, when primary season kicked off, he just couldn't get black votes in the South, and that doomed his candidacy. Of course, the Democratic Party establishment wanted to be with the Clintons, but the Democratic Party establishment also wanted the Clintons in 2008, and they got their hats handed to them because Obama could appeal to liberals and to students and that whole set, but also to black folk. So, I do think that the populist stand that Bernie represents is the future of the Democratic Party, because the status quo is not working and hasn't for a long time.

And Obama did a good job of trying to deal with the crisis aspects of what he inherited, but he was never able to deal with the chronic aspects. So, dumb wars were out. Huge financial crash, we're gonna throw a bunch of money at it, and keep the economy going, and not have another Great Depression. Okay, you get a Nobel Prize for that shit, in my point of view, and he actually did. But, that's just the crisis. Now, you gotta deal with the chronic stuff. The chronic stuff is no wage growth, nobody getting a raise for 20 years. Prisons from coast to coast are stuffed full of people who should be out here creating businesses and being entrepreneurial. The chronic stuff. No antipoverty agenda, either for poor white folks in the red states, or for poor brown folks in black and brown neighborhoods and on Native American reservations. He never could get to the chronic stuff because of all the BS from the Republicans, so that left a big hole in his legacy that Trump could run against. And, he did. Somebody is gonna have to come along, or somebodies are gonna have to come along, with a completely fresh approach the same way that Bernie did but more appealing to older brown and black people. So, you've gotta be able to get those young people as well as their parents, and that's what Obama was able to do. The Obama coalition is the right formula, but not anybody can do that.

ME: Van, will you please run for president?

VAN: Oh, heck no! I'm waiting for you, dude. We've got what, 20 more before you can? We're gonna try to hold the dike together, and then you do it. I'll back you. In order for me to run for president, I've gotta have, in my lifetime, some person that I can vote for that I have faith in. I don't see anyone other than you representing that thus far.

That's kind. There are good folks coming. My job is to encourage young people and try and tell the truth about what's going on, and try to make it safe for other people to run for office. Right now, even when good people run, they can't get heard, because the minute you become a politician, you've gotta spend half your day dialing for dollars, and you've gotta spend the other half of your day dealing with other dumb people who are in office who are mean, and if you're not bought off, they're bought off. And it's a trap.

And so, we've gotta create a big enough sense of movement and possibility among the people so that any number of people can rise up and run and be able to not just win like Obama, but also govern. I want to build a movement that can then pick any number of women and men to run rather than go out there and run and get chewed up.

ME: What gives you hope for the future of American democracy and of this country and of the planet?

VAN: Listen. People are pretty awesome, except when we suck. It's this constant foot race between our awesomeness and how much we suck. There's possibility in every generation, every decade, every year, every month, every minute for the awesome part to win out, or for the sucky part to win out. Just think about your day. Half of your day, you're doing what you're supposed to be doing, eating the right stuff, saying the right thing, then you waste a bunch of time playing a video game, yelling at your brother, and eating crap. You're the same person, it's just that choice, and strengthening the muscles for the good choice is what's making the difference.

So, look. You have two things that are game-enders: catastrophic climate change and nuclear war. And, unfortunately, we have a president that makes both of them more likely than less. So, it's a big problem, and I'm not cavalier about it, but I also know that there's an awful lot of untapped good in the country. And, I also know that, even though we had this big orange asteroid hit the Earth and knock everything out of kilter, it also cracked open the Fort Knox of "How do I get involved?"

People really want to do something. People are more awake than they've been in a long time . . . they just don't know what to do yet. And as people like you and others put forth stuff for people to do and opportunity for involvement grows, more people are gonna get in. I'm just trying to make sure that people don't become what we are opposing. I'm starting to see liberals act more like Trump than Trump. Just mean and always finding something negative in stuff, divisive, dehumanizing the Trump voters, calling them terrible names. That's not who we are.

People make bad decisions all the time. I was in San Quentin with the brothers last week. People in my community have made terrible decisions, sometimes taken people's lives or ruined them with drugs. I can find a way to forgive somebody who's committed an act of homicide, but I can't forgive a Trump voter? That doesn't make any sense. People are a product of their circumstances and once people start getting afraid and misled, they make decisions—sometimes good and sometimes bad. But you can't just sit up here, which is what the liberals are doing, and say this man is Hitler and anybody who voted for him is a Nazi.

I don't care who you voted for. You're supposed to vote for whomever you want to vote for. I'll argue with you before the vote that voting for a bigot who's a liar and has no experience in government is a bad idea. But after the vote is taken, we're all in the same country again. I'm gonna fight against you on policy, but I'm gonna fight for you as a person. If we can't have that as our fundamental approach, then Trump wins no matter what, because what Trump does is polarize and dehumanize. You can't beat polarization with polarization, and you can't beat dehumanization with dehumanization.

Your first reaction may be to do that. That's totally understandable. Somebody punches you, you want to punch them back. I get that. But damn, we've been in a food fight now for 6 months, and there's no positive sign. At a certain point, the Gandhis and the MLKs and the Ella Jo Bakers and Fannie Lou Hamers start making sense. An eye for an eye, and the whole world's blind. So, when do the leaders step up and say, "Hold on a second. I got poor, addicted, death-prone black folk in the inner cities, and you got poor, addicted, death-prone white folks out there in the red counties, and nobody's doing a damn thing for either group. When do we get together? Fine, you want to vote for Trump, go ahead. I want to vote for somebody else. But, none of them are doing anything for us." When does that happen?

I'm trying to get the Love Army going. I want to have that conversation because nobody's having that conversation. You got addicted, poor, death-prone people on Native American reservations, in the barrios, in the ghettos, in the housing projects, in Appalachia, and nobody gives a damn about any of those folks, except when it's time for them to vote. Otherwise, get the hell away from us. We don't want you in our neighborhoods, we don't want you in our schools, we don't want to do anything for you, but when it's time to vote, we'll trot you out, throw you some red meat, and tell you to vote and then go home and shut up. That's the whole agenda for both these political parties. So, I'm not stupid. You're not gonna trick me into hating some poor white dude that has fewer options than my children. What kind of idea would I be, what kind of hard-hearted person would I be, what kind of Trumplike person would I be to not be able to make any room in my heart for someone who made a bad decision, as many bad decisions as I've made?

CHAPTER 13

A Rising Generation

Uplifting the Voices of Those
Who Will Inherit the Planet

"In light of a collapsing world,
what better time to be alive than now,
because our generation gets to rewrite history."

– XIUHTEZCATL MARTINEZ

Until you see it with your own eyes, it can be difficult to grasp just how much momentum is building across this planet in the fight for change. We're up against some of the most powerful governments and industries on Earth, and, at times, it can be overwhelming. I'm terrified of issues like climate change that threaten the certainty of our futures and the stability of our planet. For a growing number of us that are brave enough to face this adversity with fierce determination and optimism, it often feels like the weight of the entire world is on our shoulders. I've certainly gone through feeling depressed, disconnected, and hopeless about the world at times. It's a lot to handle, especially being a teenager. It sucks having to choose between going to prom and the People's Climate March in D.C. Sometimes, it gets hectic trying to figure out how

I'm going to finish high school, write an album, and tour the country speaking at conferences and colleges. Days go by where part of me wishes I could just go to school, write music, hang out with my friends, and forget about being a climate warrior.

What gets me through days like these is an understanding of the bigger picture that I'm simply a small part of. It's becoming more and more clear that one of my most important roles in this movement is to open the door for and empower other leaders to stand up and be a part of this global change. As an individual, I can only do so much, but being a part of a movement is what helps lift the weight of the world off my shoulders and allow everyone to do their part. Everything I'm trying to do is based around inspiring more youth to step up as leaders in solving the crisis we're facing. In my travels, I've been blown away by how many incredible things are taking place across the planet. Young people are fighting like hell now so that generations down the road will never have to struggle in the way we have. The more I seek to spark action from my peers, the more I find myself inspired by a generation that has caught fire. They give me faith that the world we pass on to the next generation will be a planet worth inheriting.

WE WERE BORN FOR THIS

We are the largest and most diverse generation in history. The fact that many of us have grown up with people who are different from us has helped our generation become less racist and more inclusive than generations in the past. There are growing movements to support equality for all, regardless of race, class, ethnicity, gender, disability, or sexual orientation. We are the most-educated generation, which might be why we are also the most progressive. According to a University of Texas Energy poll, 91 percent of millennials believe that climate change is occurring. We are not just aware, we are bringing a fresh and unique approach to addressing global challenges. We are creative problem-solvers, and we have new tools to work with that previous generations could never have dreamed of. We are awake, connected, and equipped to leave a remarkable legacy.

We Have More Tools and Distractions Than Ever

I can see how it could be hard to focus on climate change with Snapchat filters that can put dog ears on your head. How often do you see a young person glued to their phone, endlessly lost in their apps? I'm definitely guilty of wasting hours of my time scrolling through my Instagram feed, reading stupid memes, and getting lost in random YouTube videos, rather than being productive or doing stuff that matters. It was even difficult staying on task writing this book, at times, with the influx of videos of rappers freestyling in the bathtub, with their hairless cat named Ravioli. The world is a messed-up place, and most people would rather watch cat videos and vine compilations than read articles about rising sea levels. There is a temptation for people in my generation to push aside the challenges of this life and escape into another world with social media, video games, or Netflix. On top of that, there is so much to keep up with socially and in pop culture. Even our president has become a distraction, with his endless ridiculous tweets.

"Most people walking around at the mall or on a college campus are carrying on them better technology than the entire US government had when it put a man on the moon. Each one of us is walking super power," said Van Jones.

It cuts both ways. Our greatest potential downfall is also one of our greatest advantages. Part of what gives our generation power is our access to technology and social media in ways past generations never had. While there is so much potential in these new tools, we cannot fall into the trap of being over-reliant on them. Online petitions, tweets, Instagram, and Facebook posts will never be able to replace genuine human interaction and showing up in person. So much of the passion people feel about an issue goes into online participation, and when we do that, we lose potential to engage in the movement in a real way.

That being said, social media has and can be incredibly useful for social movements. It played a major role in movements like Arab Spring, which helped overthrow dictators in the Middle East. I can't count the amount of times I've used an online tool to share an important message, persuasive article, or a video clip that has the potential to change someone's perspective. Online platforms like Uproxx, VICE, NowThis and AJ+ generate millions of views on many important issues that aren't often covered by mainstream media. Through the Internet, I'm able to stay in communication with incredible leaders around the world. Our generation has a very important choice; technology can be the distraction that derails us, or the tool that lifts us to new heights. I see this as a great challenge of our time. Can we stay on purpose and remain focused amidst the daily circus going on all around us? I believe we can enjoy all this new world has to offer, while using these tools to shift everything.

We Put Our Passions into Action

When I'm working to get people involved in the movement, I don't feel that the goal is to create more activists. I want to inspire people to bring activism into what they love to do. Whether you're an entrepreneur, poet, scientist, athlete, student, or artist, you can find ways to use what you're passionate about to have an incredible impact. Our movement desperately needs a diversity of new ideas and ways of thinking to bring forth real change. That's why we need more than traditional activist tactics. Some of the most impactful work being done in my generation is from people spreading awareness through art, music, and other creative means.

If you go back through this book, you'll see examples like Jeff Orlowski, who uses storytelling through the lens of a camera, or musicians spreading consciousness through their lyrics. Some of my biggest inspirations are from my older brothers, Frank Waln and Nahko Bear. They're able to talk about some of the most important issues facing indigenous people and our generation, while remaining authentic in their craft. We come alive when we're doing what we love. I can definitely say that for myself, as an artist using hip-hop as a tool to inspire revolution. Engaging our passions can alleviate the heaviness of the adversities we face.

We Understand the Root of the Problem

For our entire lives, many of us have felt a sense of disenfranchisement from systems of power. We look around and see that our leaders are totally disconnected and corrupted by money. As you've read in previous chapters, this is not just a Republican or Democrat problem, this is a systemic problem. It's why more young people backed Bernie Sanders in the 2016 primary than Hillary Clinton and Donald Trump combined. We found it refreshing to see a candidate who was running for the highest office in the United States who wasn't bought out by big corporations.

Young people were showing up at rallies by the tens of thousands, calling for a political revolution, just like many had for Obama in 2008. Millennials weren't afraid to elect the first black president, and they weren't afraid to elect a 70-year-old secular Jewish Democratic Socialist from Vermont. We under thirties are the only demographic that has a more favorable view of socialism than of capitalism.

Moumita Ahmed, who was the former director of Millennials for Bernie Sanders, told me why that could be the case:

> I think young people are already suffering from the current economic system that exists in our country that is based on capitalism. A lot of us are graduating with massive amounts of student loans. A lot of us don't feel like our government is taking enough action to stop climate change, which is something we're going to have to deal with and so will our children. That leaves us in a position where we are like, "Should I have kids? Should I have families? Am I even going to have drinkable water wherever I live when I'm old?" A lot of us aren't able to find jobs. Even though we are the most—educated generation in history, a lot of us end up working low-wage jobs and multiple jobs. Everything that Bernie was talking about resonated with us, because he was talking about the injustices that we are dealing with today. Because of his honesty and integrity and what he's been saying for the past 30 years and his unwavering support for working-class people, a lot of us felt comfortable joining the campaign and supporting him. We don't have a lot of elected officials caring about what young people want. They're like, you don't vote so why should we care about you? It's not

that we don't vote; it's that we haven't had many candidates who represent the issues we truly care about.

Generations before us have dug us a hole that we are fighting like hell to climb out of. Now, we need someone who is honest about the challenges we face and wants to help us confront them. We need representatives that are willing to support the voice of the people. A new study by NextGen Climate found that inaction on climate change will cost my generation $8.8 trillion. It's estimated that a child born in 2015 earning a median income will lose an average of $581,000 worth of wealth from climate change. Then, you add in student debt, which will cost the average person in my generation $113,000. As Bernie Sanders often points out, income inequality is rapidly increasing. The top one-tenth of one percent have more than doubled their share of all wealth over the past 30 years, from 10 to 22 percent. Meanwhile, politics is as corrupt as it's ever been, with wealthy corporations having more influence than ever in our political system. All of this is part of the mess we didn't create and certainly didn't ask for.

This is what made the Sanders campaign feel like a freshwater spring in the desert. In the post Citizens United world, almost every political candidate has debts to repay, mostly to their ultra-wealthy campaign financiers. Since Bernie's campaign relied entirely on grassroots contributions averaging $27, his only debt was to the people. But the Democratic Party did not embrace him or us young people who supported him. The DNC actively worked to help Hillary Clinton win the nomination, as revealed by Wikileaks through Russian hacks. It may have even affected Clinton on Election Day, as she turned out less of the youth vote than usual, despite Donald Trump being so unpopular. It didn't help that a higher percentage of youth voted for third-party candidates than other times in history.

By the 2020 presidential election, millennials will be the largest generational voting block. We can no longer be ignored. The Democrats will have a tremendous opportunity to capitalize on the unpopular Donald Trump, but to do so, they must embrace politicians who care about my generation and represent the people and not big corporations. We need someone who will back up their words with action and be partners in building a more just and livable future. Bernie Sanders showed us that it's possible to get far without corporate backers calling the shots, and I believe others in my generation will be inspired by his lead to take on the political establishment and win.

We Build Movement across Generations

One of the most valuable lessons I've learned from my father is the importance of respecting our elders. I've been able to have an impact in the world because of the support and wisdom I've received from my parents and grandparents. When my mom had the vision for the Earth Guardians movement, she helped to lay the groundwork for some of the most incredible intergenerational work. A lot of this goes down at the crew level.

Regional Earth Guardians Director Mensa Tzedse has been doing amazing things in Togo to address climate change through planting trees and empowering young people. He was inspired by the work of Nobel Prize–winning activist Wangari Maathai, who founded the Greenbelt movement, which helped plant more than one million trees in Africa. He learned from her example that, to be the best leader possible, you have to make more leaders. She said, "You cannot protect the environment unless you empower people, you inform them and you help them understand that these resources are their own, that they must protect them." Over the past 3 years, Mensa has trained more than 5,000 youth to plant more than 20,000 trees. The work is helping pull an estimated 9,000 tons of carbon in the soil and build the movement by empowering climate leaders.

We can also look at the modern divestment movement to see the way intergenerational campaigns can come full circle. Inspired by student movements to get colleges to divest from South African apartheid during the 1980s, the fossil-fuel divestment movement took flight on the Do the Math tour, which visited colleges and featured movement luminaries like Bill McKibben, Winona Laduke, Naomi Klein, Josh Fox, and Reverend Lennox Yearwood. Also featured were South African environmental and antiapartheid leaders Kami Naidoo and Desmond Tutu, whose wisdom helped the American youth in the audience better understand the subject of divestment.

In an article, Desmond Tutu wrote for the *Guardian,* entitled "We Need an Apartheid-Style Boycott to Save the Planet," he explained his reasoning. "Throughout my life, I have believed that the only just response to injustice is what Mahatma Gandhi termed 'passive resistance.' During the antiapartheid struggle in South Africa, using boycotts, divestment, and sanctions, and supported by our friends overseas, we were not only able to apply economic pressure on the unjust state, but also serious moral pressure. . . . People of conscience need to break their ties with corporations financing the injustice of climate change."

Fossil-fuel divestment makes a moral case that the fossil-fuel industry is responsible for the climate crisis, and, because of that, we must shift toward a thriving fossil-free economy. Divestment opens up the possibility for new reinvestments, particularly in community-based solutions to the climate crisis as a part of a just transition away from fossil-fuel extraction. Student leaders across the country are asking their universities, "whose side are you on?" to see if they will follow the lead of students or remain beholden to the profits of fossil-fuel CEOs.

We Are Stepping Up Our Game

Students have been rising up around the world with bold actions, awakening people to the urgency of the crisis we face. One such action was a sit-in by students at Swarthmore College in Pennsylvania in 2012, where they occupied Parrish Hall for 32 days. They only agreed to leave after the faculty voted to support the protesters' demands to divest the endowment money from fossil fuels. The sacrifice of students like those who participated in the sit-in inspired people around the world, and the movement continued to grow in size and diversity. No longer was it just students, it was now faith leaders getting their churches and mosques to divest, and union members working to divest their pension funds. In 2017, 707 institutions have committed to divest $5.45 trillion from the fossil-fuel industry, along with $5.2 billion by individuals.

Sara Blazevic was one of the student leaders who participated in the month-long sit in. She spoke to me about how escalating tactics can help shift consciousness.

Nonviolent direct action, when done skillfully, has the power to tell a story about who is responsible for a crisis and not only to lay out an argument, but to touch the hearts of those who bear witness to the action. After the sit-in at Swarthmore, our Board of Managers decided once again to rule in favor of the fossil fuel companies and in favor of endless pollution and destruction. I was deeply demoralized and felt like I had failed as an organizer, and just before graduating, too. But, then, this funny thing happened: It gradually became clear to me that, while we had lost on the particular demand of divestment, we had failed to convince a few wealthy white men to move some money from one fund into another, we had won the fight over the story across the community. In the week before my graduation, I had numerous peers and faculty members come up to me and express their shock and dismay that the board had not divested—people who I had never seen at an action, who didn't necessarily agree with all of my politics, but who had come to understand the profound moral failure of an institution like Swarthmore profiting from the destruction of our collective future. I even learned, after the fact, that one board member had remarked to another, following their last meeting with student organizers, that "maybe we are on the wrong side of history."

Divestment has shifted the narrative, but sometimes the narrative shifts on you. Now with Donald Trump as President, many divestment organizers like Sara are rethinking their strategy to reflect the urgency of the situation we find ourselves in. To confront this reality, they've formed a new group called Sunrise, which is recruiting a volunteer army for the 2018 midterm to expose the influence of fossil-fuel executives on our elections.

Sara told me, "Sunrise is part of a bigger political revolution. Across the country, a surge of teens and twentysomethings are preparing to volunteer for election campaigns or to run for office ourselves. We don't see a reason to choose between working on elections and creative protests, as it's obvious that both are needed. We're unafraid to take on wealthy elites from either political party. We call ourselves Sunrise because we know that this dark time in America will come to an end. The sun will rise again. If we focus our efforts, we could be less than 4 years away from having a true people's president and a movement strong enough to pass our agenda. Let's make it happen."

We Use Our Stories to Affect Change

Our stories are what connects us, shifts perspectives, and builds understanding. Learning to tell my story allows me to bring my message around the world. When I was at the COP21 climate talks, the historic global gathering where the Paris Agreement was signed, I worked with a group of inspiring young people from SustainUS, who really get it. SustainUS is a youth-led organization of climate leaders from around the United States, who work toward advancing justice at the UN through advocacy, direct action, and social and traditional media.

Their approach is rooted in climate justice storytelling, uplifting unheard narratives of those most affected by the climate crisis, and calling for bold action at the highest levels of decision-making. Youth should have a voice in the policy decisions that will shape our future, and through the SustainUS network and platform, young people have brought their voices to the table for more than a decade at United Nations conferences, continuing to push for stronger representation.

"Systemic change starts within and between us. We walk into those halls of power not because we believe they hold the key to climate justice, but out of a longing to disrupt and reimagine these outmoded ways of change making," says Morgan Curtis, who led the SustainUS youth delegation to COP22, the 2016 UN climate talks in Morocco. "I'll never forget the morning of the 2016 US presidential election. The world's media was waiting for us to respond as US youth. Not ready for policy analysis, we brought forward our grief and song. For it's only when we allow ourselves to *feel* the weight of this crisis that we awaken our capacity to respond."

We Aren't Afraid to Get Political

Young people are starting to understand that we can't wait any longer for those in power to suddenly start doing the right thing. Donald Trump was a huge wake-up call that everything we care about is threatened. We can clearly see the way the issues connect, from climate justice to upholding indigenous rights to access to clean water and healthy food. At a time when it's becoming clearer just how crucial it is that we come together, politicians are pitting people against one another, using racism and fear to score political points. The 2016 Republican Presidential primary was a scary example of this at work.

In September 2016, leaders from my generation decided enough is enough, and 11 people were arrested at Paul Ryan's office while demanding he withdraw his support for candidate Donald Trump. Their goal was to force the Republican Party to reckon with their politics of hate. Out of the action would emerge the political force known as #AllofUs. They continued to organize events to reveal the GOP's strategy of using racism to divide people in order to distract us from their policies, which are an attack on working-class people, which further widens economic inequality.

They weren't just confronting Republicans, though. After Trump surprised many by beating Clinton in the 2016 election, #AllofUs was the first to take action against establishment Democrats who wouldn't take a stand to oppose Trump. The reality television star turned United States President was able to scapegoat people of color because the democratic establishment was corrupt and refused to name the billionaire class as the real culprit. The establishment took young voters for granted, and wrote off white working-class voters. Their decision to look the other way as Wall Street bankers and corporate CEOs rig the economy for themselves has had disastrous consequences for our democracy and country. In addition to calling out the failures that led to Trump, they began to lay the groundwork for a new kind of leadership. The group formed a new PAC called WeWillReplaceYou. The name was a warning for Democrats to resist Trump's agenda of hatred and greed and fight for all Americans, or risk facing a primary challenge.

"We believe the American people are looking for a new idea of ourselves as a nation," Yong Jung Cho, cofounder of #AllofUs, told me: "This is a new political movement, led by a multi-racial group of millennials, to create an America that's actually for all of us—not the ruling class. We're putting pressure on politicians to defend our democracy and our rights. It's time to support a new generation of political leaders to run for office who will put forth a bold agenda that works for all Americans—criminal justice reform, a clean energy economy, health care, college, jobs, and housing for all."

We See Power in the Crowd

The concept of the hive-mind is being implemented in powerful ways by my generation. The hive-mind is the idea that when you allow for a variety of people's input, it can lead to amazing things. The Hive program, created by Ideas For Us, is a great example. It's a way of bringing together all kinds of people from students to entrepreneurs to elected officials to crowdsource community solutions. Out of this model came fleet farming, the urban agriculture solution I discussed in the food chapter, a program that has been so successful in its spread around the world. In Uganda, they have taken this concept a step further by using vertical gardens to maximize space in an urban environment. The initiative, called micro urban gardening, won both the Pride Uganda Award and the MIT Climate Colab.

My friend Chris Castro, who I met back at the Rio +20 when I was 12, founded Ideas For Us and told us about the project. "What we've seen is that giving the youth not only a voice but strategies to organize themselves to create projects they feel are going to address these challenges at the local level is critical. It's where the hive has really started to blossom at different schools, whether it's high schools, colleges, or even rural communities, they use human-centered design to come up with solutions to the critical problems."

In addition to crowdsourcing solutions, Ideas For Us is crowd funding for the projects. They call it the Soup, which is based off the Detroit Soup, a kind of micro granting dinner. Because they have so many great ideas coming out of the Hive, they can't fund them all. So, people will go to a dinner, buy a bowl of soup, and vote for a project. At the end of the night, the project with the most votes gets the funding.

Crowdfunding has been an amazing tool that I've used to help to put ideas into action. From Kickstarting my album, to funding the Earth Guardians delegation to Paris for COP 21, to providing the funding for our first RYSE training, my network has always come up clutch. Not only does crowd-funding help us get funds for a project, it helps spread the word about our work, and allows our community to feel connected and invested in our projects. Crowdsourcing plus crowdfunding equals innovative change and ideas brought to life.

We Are "Solutionaries"

Some young people don't even need funding to put their vision into action. Take William Kamkwamba, who grew up in a poor rural town in the Eastern African country of Malawi. His story is an example of the ingenuity and resilience of my generation. A year-long drought struck his community, resulting in severe famine that meant he and his family could no longer afford to keep him in school. Despite the terrible situation, William refused to let it bury him. He became a seed of inspiration for people around the world.

He went to the library and began researching renewable energy. Even though he spoke almost no English, he was able to learn how to build a wind turbine from the diagrams. He didn't have the materials the book said he needed, so he went to a scrap yard to find things he could substitute. He used items like a tractor fan and an old bicycle frame to build two wind turbines—one that provided electricity and one that pumped water for the dry farm fields.

When he had the idea, other people in the village, and even his own mother, thought he was crazy. At the age of just 14, he was able to help solve multiple problems facing his community. He provided water for his drought-stricken community that is heavily reliant on agriculture and electricity for a community where it was scarce. Malawi is a place that is likely to be more affected by climate change than others, so extreme weather events like drought and floods are likely to increase. Scientists' fear that that crop yields in sub-Saharan Africa could fall as much as 90 percent by the year 2100 due to increasingly severe weather.

The electricity for his community was also crucial and was done in a way that is a model for the future. Many developing nations need power for education, health, and communication, but using fossil fuels would further exacerbate problems with water and climate that already plague these same regions. He found a solution and did it all with salvaged materials laid to waste in a dump. This is the kind of resourcefulness my generation possesses. He could've waited for an NGO to come and help, but instead, he solved the problem himself in spite of all the challenges he faced.

TOOLS FOR REVOLUTION

To be "solutionaries," you have to take the knowledge, stories, and strategies that you've learned in this book and act in a way that resists injustice and build solutions. But, nobody has ever created change alone. Someone must plant the first seed. It takes an organized community to grow the garden of social change. At Earth Guardians, we've been working to develop our community through our Crews and RYSE Youth Council. Here are some tools we'd like to pass on to help you organize, strategize, and win.

The foundation of all social movements is people power, but we need to understand power and the way it works in society to build it. There are typically three types of power we talk about in organizing: power over, power together, and power within.

Power Over

Presidencies, dictatorships, bosses, or even parents are often a classic representation of power over, a form of control where people and institutions wield authority over others. This type of influence gives many of us a negative feeling about power. So, often, we give our power away to these authorities, because we feel that we don't have any other choice or because we don't know any other way. Some expect those in power to solve the problems for them. We can't forget that many of these elected officials have corporations and other big funders with power over *them*. Unless we organize, big-money interests will get their way over the interests of the people. As Frederick Douglass once said, "Power concedes nothing without a demand. It never did and it never will." That couldn't be more true in this day and age.

Power Together

As organizers, this is the kind of power we're trying to build. It is one that shares power toward a common vision. When we organize, and when we build movements, we focus on building and leveraging all the power in our communities to reach specific goals. Winning campaigns takes skill, strategy, perseverance, and the involvement of many different stakeholders. This is why we build coalitions of organizations with different areas of focus and expertise. Learning to leverage the power of these coalitions is crucial for achieving our goals.

Power Within

One way to recognize our personal power is by getting in touch with our stake or our personal motivation. What are the personal experiences that lead us to this work? One person's stake might be that they want to stop a fracking well that is right next to their home because their children are getting sick, while another person's stake in raising their voice is because they were bullied and it's the first time in their life that they feel empowered to stand up for themselves. As you transform and understand your story and why you are motivated to be active, your stake will change as well. Understanding your motivation in this work helps in connecting with your internal power and supports you in building shared power with others.

The way we understand power has immense implications for the way we choose to organize. Even with a leader in a position of power, history shows us that change only comes from the bottom up. It often takes continued pressure to hold our public officials accountable. Real revolutionary change often comes from building shared and strategic people power. Below are some tools to help you build the good kind of power—community based—to create successful campaigns.

SPECTRUM OF ALLIES

To be an effective changemaker, we must understand the social and political landscape in which we're organizing. There is a different spectrum of support everywhere we go, and a variety of viewpoints that people hold about an issue in a community. Understanding where members of the public fall on the range of support can help us understand who we need to move and how. We need to first assess which side people are on, and can we shift them toward us. Here is the range we should consider:

Active Allies

This is your base, your organizers, the people you don't need to move, but are critical to collaborate and plan with. Some organizing can be too focused on this section of the spectrum, creating actions with the main appeal to those already engaged. If we are to move the needle, it's important to break out of this, and think of what would appeal to the broader community outside your immediate circle.

Passive Allies

These are the folks that we need to activate, because they agree with you but aren't actively engaged. They could be a friend, a family member, a coworker, or a classmate. They may like or share a Facebook post or sign a petition, but are unlikely to take more significant action unless they are moved to do so. You might want to invite them to a meeting or see if there is a way that they can use their skills or passions to help with the campaign.

Neutral

These people are undecided on how they feel about the issue. These are people you can move into passive allies, by shifting the narrative. Through media campaigns, education, and large demonstrations, neutrals can be swayed to take a side on an issue that they were previously unaware of. You might start by asking them to sign a petition or take a smaller action. Once they have taken a side, you might be able to move them into becoming active.

Passive Opposition

They aren't on your side, but they can be swayed. While they might be more likely to side with your opposition, they might also be moved to neutral, if you can change public opinion. Think of the protests to Trump's Muslim travel ban. On the day that he enacted the policy, polls had him at 48 percent approval rating, within just 2 days, his approval rating had plummeted four points to 44 percent. At the same time, the percentage of people who disapproved did not increase at all. Bold, swift action to fight an unjust law had caused passive opposition to reevaluate their support for the President's policies. While they didn't immediately move to our side, now they can be swayed into passive support. This section is best approached indirectly rather than directly, or you might piss them off and move them into active opposition.

Active Opposition

They are on the opposite side of the issue than you are and rarely move. There are a few exceptions, like the story told in the chapter on Standing Rock about Governor George Wallace, but that's often many years down the road, because public opinion has shifted. Unless they are a target like Wallace or Trump, active opposition are best ignored. You don't want to play into their narrative or waste time arguing with people who will likely never be on your side. There are exceptions, and you can strive to find middle ground. Sometimes, people that you assume would be opposition, like a government official, might actually be a passive ally who can be activated. An example of this came when Bristol County District Attorney Sam Sutter dropped all charges against Jay O'Hara and Ken Ward, who blockaded a coal ship with a lobster boat. Someone might assume Sutter was in a position of active opposition, but he was actually an ally. He made a public statement about the importance of taking bold action on climate and later marched alongside O'hara at the People's Climate March. Turning government officials and industry workers into allies is a key strategy to winning campaigns.

I first heard about the Spectrum of Allies at Wildfire training with Joshua Kahn Russell, Sophia Campos, and Luke Nephew. They told us about how the Spectrum of Allies was used in successful past campaigns like the Student Nonviolent Coordinating Committee with Freedom Summer during the Civil Rights Movement. They saw that they had passive allies at colleges in the North, so they sent buses to bring them down South and turn them to active allies. That summer, many of the students saw the horrific violence of racial oppression and wrote to their parents about what they'd seen. Then, their families who may have been neutral or even passive opposition were becoming passive allies. Think about what actions you can take that will move people from multiple segments of the spectrum toward you.

PUBLIC NARRATIVE

One powerful tool for moving people and building strong movements is telling our stories and how it relates to the current moment. This is a tool that's been used in movements going way back, but Marshall Ganz, an organizer in the Civil Rights Movement and Farmworkers Movement of California, helped create a model that breaks it down into three elements: the story of self, the story of us, and the story of now. Everyone from the Obama campaign to PowerShift has used this as a strategy. Organizations like Wellstone Action use it as a tool for empowerment in trainings. Stories engage our heart, demonstrate our values, and can establish an emotional connection to the issues and the movement. It's a critical element to a successful campaign.

Story of Self

All of us have compelling stories, but the best stories are about challenges we face, especially where we have to make a choice, and from that choice, we learn something about ourselves and our values.

A good way to start to build our own public narrative is by having each member of the group answer the following questions.

What was a pivotal challenge you faced in your life? Why was it so challenging?

What was a choice you made as a result of that challenge?

Why did you make that choice?

What was the outcome of your choice? What did it teach you?

Story of Us

After you've told your personal story, connect to a larger story of what's going on in your community or the world. Find the commonalities between your own story and others around you. Try these questions to help you with this part of the story.

Who is the "us?"
What collectively are you passionate about?
What are the core values that guide these passions?
What is the collective purpose that can be extended beyond the group you are currently with?

Story of Now

The final part, the story of now, is where you establish urgency. This where you share how the story relates to the present moment. This is the opportunity to get people pumped about working together to accomplish our goals and achieve a collective vision. To get yourself started on this, you might ask yourself:

What is the present conflict that your community or the world is facing?
What's at stake for you and others?
What gets you fired up to take action?

Campaign Strategy

As we build public support for an issue, the most powerful thing we can do is create highly strategic campaigns by choosing creative tactics, picking useful targets, setting goals, and escalating our campaigns toward a shared victory.

Choosing a Campaign Target

In applying people power, it's important to make sure every campaign has a clear target. Generally this is the person who has the most power or influence over a decision. It's best if this is a single individual, rather than an entire body. For example, during the Keystone XL fight, activists chose to target President Obama, even though the State Department was doing the review, because he had executive power and was seen as a movable target. In general, people in charge like to convince us that the institutions we are dealing with are not made up of people that can be swayed or influenced. It is imperative to have a clear sense of who the influential players are. In a model where you have a campaign target, your primary goal is still to build public support. The target is someone you can channel movement energy at and around to change their position to represent the view of the people.

Secondary Targets

There are a lot of other people around a decision maker whom you may also want to influence. You should only ever pick one target for your campaign, but it's certainly true that you should still find other ways to engage other people who might impact the decision. This group of people are called secondary targets. While they might not be your primary focus, secondary targets are still of value. They are often more accessible to us and with enough pressure, we can get our secondary targets to influence our primary targets.

Goal Setting

Creating change requires us to set goals that are as refined and accurate as possible. Clear and precise goals help us to move our campaigns forward with clear benchmarks of success. In setting goals, we often use the acronym SMART, which stands for:

- Specific: The goal should clearly explain the purpose of the campaign (i.e., Put solar power on this specific high school or get pesticides out of public parks).

- Measurable: We can clearly see when we've obtained our goal and how far we have to go to get there.

- Agreed upon: Everyone understands the goals fully and consensus is formed.

- Realistic: Make sure the goal is attainable.

- Time-Based: Make sure that you have enough time to reach the goal, but not too much time.

Timeline

Once we have goals set we can make a timeline backwards to see how we can get there. By starting with where we ultimately want to get to we can understand what we need to achieve along the way to win. These timelines can help us see our long-term, medium-term, or short-term goals.

Sustaining Momentum

To grow sustainably, we have to be able to capture the energy generated from crucial moments in the campaign. A common problem is when people turn out to an action wanting to get involved, and then never hear from the organizers again. Organizations tend to grow through personal relationships and broader engagement such as meetings. It's ideal to combine these approaches—everyone who comes to a meeting or an action should have a real relationship with an organizer or a leader, and in-depth leadership development can happen through these personal relationships. We know that we're in a stage of momentum when people we don't even know are showing up to our actions and meetings because our issue is hot, and there's hype around it.

THE ACT-RECRUIT TRAIN CYCLE

The Act-Recruit-Cycle is one way to think about continually building our base. This gives us a structured way to absorb the momentum of big moments. We do this through recruiting people out of actions and into training. This will give our new recruits the skills and relationships that empower them to stay committed to a campaign. Offering people the opportunity to take the next step beyond just showing up to an event or action can help your movement grow.

THE TACTIC STAR

We love the following tool known as a tactic star, originally developed by Beyond the Choir to help walk through the components of a successful action. There are 9 areas. Go through each individually and check them off to ensure that your action tactics line up with your strategy. As you're planning your action, this can be a checklist to make sure you have everything covered.

After you run through these steps to make your action happen, it's not over. It's important, while it's still fresh, to celebrate what you accomplished and later debrief. Here are some questions you should ask when debriefing your action.

- What were the actions highlights?
- Where is there room for improvement?
- How can we involve more people in the next action?
- How did it affect our target?
- Did we meet our goals?
- What are some next steps?

GROWING THE REVOLUTION

Combining all of these factors and elements give us the strength to plant the roots of a revolution. Once we have a foundation of essential tools we can draw from, we can spread the necessary seeds of change, and take proper care to grow it into something big and beautiful. We, the people, are far from powerless, but the systems of oppression we are resisting are adamant in destroying our futures, lives, and cultures in the name of profit and power. It will take building an immense amount of people power to win demands that align with our vision of victory for the future. When we implement capacity-building tools in line with an understanding of the terrain we are organizing on, we can create sustained waves of momentum, and have our organizations come out stronger than before. When we frame our actions as moments of victory, we can always make sure that we are telling the story that this political moment requires. We need to organize our communities with more passion and skill than ever; our very survival depends on it.

Three Fundraising Tips from Pearl Gottschalk

One of the biggest challenges Earth Guardians has faced over the years is finding the funding to carry out our vision and build our organization. We're often so focused on taking the steps to make change in the world that we forget about the other part of that—generating the funds to make it all happen. Luckily, we have incredible people like my friend Pearl in our network. She has spent time on the grant-giving side of things and knows what it's like to be approached in a good way. She recently joined the Earth Guardians board and helped us reframe our approach to fundraising.

Tip # 1: Be authentic and find your uniqueness.

What makes your organization unique? What will stick out in the mind of a potential funder that might hear dozens of funding pitches every day? These are things to think about as you hone your pitch to funders. Remember, if you're talking with a funder in person, you want your pitch to be as succinct and relevant as possible. So, doing the groundwork to think about why your project is different, interesting, and effective is critical. This will also help you understand where you should focus when writing grants.

Tip # 2: Build personal relationships.

Nothing can replace the importance of genuine human interaction and connection. Relationships are a two-way street, so in addition to sharing what your passionate about, ask questions to find out about a prospective funder's journey and passions. They may tell you something that can be useful in your fundraising ask. For instance, you might be an environmental organization that works on advocacy, education, and direct action. From a conversation, you might learn that your funder is particularly passionate about environmental education. Now, you can focus your ask around this specifically and increase your chances of getting funded.

Tip # 3:
Align your vision and ask from gratitude.

So many of us come from a place of dread when it comes to fundraising. Realigning this is crucial and requires that we connect deeply to our vision and purpose. Take a moment to visualize where you are going with your project or organization. Feel the good fortune and excitement of having such a noble cause that you can help actualize. That feeling of gratitude for the opportunity to engage in such important work is the same attitude you should feel when fundraising. When you approach a potential funder, know that you are offering them an opportunity to share in this same powerful feeling of purpose.

THREE SOCIAL MEDIA TIPS FROM JADE BEGAY

My sister in the movement Jade has been working with Indigenous Rising Media and 350.org to support front-line resistance like the water protectors at Standing Rock. She is incredibly knowledgeable when it comes to getting out your message online. I want to pass along a few tips she offers.

1. Plan and focus.

Before you begin sharing content on your social platforms, take time to plan, research your issue, and learn which social media channel will best serve your goals. While Facebook is great for community organizing and live streaming, twitter is great for engaging media and politicians, and Instagram is best for visual storytelling.

Research your issue and riff off of hashtags that are already getting lots of attention, this will get your platform engaged in a conversation that is already happening.

Plan your posts around current events. For example, if you are a youth organization, mark your calendars for "World Youth Day" and follow hashtags that are relevant to your issues to stay up-to-date on news and events.

2. Share stories and solutions, not statistics.

Without a doubt, humans relate more to stories than statistics, so, when creating posts for social media, find ways to include personal experiences rather than posting numbers. Just as we engage better with stories, we also engage better with solutions. While it's critical to talk about the urgency of an issue, ultimately, we want to get our audience to get involved, and we don't want to push them away by causing them to feel overwhelmed. So, if you focus on solutions, your audience might feel more inspired to be a part of that.

3. Inspire and give action items.

Be discerning when choosing the image for your social media post. Does your photo create a feeling of sadness or despair, or does it create a feeling of inspiration and curiosity? Environmental and social injustices are real, and we cannot overlook the grief that these issues cause us and our communities, however, with social media, we want to inspire action, so choosing images and messages that bring out our strong emotions such as courage and hope will be more engaging. Finally, always be sure to include an action item, whether it's a suggestion to donate, to share a post, to sign a petition, or to attend an event. While we inspire people with stories and solutions, we also want to provide a way for them to get involved.

In the tools outlined above, you should find a variety of ways to get involved, engage, connect, and create movements that can help save the planet. But don't stop there. If you want to go deeper into organizing skills and strategies, there are many awesome resources out there. You can also find a downloadable guide to action at www.earthguardians.com.

WE RISE

The more I do this work, the more I realize that we're not alone. I've had patches where I feel isolated, but like the tide of the ocean ebbs and flows, so has my experience of this movement. I realize now that I am part of a generation that is actively engaged in building the world we want to see from the bottom up. As I tour around to colleges and high schools, I am constantly blown away by the knowledge and wisdom of the youth climate justice movement. I learn things from them that you don't hear about in the corporate media or in school. People are getting more creative and more innovative with their actions, reaching across barriers and pulling people onto our side, while our network of allies grows. Every day, we are becoming a more compassionate and diverse movement.

We are not just rising, we are winning. We have the system on the ropes in the courts, on the streets, on college campuses, and, soon enough, at the ballot box. I don't need statistics or pundits to tell me that, because I feel it when I'm with students fighting for divestment on their campuses, I felt it when I was at Standing Rock, and I feel it when I talk with amazing youth leaders taking action around the world. We see that a world in crisis offers us an opportunity to build a more just one in its place. More than ever, we understand the intensity of the opposition we face. We have all the tools we need to solve this challenge, but we can't do it alone. We need everybody regardless of age, race, or religion to join us. We don't just want your encouragement; we want your courage, your passion, and your energy. The time has come for us to put aside everything that divides us and rise together like the oceans to turn the tides.

REFERENCES

Chapter 3: Composing Revolution

"Biography: Kathy Jetnil-Kijiner," Poetry Foundation, www.poetryfoundation.org/poems
-and-poets/poets/detail/Kathy-jetnil-kijiner.

"Musical Responses to September 11th: The List of Allegedly 'Banned' Songs," *Free Muse*, December 9, 2004, http://freemuse.org/archives/5679.

Chapter 4: Moving from Crisis to Opportunity

Fang, Lee. "How Big Business is Buying the Election." The Investigative Fund, August 30, 2012, www.theinvestigativefund.org/investigations/politicsandgovernment/1689 /how_big_business_is_buying_the_election.

Grenoble, Ryan. "Neil deGrasse Tyson Reveals Humorous Plan to Grab Donald Trump's Attention." *Huffington Post*, November 18, 2016, www.huffingtonpost.com/entry /neil-degrasse-tyson-grab-trump-attention_us_582f5243e4b030997bbf3a3f.

Hulac, Benjamin. "Tobacco and Oil Industries Used Same Researchers to Sway Public." *ClimateWire*, July 20, 2016, www.scientificamerican.com/article/tobacco-and -oil-industries-used-same-researchers-to-sway-public1.

McKibben, Bill. "What Exxon Knew About Climate Change." *New Yorker*, September 18, 2015, www.newyorker.com/news/daily-comment/what-exxon-knew-about -climate-change.

Ocean Portal Team. "Gulf Oil Spill." The Ocean Portal, http://ocean.si.edu/gulf-oil -spill.

Reynolds, Emma. "Welcome to the Madhouse: Scientist Says Trump Could Destroy the World." News.com.au, February 10, 2017, http://www.news.com.au/technology /environment/climate-change/welcome-to-the-madhouse-scientist-says-trump-could -destroy-the-world/news-story/0e31691ab55a520800cef7dbd289fdad.

Sharp, Tim. "Superstorm Sandy: Facts About the Frankenstorm." LiveScience, November 27, 2012, www.livescience.com/24380-hurricane-sandy-status-data.html.

Sutter, John. "Trump Doesn't Represent American Views on Climate Change: A Visual Guide." *CNN*, January 18, 2017, www.cnn.com/2017/01/18/politics/sutter-american -climate-opinions-trump.

Thompson, Andrea. "Climate Experts Weigh In on Trump's Election Win." *Climate Central*, November 9, 2016, www.climatecentral.org/news/what-climate-experts -think-of-trumps-win-20860.

Viñas, Maria-José and Carol Rasmussen. "Warming Seas and Melting Ice Sheets." NASA, August 26, 2015, www.nasa.gov/feature/goddard/warming-seas-and-melting-ice -sheets.

Welch, Craig. "Climate Change Helped Spark Syrian War, Study Says." *National Geographic*, March 2, 2015, http://news.nationalgeographic.com/news/2015/03/150302 -syria-war-climate-change-drought.

www.countable.us

www.indivisibleguide.com/guide

Chapter 5: Holding Back the Sea

"50 Simple Things: A Carbon-Cutting Action Guide," Earth Guardians.org, www .earthguardians.org/50simplethings.

DeChristopher, Tim. "Posing As a Bidder, Utah Student Disrupts Government Auction of 150,000 Acres of Wilderness for Oil & Gas Drilling." *Democracy Now* video, 31:40, December 22, 2008, www.democracynow.org/2008/12/22/posing_as_a _bidder_utah_student.

Farrell, Bryan. "Tim DeChristopher: This is What Hope Looks Like." *Waging Nonviolence*, July 26, 2011, https://wagingnonviolence.org/feature/tim-dechristopher -this-is-what-hope-looks-like.

"Increased Flooding Risk: Global Warming's Wake-Up Call for Riverfront Communities," National Wildlife Federation, 2009, www.nwf.org/~/media/PDFs/Global-Warming /NWF_FloodReport_optimized.ashx.

"The Mandel Visit: Excerpts from Mandela Speech to Joint Meeting of Congress," *New York Times*, June 27, 1990, www.nytimes.com/1990/06/27/world/the-mandel-visit -excerpts-from-mandela-speech-to-joint-meeting-of-congress.html?pagewanted=all.

"Wildfires," Insurance Information Institute, www.iii.org/fact-statistic/wildfires.

Chapter 6: Wilderness Warriors

Batsakis, Anthea. "Nina Gualinga is Winning the Fight Against Oil Companies to Protect the Amazon." 1 Million Women, November 20, 2015, www.1millionwomen.com.au /blog/nina-gualinga-winning-fight-against-oil-companies-protect-amazon.

"Conflict Palm Oil," Rainforest Action Network, www.ran.org/palm_oil#.

"Crude: The Incredible Journey of Oil," *ABC Science* video, 29:04, May 24, 2007, www.abc.net.au/science/crude.

"Fight for the Forests," *TakePart* video, 3:05, www.takepart.com/forests/index.html.

Goodman, David. "Deep in the Amazon, a Tiny Tribe is Beating Big Oil." *Yes! Magazine*, February 12, 2015, www.yesmagazine.org/issues/together-with-earth/deep-in-the -amazon-a-tiny-tribe-is-beating-big-oil.

Gualinga, Nina. "Indigenous Voices: A Call to Keep the Oil in the Ground." *Huffington Post*, February 11, 2015, www.huffingtonpost.com/amazon-watch/indigenous-voices -a-call-to-keep-the-oil-in-the_b_6312368.html.

Hill, David. "Ecuador's Leading Environmental Group Fights to Stop Forced Closure." *The Guardian*, January 7, 2017, www.theguardian.com/environment/andes-to-the -amazon/2017/jan/07/ecuadors-leading-environmental-group-fights-forced-closure.

"Indigenous Group Brings 'Canoe of Life' 6,000 Miles from Amazon to Paris to Call for Climate Action," *Democracy Now* video, 59:04, December 11, 2015, www.democracy now.org/2015/12/11/indigenous_group_brings_canoe_of_life.

Kodas, Michael. "Indonesia is Still Burning." *TakePart*, April 18, 2016, www.takepart .com/feature/2016/04/18/palmoil.

"Orang-utans," World Wide Fund for Nature, http://wwf.panda.org/what_we_do/endangered _species/great_apes/orangutans.

"Rainforest Stats," Save the Amazon Coalition, www.savetheamazon.org/rainforeststats.htm.

Silber, Susan and William Velton. "Fact Sheet: Rainforest Animals." Rainforest Action Network, www.ran.org/fact_sheet_rainforest_animals.

Vidal, John. "UN Environment Programme: 200 Species Extinct Every Day, Unlike Anything Since Dinosaurs Disappeared 65 Million Years Ago." *Huffington Post*, May 25, 2011, www.huffingtonpost.com/2010/08/17/un-environment-programme -_n_684562.html.

"What are Carbon Sinks?" Fern, www.fern.org/campaign/forests-and-climate/what -are-carbon-sinks.

Chapter 7: Troubled Waters

Associated Press, The. "Greenpeace, 'Xena' Actress Lawless Try to Stop Drilling Ship From Leaving Port." *Denver Post*, February 23, 2012, www.denverpost.com/2012/02/23 /greenpeace-xena-actress-lawless-try-to-stop-drilling-ship-from-leaving-port.

Belfield, Sarah. "Great Barrier Reef: No Buried Treasure." Geoscience Australia, February 8, 2002, http://web.archive.org/web/20071001045912/http://www.ga.gov.au /media/releases/2002/1013133456_20385.jsp.

"Billion Oyster Project," www.billionoysterproject.org.

"*Chasing Coral*: An Exposure Labs Production," www.chasingcoral.com/#film.

"Dispersants," Center for Biological Diversity, www.biologicaldiversity.org/programs /public_lands/energy/dirty_energy_development/oil_and_gas/gulf_oil_spill/dispersants .html.

Griffin, Drew, Nelli Black, and Curt Devine. "5 Years After the Gulf Oil Spill: What We Do (and Don't) Know." *CNN*, April 20, 2015, www.cnn.com/2015/04/14/us/ gulf-oil-spill-unknowns.

Grobar, Matt. "'Chasing Coral' Director Jeff Orlowski on 'Very Real' Dangers of Climate Change—Sundance Studio." *Deadline*, January 25, 2017, http://deadline.com/2017/01/ chasing-coral-sundance-netflix-jeff-orlowski-video-interview-1201894026.

"How Does Climate Change Affect Coral Reefs?" Teach Ocean Science, www.teach oceanscience.net/teaching_resources/education_modules/coral_reefs_and_climate _change/how_does_climate_change_affect_coral_reefs.

Jansen, Lesa and Brianna Kellar. "Markey: Spillcam was Game-Changer in BP Disaster Response." *CNN*, April 20, 2011, www.cnn.com/2011/POLITICS/04/20 /markey.bp.

Macalister, Terry. "Shell Abandons Alaska Arctic Drilling." *The Guardian*, September 28, 2015, www.theguardian.com/business/2015/sep/28/shell-ceases-alaska-arctic -drilling-exploratory-well-oil-gas-disappoints.

Mora, Camilo et al. "The Projected Timing of Climate Departure from Recent Variability." *Nature* 502 (October 2013): 183–87. doi: 10.1038/nature12540.

Ocean Portal Team. "Gulf Oil Spill." The Ocean Portal, http://ocean.si.edu/gulf-oil-spill.

Pennington, James. "Every Minute, One Garbage Truck of Plastic is Dumped Into Our Oceans. This Has to Stop." World Economic Forum, October 27, 2016, www.weforum.org/agenda/2016/10/every-minute-one-garbage-truck-of-plastic-is-dumped-into-our-oceans.

Rothman, Lily. "What Caused the Worst Oil Spill in American History." *Time*, April 20, 2015, http://time.com/3818144/deepwater-horizon-anniversary.

"Seismic & Sonar Testing," Greenpeace, www.greenpeace.org/usa/oceans/save-the-whales/seismic-sonar-testing.

Singer, Lauren. "2 Steps to Zero Waste." trash is for tossers (blog), www.trashisfortossers.com/p/the-steps.html.

"The Be Straw Free Campaign," NPS Commercial Services, www.nps.gov/commercial services/greenline_straw_free.htm.

Wang, Marian. "In Gulf Spill, BP Using Dispersants Banned in U.K." *ProPublica*, May 18, 2010, www.propublica.org/blog/item/In-Gulf-Spill-BP-Using-Dispersants-Banned-In-UK.

"We are Sea Shepherd," www.seashepherd.org.

Worm, Boris et al. "Rebuilding Global Fisheries." *Science* 325, no. 5,940 (July 2009): 578. doi: 10.1126/science.1173146.

http://www.trashisfortossers.com/p/the-steps.html

Chapter 8: Future Food

Ahmed, Beenish. "Behind India's 'Epidemic' of Farmer Suicide." ThinkProgress, April 17, 2015, https://thinkprogress.org/behind-indias-epidemic-of-farmer-suicides-fa820ad674f3#.za3l3wow.

"Biography," DJCavem.com, http://djcavem.com/biography.

De Schutter, Olivier. "Eco-Farming Can Double Food Production in 10 Years, Says New UN Report." United Nations Human Rights Office of the High Commissioner, March 8, 2011, www.srfood.org/images/stories/pdf/press_releases/20110308_agroecology-report-pr_en.pdf.

Herrera, Dave. "From Tough Time, DJ Cavem Moetavation Built Conscious Lines." *Westword*, September 20, 2012, www.westword.com/music/from-tough-times-dj-cavem-moetavation-built-conscious-lines-5118025.

Herreria, Carla. "Kauai's Anti-GMO Regulation Challenged by Big-Ag Lawsuit." *Huffington Post*, January 25, 2014, www.huffingtonpost.com/2014/01/14/kauai-anti-gmo-lawsuit_n_4593043.html.

http://ngm.nationalgeographic.com/2011/07/food-ark/food-variety-graphic

Knoblauch, Jessica. "Pesticides in Paradise." *Earthjustice*, Spring 2015, http://earthjustice.org/features/pesticides-in-paradise.

McNeil, Maggie. "US Organic Sales Post New Record of $43.3 billion in 2015." Organic Trade Association, May 19, 2016, www.ota.com/news/press-releases/19031.

Mercola, Joseph. "How GMOs Contribute to Environmental Damages." Mercola.com, March 5, 2013, http://articles.mercola.com/sites/articles/archive/2013/03/05/gmo -affects-climate-change.aspx.

Perkins, Sid. "Antiburp Compound Could Reduce Methane Emissions from Cows." *Science*, July 31, 2015, www.sciencemag.org/news/2015/07/antiburp-compound-could -reduce-methane-emissions-cows.

Philpott, Tom. "No, GMOs Didn't Create India's Farmer Suicide Problem, But..." *Mother Jones*, Spetember 30, 2015, www.motherjones.com/tom-philpott/2015/09 /no-gmos-didnt-create-indias-farmer-suicide-problem.

"Real Food Challenge," www.realfoodchallenge.org.

Rieff, David. "Where Hunger Goes: On the Green Revolution." *The Nation*, February 17, 2011, www.thenation.com/article/where-hunger-goes-green-revolution.

Roshmann, Michael. "Suicide Rate of Farmers Higher than Any Other Group." *Farm & Ranch Guide*, August 5, 2016, www.farmandranchguide.com/entertainment /country_living/farm_and_ranch_life/suicide-rate-of-farmers-higher-than-any-other -group/article_e1ee8bfc-5b13-11e6-a1cc-cfffc7592815.html.

Schwartz, Judith D. "Soil as Carbon Storehouse: New Weapon in Climate Fight?" Yale Environment 360, March 4, 2014, http://e360.ale.edu/features/soil_as_carbon _storehouse_new_weapon_in_climate_fight.

Sergio, Maggie. "GMO & Pesticide Experiments in Hawaii: The Poisoning of Paradise." *Huffington Post*, July 2, 2013, www.huffingtonpost.com/maggie-sergio/gmo-pesticide -experiments_b_3513496.html

Shiva, Vandana. "Seeds of Suicide and Slavery versus Seeds of Life and Freedom." *Aljazeera*, March 30, 2013, www.aljazeera.com/indepth/opinion/2013/03/20133 2813553729250.html.

Shiva, Vandana. "The Seeds of Suicide: How Monsanto Destroys Farming." Global Research, March 9, 2016, www.globalresearch.ca/the-seeds-of-suicide-how-monsanto-destroys -farming/5329947.

"Suzy Amis Cameron," www.suzyamiscameron.com.

"The Science," 350.org, https://350.org/about/science.

"Vandana Shiva," *Wikipedia*, https://en.wikipedia.org/wiki/Vandana_Shiva.

Venkat, Vidya. "Bt Cotton Responsible for Suicides in Rain-Fed Areas, Says Study." *The Hindu*, June 24, 2015, www.thehindu.com/news/national/bt-cotton-responsible-for -suicides-in-rainfed-areas-says-study/article7337684.ece.

Vermeulen, Sonja J., Bruce M. Campbell, and John S.I. Ingram. "Climate Change and Food Systems." *Annual Review of Environment and Resources* 37 (November 2012): 195–222. doi: 10.1146/annurev-environ-020411-130608.

Chapter 9: The True Cost of Fossil Fuels

Associated Press, The. "A Timeline of the Keystone XL Oil Pipeline." *Salon*, January 24, 2017, www.salon.com/2017/01/24/a-timeline-of-the-keystone-xl-oil-pipeline.

Carrington, Damian. "Fossil Fuel Divestment Funds Double to $5tn in a Year." *The Guardian*, December 12, 2016, www.theguardian.com/environment/2016/dec/12 /fossil-fuel-divestment-funds-double-5tn-in-a-year.

"Citizen's Climate Lobby," http://citizensclimatelobby.org.

Coady, David, Ian Parry, Louis Sears, and Baoping Shang. "How Large are Global Energy Subsidies?" IMF Working Paper, 2015, www.imf.org/external/pubs/ft/wp/2015 /wp15105.pdf.

"Death and Disease from Power Plants," Clean Air Task Force, www.catf.us/fossil /problems/power_plants.

Epstein, Paul R. et al. "Full Cost Accounting for the Life Cycle of Coal." *Annals of the New York Academy of Sciences* 1219 (February 2011): 73–98. doi: 10.1111/j.1749 -6632.2010.05890.x.

Fenberg, Steve. "Top 10 Lies About Municipalization: Mythbusters!" RenewablesYes.org, www.renewablesyes.org/?page_id=2401.

Friedman, Lisa. "Coal-Fired Power in India May Cause More Than 100,000 Premature Deaths Annually." *ClimateWire*, March 11, 2013, www.scientificamerican.com/article /coal-fired-power-in-india-may-cause-more-than-100000-premature-deaths -annually.

Groeger, Lena. "How Safe Are America's 2.5 Million Miles of Pipelines?" *ProPublica*, November 16, 2012, www.scientificamerican.com/article/how-safe-are-americas -2-5-million-miles-of-pipelines.

Hirji, Zahra. "Unique Hazards of Tar Sands Oil Spills Confirmed by National Academies of Sciences." InsideClimate News, December 9, 2015, https://insideclimatenews.org /news/09122015/unique-hazards-tar-sands-oil-spills-dilbit-diluted-bitumen-confirmed -national-academies-of-science-kalamazoo-river-enbridge.

Morris, Monique W. (ed.) "Coal Blooded: Putting Profits Before People, Executive Summary." NAACP, April 2016, www.naacp.org/wp-content/uploads/2016/04/Coal _Blooded_Executive_Summary_Update.pdf

"Renewable Electricity Subsidies," Global Subsidies Initiative, www.iisd.org/gsi /renewable-electricity-subsidies.

"Statement by the President on the Keystone XL Pipeline," The White House Office of the Press Secretary, November 6, 2015, https://obamawhitehouse.archives.gov/the -press-office/2015/11/06/statement-president-keystone-xl-pipeline.

Swift, Anthony. "Nebraska's Court Ruling Deeming Keystone XL's Route Void is a Win for Landowners, Water, and Climate." NRDC Expert Blog, February 21, 2014, www.nrdc.org/experts/anthony-swift/ nebraskas-court-ruling-deeming-keystone-xls-route-void-win-landowners-water.

"Tens of Thousands Rally to Stop Keystone XL Pipeline & Urge Obama to Move 'Forward on Climate,'" *Democracy Now* video, 25:57, February 18, 2013, www.democracynow .org/2013/2/18/tens_of_thousands_rally_to_stop.

"Thousands Surround Obama's White House: 'Stop Keystone XL!'" *Common Dreams*, November 18, 2012, www.commondreams.org/news/2012/11/18/thousands -surround-obamas-white-house-stop-keystone-xl.

"Top 10 Facts About the Alberta Oil Sands," DeSmogBlog (blog), www.desmogblog.com /top-10-facts-canada-alberta-oil-sands-information.

"What Are Tar Sands?" Union of Concerned Scientists, www.ucsusa.org/clean-vehicles /all-about-oil-what-are-tar-sands#.WNQuYRLyvdc.

Wong, Edward. "Coal Burning Causes the Most Air Pollution Deaths in China, Study Finds." *New York Times*, August 17, 2016, www.nytimes.com/2016/08/18/world/asia /china-coal-health-smog-pollution.html.

Chapter 10: Fracking for Fool's Gas

Appunn, Kerstine. "Germany's Greenhouse Gas Emissions and Climate Targets." Clean Energy Wire, February 1, 2017, www.cleanenergywire.org/factsheets/germanys -greenhouse-gas-emissions-and-climate-targets.

Arvesen, Amelia. "First Lawsuit Filed in Connection with Deadly Firestone House Explosion." *Daily Camera*, May 15, 2017, www.dailycamera.com/news/ci_30990482 /first-lawsuit-filed-connection-deadly-firestone-house-explosion.

Beans, Laura. "Colorado Governor Admits No One Wants Fracking in Their Backyard." EcoWatch, July 30, 2013, www.ecowatch.com/colorado-governor-admits-no-one -wants-fracking-in-their-backyard-1881782455.html.

Chow, Lorraine. "Solar Employs More Workers than Coal, Oil, and Natural Gas Combined." EcoWatch, January 17, 2017, www.ecowatch.com/solar-job-growth-2197574131 .html.

"COGCC Hearing," YouTube video, 12:01, posted by "Earth Guardians," April 30, 2014, www.youtube.com/watch?v=HV6Zy7RGNwY&list=PLVbQKnMSQUosnpjjO8oUfctc Gcr12SX6W&index=6.

Crowe, Elizabeth et al. "When the Wind Blows: Tracking Toxic Chemicals in Gas Fields and Impacted Communities." Coming Clean Inc., June 2016, http://comingcleaninc .org/wind-blows.

Dyer, Joel, Matt Cortina, and Elizabeth Miller. "Who Killed the Vote on Fracking?" *Boulder Weekly*, October 2, 2014, www.boulderweekly.com/news/who-killed-the -vote-on-fracking.

Elliott, Dan. "Front Range Flunks on Air-Quality Group's Ozone Report Card." *The Gazette*, April 20, 2016, http://gazette.com/front-range-flunks-on-air-quality-groups -ozone-report-card/article/1574508.

Finley, Bruce. "Colorado Appeals Court Says State Must Protect Health and Environment Before Allowing Oil and Gas Drilling." *Denver Post*, March 24, 2017, www.denverpost .com/2017/03/23/colorado-appeals-court-state-must-protect-health-environment.

"Frequently Asked Questions: What is US Electricity Generation by Energy Source?" US Energy Information Administration, www.eia.gov/tools/faqs/faq.php?id=427&t=3.

Gold, Russell and Tom McGinty. "Energy Boom Puts Wells in America's Backyards." *Wall Street Journal*, October 25, 2013, www.wsj.com/articles/energy-boom-puts -wells-in-america8217s-backyards-1382756256.

Goodell, Jeff. "The Big Fracking Bubble: The Scam Behind Aubrey McClendon's Gas Boom." *Rolling Stone*, March 1, 2012, www.rollingstone.com/politics/news /the-big-fracking-bubble-the-scam-behind-the-gas-boom-20120301.

Greeley Tribune, The. "Weld County Infant Mortality Rate Runs Twice as High as Neighboring Counties." *Denver Post*, August 29, 2016, www.denverpost.com/2016 /08/29/weld-county-infant-mortality-rate.

Hauter, Wenonah. *Frackopoly* (New York: The New Press, 2016): 78.

"Hickenlooper: Suspending EPA's New Ozone Standard 'Would be a Great Idea,'" Energy Policy Center, April 1, 2016, http://energy.i2i.org/2016/04/01/hickenlooper -suspending-epas-new-ozone-standard-%E2%80%98would-be-a-great-idea%E2%80%99.

Hickman, Leo. "'Fracking' Company Targets US Children with Colouring Book." *The Guardian*, July 14, 2011, www.theguardian.com/environment/blog/2011/jul/14 /gas-fracking-children-colouring-book.

Howarth, Robert W. "Methane Emissions and Climatic Warming Risks from Hydraulic Fracturing and Shale Gas Development: Implications for Policy." *Energy Emission Control Technologies* 3 (October 2015): 45–54. doi: 10.2147/EECT.S61539.

http://research.noaa.gov/News/NewsArchive/LatestNews/Tabld/684/ArtMID/1768 /ArticleID/10000/Oil-and-Gas-Wells-Contribute-Fuel-for-Ozone-Pollution.aspx.

Kelly, David. "Study Shows Air Emissions Near Fracking Sites May Pose Health Risk." *CU Anschutz Today*, March 19, 2012, www.cuanschutztoday.org/health-impacts -of-fracking-emissions.

Kunze, Conrad and Paul Lehmann. "The Myth of the Dark Side of the Energiewende." *Energy Post*, February 17, 2015, http://energypost.eu/energiewende-dark-side.

Lewis, Renee. "New Study Links Fracking to Birth Defects in Heavily Drilled Colorado." *Aljazeera America*, January 30, 2014, http://america.aljazeera.com/articles/2014/1/30 /new-study-links-frackingtobirthdefectsinheavilydrilledcolorado.html.

Martinez, Xiuhtezcatl. "Why Would People from the Oil & Gas Industry Bully 10 and 13 Year Old Kids?" Our Children's Trust (blog), May 10, 2013, www.ourchildrenstrust .org/blog/2016/6/27/why-would-people-from-the-oil-and-gas-industry-bully-10-and-13 -year-old-kids.

"Multistate Summary," The Endocrine Disruption Exchange, January 27, 2011, http://endocrinedisruption.org/assets/media/documents/Multistate%20summary%20 1-27-11%20Final%20with%20letterhead%2012-07-16.pdf.

Nearing, Brian. "Prize to Fuel Anti-Fracking Fight." *Times Union*, March 27, 2012, www.timesunion.com/local/article/Prize-to-fuel-anti-fracking-fight-3433911.php.

Pantsios, Anastasia. "Breaking: Cuomo Bans Fracking in New York State." EcoWatch, December 17, 2014, www.ecowatch.com/breaking-cuomo-bans-fracking-in-new-york -state-1881990932.html.

Prendergast, Alan. "Fracking Interests, Xcel Spend More Than $1 Million Combined on Ballot Issues." *Westword*, November 4, 2013, www.westword.com /news/racking-interests-xcel-spend-more-than-1-million-combined-on-ballot-issues -5834387.

Quinn, Megan. "Broomfield Fracking: Recount Finds 5-Year Ban Wins by 20 Votes." *Daily Camera*, December 3, 2013, www.dailycamera.com/broomfield-news /ci_24649390/broomfield-fracking-recount-finds-5-year-ban-wins.

Romm, Joe. "More Bad News for Fracking: IPCC Warns Methane Traps Much More Heat Than We Thought." ThinkProgress, October 2, 2013, https://thinkprogress .org/more-bad-news-for-fracking-ipcc-warns-methane-traps-much-more-heat-than-we -thought-9c2badf392df.

Samuelson, Kate. "Renewable Energy is Creating Jobs 12 Times Faster than the Rest of the Economy." *Fortune*, January 27, 2017, http://fortune.com/2017/01/27/solar-wind-renewable-jobs.

Solotaroff, Paul. "What's Killing the Babies of Vernal, Utah?" *Rolling Stone*, June 22, 2016, www.rollingstone.com/culture/features/fracking-whats-killing-the-babies-of-vernal-utah-20150622.

Spear, Stefanie. "Frack Free Colorado Rally and Concert Promotes a Renewable Energy Future." EcoWatch, October 24, 2012, www.ecowatch.com/frack-free-colorado-rally-and-concert-promotes-a-renewable-energy-futu-1881654243.html.

Spiegelman, Annie. "Living Downstream: Steingraber Documentary Puts Moral Imperative on Banning Cancer-Causing Chemicals. *Huffington Post*, May 25, 2011, www.huffingtonpost.com/annie-spiegelman/post_1069_b_764862.html.

Steingraber, Sandra. "Pledge to Resist Fracking: Writer-Biologist Sandra Steingraber Issues a Call for Action and a Warning to the Gas Industry." Alternet.org, August 29, 2012, www.alternet.org/fracking/pledge-resist-fracking-writer-biologist-sandra-steingraber-issues-call-action-and-warning.

Turner, A.J. et al. "A Large Increase in US Methane Emissions Over the Past Decade Inferred from Satellite Data and Surface Observations." *Geophysical Research Letters* 43, no. 5 (March 2016): 2,218–24. doi: 10.1002/2016GL067987.

Wolfgang, Ben. "I Drank Fracking Fluid, says Colorado Gov. John Hickenlooper." *Washington Times*, February 12, 2013, www.washingtontimes.com/blog/inside-politics/2013/feb/12/colorado-gov-hickenlooper-i-drank-fracking-fluid.

http://www.huffingtonpost.com/annie-spiegelman/post_1069_b_764862.html

http://wwwtimesunion.com/local/article/Prize-to-fuel-anti-fracking-fight-3433911.php

Chapter 11: From Protestors to Protectors

Almendrala, Anna. "Native American Youth Suicide Rates are at Crisis Levels." *Huffington Post*, December 19, 2016, www.huffingtonpost.com/entry/native-american-youth-suicide-rates-are-at-crisis-levels_us_560c3084e4b0768127005591.

Beaumont, Hilary. "Case Closed, Case Opened." *Vice News*, November 28, 2016, https://news.vice.com/story/attempted-murder-charges-dropped-against-standing-rock-protestor.

Capehart, Jonathan. "George Wallace's Daughter: From Segregation to 'Making Things Right.'" *Washington Post*, March 8, 2017, www.washingtonpost.com/blogs/post-partisan/wp/2017/03/08/george-wallaces-daughter-from-segregation-to-making-things-right/?utm_term=.1d2b2d0cdb13.

"Dakota Access Pipeline: An On-the-Ground View from a Young Protestor," GreatLakesNow, November 3, 2016, www.greatlakesnow.org/2016/11/dakota-access-pipeline-an-on-the-ground-view-from-a-young-protestor.

"Dakota Access Pipeline Company Attacks Native American Protesters with Dogs and Pepper Spray," *Democracy Now* video, 7:46, September 4, 2016, www.democracynow.org/2016/9/4/dakota_access_pipeline_company_attacks_native.

Elbein, Saul. "The Youth Group That Launched a Movement at Standing Rock." *New York Times*, January 31, 2017, www.nytimes.com/2017/01/31/magazine/the-youth -group-that-launched-a-movement-at-standing-rock.html.

Evans, Bo. "Chase Iron Eyes Among 76 Arrested After DAPL Protesters Attempt to Set Up New Camp on Private Land." *KFYR-TV/West Dakota FOX*, February 1, 2017, www.kfyrtv.com/content/news/Law-enforcement-makes-arrests-after -DAPL-protesters-attempt-to-set-up-new-camp-on-private-land-412490153.html.

Hampton, Liz and Valerie Volcovici. "Top Executive Behind Dakota Access Has Donated More Than $100,000 to Trump." *Reuters*, October 26, 2016, www.reuters.com/article /us-usa-election-trump-dakota-access-idUSKCN12Q2P2.

Mufson, Steven. "Pipeline Spill by Dakota Access Company Could Have a 'Deadly Effect.'" *Washington Post*, May 8, 2017, www.washingtonpost.com/news/energy -environment/wp/2017/05/08/pipeline-spill-by-dakota-access-company-could-have-a -deadly-effect/?utm_term=.920d2b031610.

Raphael, T.J. "Bismarck Residents Got the Dakota Access Pipeline Moved Without a Fight." *Public Radio International*, December 1, 2016, www.pri.org/stories/2016-12-01 /bismarck-residents-got-dakota-access-pipeline-moved-without-fight.

"'Segregation Forever': A Fiery Pledge Forgiven, But Not Forgotten" on *NPR Radio Diaries*, January 10, 2013, www.npr.org/2013/01/14/169080969/segregation -forever-a-fiery-pledge-forgiven-but-not-forgotten.

van Gelder, Sarah. "Veteran Wesley Clark Jr.: Why I Knelt Before Standing Rock Elders and Asked for Forgiveness." *Yes! Magazine*, December 22, 2016, www.ecowatch.com /veterans-standing-rock-elders-2160559817.html.

http://earthjustice.org/news/press/2017/in-victory-for-standing-rock-sioux-tribe-court -finds-that-approval-of-dakota-access-pipeline-violated-the-law

Chapter 12: Justice, Not Just Us

"A New Movement for a New Century: 2008 Annual Report," Green For All, https://web .archive.org/web/20090305142903/http://greenforall.org/resources/green-for-all-2008 -annual-report.

"Black Lives Matter Stands in Solidarity with Water Protectors at Standing Rock," Black Lives Matter, http://blacklivesmatter.com/solidarity-with-standing-rock.

"History: What is the Peoples Climate Movement, and Where Did It Come From?" Peoples Climate Movement, https://peoplesclimate.org/history.

Jegroo, Ashoka. "Why Black Lives Matter is Fighting Alongside Dakota Access Pipeline Protesters." *Fusion*, September 13, 2016, http://fusion.kinja.com/why-black -lives-matter-is-fighting-alongside-dakota-acc-1793861838.

"Meeting Hosted by Southwest Network for Environmental and Economic Justice (SNEEJ), Jemez, New Mexico, December 1996: Overview," Natural Resources Defense Council, March 16, 2016, www.nrdc.org/resources/jemez-principles -democratic-organizing.

Mock, Brentin. "350.org Challenges Climate Activists to Stand Up for Ferguson." *Grist*, August 22, 2014, http://grist.org/politics/350-org-challenges-climate-activists -to-stand-up-for-ferguson.

Sheth, Sonam and Skye Gould. "5 Charts Show How Much More Men Make Than Women." *Business Insider*, March 8, 2017, www.businessinsider.com /gender-wage-pay-gap-charts-2017-3/#the-gender-wage-gap-varies-widely-depending -on-the-state-1.

Smith, Brendan, Jeremy Brecher, and Kristen Sheeran. "Where Should the Divestors Invest?" *Common Dreams*, May 17, 2014, www.commondreams.org/views/2014/05/17 /where-should-divestors-invest.

Smith, Deirdre. "Why the Climate Movement Must Stand with Ferguson." 350.org, August 20, 2014, https://350.org/how-racial-justice-is-integral-to-confronting -climate-crisis.

"Van Jones Credits Omega as Inspiration for His Green Jobs Initiative," Omega, 2014, www.eomega.org/omega-in-action/feature/van-jones-credits-omega-as-inspiration-for -his-green-jobs-initiative.

Zinshteyn, Mikhail. "College Graduation Rates Rise, But Racial Gaps Persist and Men Still Out-Earn Women." *The Hechinger Report*, May 26, 2016, http: //hechingerreport.org/college-graduation-rates-rise-racial-gaps-persist-men-still-earn -women.

Chapter 13: A Rising Generation

"15 Economic Facts about Millennials," The Council of Economic Advisers, October 2014, https://obamawhitehouse.archives.gov/sites/default/files/docs/millennials /report.pdf

"Climate Change Case Study: Malawi," Trócaire, www.trocaire.org/sites/default/files /resources/policy/malawi-climate-change-case-study.pdf.

Kirshenbaum, Sheril. "Millennials' Views on Climate Change May Influence the 2016 US Presidential Election." *Scientific American*, October 27, 2016, https://blogs .scientificamerican.com/plugged-in/millennials-views-on-climate-change-may-influence -the-2016-u-s-presidential-election.

"Millennials Most Progressive Generation in 50 Years," CivicYouth.org, September 2009, 6–7, http://civicyouth.org/wp-content/uploads/2009/08/v6.i2.3.pdf.

"Millennials on Track to Be the Most Educated Generation to Date," Pew Research Center, March 17, 2015, www.pewresearch.org/fact-tank/2015/03/19/how-millennials -compare-with-their-grandparents/ft_millennials-education_031715.

NextGen Climate. "The Price Tag of Being Young: Climate Change and Millennials' Economic Future." Demos, August 22, 2016, www.demos.org/publication/price -tag-being-young-climate-change-and-millennials-economic-future.

Phillips, Ari. "How 2 Guys, a Lobster Boat, and a District Attorney Just Made Climate History." ThinkProgress, September 10, 2014, https://thinkprogress .org/how-2-guys-a-lobster-boat-and-a-district-attorney-just-made-climate-history -ec360cc83ae2.

Richmond, Emily, Mikhail Zinshteyn, and Natalie Gross. "Dissecting the Youth Vote." *The Atlantic*, November 11, 2016, www.theatlantic.com/education/archive/2016/11 /dissecting-the-youth-vote/507416.

"The Passing of Nobelist Wangari Maathai: 'You Cannot Protect the Environment Unless You Empower People,'" ThinkProgress, September 26, 2011, https://thinkprogress .org/the-passing-of-nobelist-wangari-maathai-you-cannot-protect-the-environment -unless-you-empower-people-22824c632d8.

Tutu, Desmond. "We Need an Apartheid-Style Boycott to Save the Planet." *The Guardian*, April 10, 2014, www.theguardian.com/commentisfree/2014/apr/10/divest -fossil-fuels-climate-change-keystone-xl.

ACKNOWLEDGMENTS

I dedicate this book to all the youth who don't have a voice, and future generations. We Rise for them!

Writing this book has been such an incredible journey and learning experience for me, and I definitely couldn't have written it without the support of so many.

First of all, I'd like to thank my mama for laying the groundwork of my activism and never faltering in her belief in me. She works harder and has sacrificed more than anyone I know. She has poured everything into the vision that this world can be healed if we lift up the voices of the youth. Her unwavering dedication to this movement has made her my hero. My greatest hope is to make her dreams for the world she envisions comes to fruition. Thank you for being the best mother a young wild boy could ask for. All moms out there could definitely take a page out of her parenting book.

I wanna say thanks to mi papa for teaching me to work hard and for showing me the importance of staying connected to my roots in order to find my way. It's because of everything my father taught me that I am the person I am today. Carrying my culture with me in my name and my lineage is the greatest honor as an ambassador for the youth and our people. *Gracias por enseñar me como ser un guerrero.* Thank you for showing me how to be a warrior.

So much gratitude to my grandfathers, Xolotl and Makasha, warriors from two different worlds, whose perspectives have taught me so much.

I want to thank my friend and partner in crime Russell Mendell for working tirelessly by my side to help me craft this book and provide this project with his vast knowledge and experience as an organizer and leader. I have learned so much from him. A shout-out to my boy Bernie Sanders who was present for pretty much the entire creation of the book in the form of a 6-inch action figure.

To Justin Spizman, the "Georgia Author of the Year," and a great book architect. You kept me on task during the writing of this book, showed never-ending patience, and provided a gentle nudge when I needed it. I appreciate how much time, energy, and effort you put into keeping this project on track and helping me find my voice as an author.

A shout-out to Kendrick Lamar, Joey Bada$$, and Logic for dropping really lit and inspiring albums that became the soundtrack of my writing process.

A shout-out to the Earth Guardians team: Russell, Michaela, Daniel, Christian, Aidan, and my mama, for helping with research and pulling together important resources for the book. I am so grateful to Brooke Losey who helped so much with web support to launch my book out into the world.

Thank you to the Rodale team; Jennifer Levesque, Gail Gonzales, Yelena Nesbit, Angie Giammarino, Nicole Barnhart, Amy King, and Kate Bittman with Bitty Media for the incredible opportunity and the doors they opened that made it possible for me to write this book.

Sending deep gratitude to all of the amazing people whom I have crossed paths with on this journey who agreed to share their knowledge and stories in this book through our interviews. I have been inspired and learned so much from each and every one of you.

I am so deeply honored by all of you who have provided endorsements for this, my first book: Leonardo DiCaprio, Mark Ruffalo, Winona LaDuke, Shailene Woodley, and Paul Hawken.

And last but not least, to the Earth that gives us life. May this book be an inspiration and guide for many and may it offer the reflections and support to help guide us toward a healthy, just, sustainable world.

INDEX

Boldface references indicate photographs.